WHEN
GOD
HAD A
WIFE

"A book that blows the lid off one of the most ancient cover-ups in the world—the existence of a feminine deity every bit as important as the masculine Yahweh. This is a book that all should read—it is powerful, thought-provoking, and wonderfully contentious. The scholarship of the writers is evident on every page. So read on and be prepared to be astounded and diverted. Your world may never look the same again."

JOHN MATTHEWS, COAUTHOR OF *TEMPLES OF THE GRAIL* AND *THE LOST BOOK OF THE GRAIL*

"Picknett and Prince, long known for profoundly unsettling religious and historical revelations, have excelled themselves with this story of the little-known Israelite goddesses—their rise, fall, and, unexpectedly, their rise again. But now we are also faced with another deeply uncomfortable cover-up—that of the priestesses who celebrated the goddess even from within Christ's own circle. A major book and a gripping read."

GRAHAM PHILLIPS, AUTHOR OF *THE VIRGIN MARY CONSPIRACY* AND *THE CHALICE OF MAGDALENE*

"What I like about this book is the referencing to external scholarship and the clarity of presentation. The finding of an 8th-century-BCE inscription at Kuntillet Ajrud, read as 'Yahwe (God) and his Ashera,' supports the authors' contention that God had a consort."

ROBERT FEATHER, AUTHOR OF *THE SECRET INITIATION OF JESUS AT QUMRAN*

PRAISE FOR OTHER WORKS BY
LYNN PICKNETT AND CLIVE PRINCE

"Lynn Picknett and Clive Prince . . . specialize in topics that challenge established and cultural history."

FORTEAN TIMES

"Lynn Picknett and Clive Prince . . . hold as good a claim as any to be the model for Robert Langdon, for their book stands at the heart of *The Da Vinci Code*'s ideas."

MICHAEL HAAG, JAMES MCCONNACHIE, AND
VERONICA HAAG, AUTHORS OF *THE ROUGH
GUIDE TO THE DA VINCI CODE*

"[Picknett and Prince] provide credible explanations for incredible topics."

IAN PUNNETT, WEEKEND HOST ON *COAST TO COAST AM*

"*Turin Shroud* is a book to which all the tabloid adjectives truly apply. It really is astonishing, gruesome, shocking, and sensational. It even appears to be true."

WASHINGTON TIMES

"[In *The Masks of Christ* Picknett and Prince] strike boldly and unreservedly against what they see as the mythos that transformed the historical Jesus into a God. . . . Studying the traditions and tensions that surrounded the early Christians and filtering these through the lens of skepticism, they create a picture that is both challenging and disturbing."

PUBLISHERS WEEKLY

"Finally a comprehensible and instructive history of the myth of the 'royal blood' and supposed descendants of Jesus [*The Sion Revelation*]."

JAVIER SIERRA, AUTHOR OF *THE SECRET SUPPER*

WHEN GOD HAD A WIFE

The Fall and Rise of the Sacred Feminine
in the Judeo-Christian Tradition

LYNN PICKNETT
and CLIVE PRINCE

Bear & Company
Rochester, Vermont

Bear & Company
One Park Street
Rochester, Vermont 05767
www.BearandCompanyBooks.com

Text stock is SFI certified

Bear & Company is a division of Inner Traditions International

Cataloging-in-Publication Data for this title is available from the Library of Congress

ISBN 978-1-59143-370-5 (print)
ISBN 978-1-59143-371-2 (ebook)

Printed and bound in the United States by Lake Book Manufacturing, Inc. The text stock is SFI certified. The Sustainable Forestry Initiative® program promotes sustainable forest management.

10 9 8 7 6 5 4 3 2 1

Text design and layout by Priscilla Baker
This book was typeset in Garamond Premier Pro with Futura and Hermann used as display typefaces

To send correspondence to the authors of this book, mail a first-class letter to the authors c/o Inner Traditions • Bear & Company, One Park Street, Rochester, VT 05767, and we will forward the communication, or contact the authors directly at **www.picknettprince.com**.

To the new arrivals, and looking toward
a more goddess-friendly future:
Isaac Samuel Braun
Leonardo Milani-Ferris
Aurora Elizabeth Beskin Schofield
Ada Iona Fearnley Hanison

Contents

Acknowledgments

Our heartfelt thanks are due to many people:

Bali Beskin, whose friendship, inspiration—and drive—made this book possible. And special thanks, too, to Geraldine Beskin and Dr. Stephen Schofield, also of the magickal Atlantis Bookshop, London. Thank you for all the giggles, deep discussions, special evenings, fascinating introductions—and certain very big birthdays.

Our lovely friend Carina Fearnley, for being such an amazingly supportive, kind, and fun star. Thanks, too, to her partner Jack Hanison.

As ever, our agent Jeffrey Simmons, for believing in this book.

The team at Bear & Company for making it real: Jon Graham, John Hays, Patricia Rydle, Jennie Marx, Kelly Bowen, Erica B. Robinson, Eliza Burns, and Manzanita Carpenter Sanz.

The effervescent, funny, and kind Helen Scott, whose light shone so brightly in our darkest days, and who has been taken from us so tragically. She will always be much missed.

For always being there for us, with helpful suggestions, jolly distractions, fabulous conversations, and genial generosity:

Debbie and Yvan Cartwright; Jane Lyle; Mike Wallington; Javier and Eva Sierra; Sheila Taylor; Keith Prince; Chris Murray; Sinziana Paduroiu; Graham Phillips; Karine Espareil; John and Judith Rimmer, Kevin and Noyumi Murphy, Trevor Pyne, and all our fellow Magonians; Gary Lachman; Hannah Johnson and Stu Braun; John and Caitlín Matthews; Andrew Collins; Magister Cygnus; Sharon and Phil Jagger; Dan O'Connell; Eleanor Julie and Iain Duxbury Wilson; Moira Hardcastle; Greg Rattey; Bobby Sullivan; Steffi Grant; the late great Guy Lyon Playfair; Mike Playfair; Ashley Brown; Stewart Ferris and Katia Milani; Heather Couper; Nigel Henbest; the late, fabulous Ian Dougan; Chris Warwick; Carrie Kirkpatrick; Dr. Robert Feather; Sheila Andrews and Darren Roberts; Tessa Harris; Veronica and Allan Goodroad; Stu Barker; Mark Friedman; Jean and Jim Bodie; Ronald Hendrickson; Max D. Crapo; Ellie Chamberlain; Jack Sarfatti; Sally Morgan; Bruce Burgess; David Elkington; Dwina Gibb; Ken Graydon; Joy and Chris Millar; Caroline Brown; Kimberley Humberstone; and Robbie Bridgstock.

For invaluable research assistance, the staff at the British Library.

INTRODUCTION

Bringing Her Back Home

Every book represents a new and exciting journey, not just for the reader, but also for the authors themselves. In our case *When God Had A Wife* not only took us into unexplored territories—which we would expect— but also revisited some of the key themes of our previous books. But this time we found a sharper message and many more tantalizing questions, some very big indeed. After all, few nonfiction topics can be quite as intriguing as the deliberate near eradication of the sacred feminine in the two great religions of Judaism and Christianity. But surely even more astonishing is the fact that they had a goddess figure in the first place!

As some readers will know, this theme has been close to our hearts for decades, but there was more to investigate, more loose ends to tie up, more revelations to uncover. The goddess never yields her secrets easily, but she allows glimpses, often through the most unlikely sources. It is never impossible to trace her survival, though there are still those who hate that ancient cover-ups are being exposed, and especially loathe the comeback of the goddess.

We know how the patriarchies react because we have already felt the cold wind of their disapproval, and the even sharper bite of real hostility. Indeed, this book is something of a prequel to our controversial *The Masks of Christ: Behind the Lies and Cover-Ups About the Man Believed to Be God* (2008), which in turn dug deeper into subjects at the heart of our *The Templar Revelation: Secret Guardians of the True Identity of Christ* (1997, revised and updated 2007). This book also fits snugly into the arc of Lynn's solo works, *Mary Magdalene: Christianity's Hidden Goddess* (2003) and *The Secret History of Lucifer: The Ancient Path to Knowledge and the* Real *Da Vinci Code* (2005).

This book sees us return to the sacred feminine in the Hebrew religion, which we touched on in both earlier books (especially *Templar Revelation*) because it was so central to their main subject—Jesus and the origins of Christianity. But now even we are amazed at the extent and clarity of the whole picture as we reconstructed it, excitedly piece by piece.

In the decade after *Masks of Christ* our ongoing research has revealed Christ himself was heavily involved with the holy feminine, which helps explain some of his enduring mysteries. These include the strange mix of Jewish and pagan—especially Egyptian—elements in his mission. Previously our attempts to reconcile them stopped short of completely closing the gap. Now we hope we have done just that, shedding further light on our previous conclusions, especially those in *Templar Revelation*.

What were once maddeningly elusive pieces are now back in the puzzle, and the picture is startlingly different.

We were not, however, alone on this journey.

KNOWLEDGE IS POWER

One might feel a profoundly spiritual and emotional response to the goddess, but this is not doing her complete justice. Spirit is powerful, but it is not everything. We only know her names, titles, and attributes and what she meant to which ancient peoples through the accumulation of hard facts. We have always loved the goddess, but sometimes she is lost and needs finding with both the heart *and* mind.

Over the years we have come to respect the archaeologists who excavated ancient sites, the academics who painstakingly analyzed data, and the professors whose landmark research has been ignored for decades. Part of our mission is to build a bridge between the "Mind, Body, and Spirit" (MBS) community and academics. We realize the time is right to share the curious, not always easy, crossover between their discoveries and ours.

(Lynn discovered the value of research the hard way: As a girl she fell into the clutches of a world-famous cult, experiencing the euphoria of conversion. But discovering the truth about the cult's founder and its historical claims soon brought her down to earth. As the Bible says, "the truth shall make you free.")

Sadly but understandably, there has been great distrust between the two communities. The MBS side often regards academia as over-conservative, obsessed with cold facts, and far too materialistic. Scholars tend to dismiss the MBS community as naive, basing their worldview on wishful thinking and oversimplification. To us, however, both sides are partly wrong, and both sides are partly right. It's time to bring them together in the spirit of mutual respect.

While we personally are by no means skeptical about the unexplained or the spiritual realm—not to mention information from outside academe—we have always realized that data from *all* sources must be checkable; otherwise any case stands little chance of being totally persuasive.

For that reason, we are careful to base our books on factual sources, although, given the incompleteness of the historical record, we sometimes have to speculate—just as academics do, in fact!

We now realize how much bringing together all the data from different disciplines, as we do here, reinforces the most cherished alternative ideas about the divine feminine in the ancient world. One of our biggest surprises about goddess research is that both the MBS and academic camps are pushing in the same direction, even if they don't know it.

By assembling all the latest research and discoveries on subjects such as the ancient Israelite worship of Asherah, the significance of the female Wisdom in Judaism, and the central, but unrecognized, place of her new form of Sophia in the Jesus story, we show it is all part of the same narrative. And what a story it is . . .

And now for the first time, it is presented in one, easily accessible book.

This book returns their own lost goddess to Judaism and Christianity, the two religions that have underpinned Western civilization. Her return will be a lightning strike against misogyny and much abuse, bringing with her both new and ancient freedoms for all people.

This time she will not be ignored. This time she is here to stay.

1
Out of Egypt

To modern Jews and Christians certain aspects of their faiths go unchallenged, hallowed as they are by many centuries of unquestioning belief. Indeed, to most believers it is virtually blasphemy to question that God is and always was the one and only true deity, and that only pagans and idolaters worship a pantheon of many, horribly fake gods. Add to this the idea that God, always resolutely male, ruled alone, and you have the outline of what the Judeo-Christian tradition has insisted upon, not always peaceably, over the millennia. But just how true is all that? Did the forefathers of today's Jews really worship Yahweh alone? Just who was he? And did he, as this book's title suggests, really have a female consort? Did Yahweh once have a wife—and if so, what happened to her?

The truth is that, just like the story of other ancient peoples, over the course of many centuries the Israelites' history had shifted and changed considerably, together with their beliefs. To find the answers to our questions we need to dig deep, to investigate—at times forensically and certainly always fearlessly—and take nothing for granted, even the pronouncements of respected academics, who can be too beguiled by their own agendas and fashionable memes.

We need to uncover just who the Israelites really were, and how the hard evidence matches—or doesn't—their alleged story as given in the Hebrew Bible (the Old Testament to Christians). We need to sift through the often fragmentary and sometimes even contradictory evidence concerning, for example, the Exodus from enslavement in Egypt—a very hot topic among scholars today, many of whom simply deny it ever happened.

Everything we discover about the long and vexed history of the ancient Israelites will help provide a fuller picture of the setting against which God's hold on their hearts and minds crystalized. Because only then can we begin to understand how he could have had a wife—for there is no doubt that he did—who was worshipped in her own right for centuries, and then lose her. And surely with her loss went much respect, not only for the divine feminine, but also for ordinary women. Recovering the truth about her, and reestablishing her prominence, will present new opportunities for personal empowerment to all women, not just Jews and Christians.

IN THE BEGINNING

Most people think that today's Judaism, with a few superficial differences, is basically the same as the religion that is described in the Hebrew Bible. That simply isn't true. Judaism was the religion of just one of the twelve tribes of Israel, Judah—the linguistic origin of *Jew* and *Judaism*—and differed very dramatically from the previous faith of Moses's day.

While the Hebrew Bible is the foundation text of the Jewish religion, it really tells the story of the *emergence* of Judaism from the earlier Israelite beliefs and practices. It is more accurate to use the terms "Israelites," "people/children of Israel" or "Hebrews" when delving into the Bible. *Hebrew* is an alternative term used occasionally in the Old Testament for the Israelites. It comes from a verb meaning "to cross over," although exactly what this was meant to convey remains a mystery. In the Hebrew Bible it appears when the Israelites are talking about themselves in relation to other peoples—as in the early part of

Exodus, while they are still in Egypt. Hebrew became the name for the Israelite language much later—around the second century BCE.

The pivotal moment—the true beginning of Judaism—is not generally well known. This took place some eighty years after the return from Exile in Babylon—in the mid-fifth century BCE—when the governor of Jerusalem, Nehemiah, and the priest-scribe Ezra set about a root-and-branch regeneration of the religion, codifying it in the form of scrolls to be read out at public gatherings and relating it to the people's legendary past.

The unfolding narrative in the Hebrew Bible tells the stories that underpin not just Western religion but our entire culture—often the first that children learn about their faith—the Garden of Eden; the Flood; the Patriarchs, beginning with Abraham, who made a covenant with God; the twelve sons of Jacob (renamed Israel) who were the progenitors of the twelve tribes; Joseph (with his famous multicolored coat) and the sojourn in Egypt; the Exodus under Moses and, after forty years wandering in the wilderness, the conquest of the Promised Land. Then there's the foundation of the Kingdom of Israel; the golden age of Solomon; the eventual fall of Jerusalem and destruction of Solomon's magnificent Temple—followed by the Jews' traumatic Captivity in Babylon, then their triumphant return after fifty years in Exile and the building of a new Temple. For Christians, the Old Testament history also sets the scene for the incarnation of Jesus Christ.

That's the whistle-stop version of the Bible story. But did it really happen like that?

For most of the West's story, the Bible was regarded *as* history, largely because there were no other sources to check it against. And as it was fervently believed to be nothing less than God's word there was no reason to doubt it.

When people did start to think critically about the texts of the Hebrew Bible, it soon became apparent they simply could not have been written when Jewish tradition or Church dogma claimed. For example, the first five books of the Old Testament, the Pentateuch (Greek for "five scrolls"), were believed to be by Moses himself. But as they describe his own death and burial, this was somewhat unlikely. And asides mentioning that certain practices were still like that "to this day" reveal that the books were written some time after the event.

In the seventeenth century CE, it dawned on scholars that, for various reasons, the books describing the origins of the Israelites had to have been written—at least in today's form—after the return from the Exile in Babylon. In the 1600s, the metaphysical Dutch philosopher Baruch Spinoza—who had already been shunned by his Jewish community in Amsterdam because of his daring heretical thinking—suggested that the books of the Pentateuch were actually the work not of Moses, but of Ezra himself.

It transpires that Spinoza was essentially correct, although there were several phases to this process of compiling a canon, the first being a couple of hundred years before Ezra, during a period of reform of the religion started by Judah's King Josiah (ca. 650–609 BCE).

According to the biblical account a pivotal event happened in 621 BCE. During rebuilding work in the Temple of Solomon a hitherto unknown "Book of the Law" written by Moses was discovered, setting out the obligations and practices of the religion. This is what became Deuteronomy—the "Second Law"—or more likely an early form of it.

Josiah, alarmed that—however innocently—he and his people had not managed to keep to the rules set down by God and imparted to Moses, set about reforming the religion in accordance with this newly discovered book. He duly purged the religion and the practices of the Temple of anything not sanctioned in the newfound book, and under him work started on compiling an officially endorsed canon. The books of Judges, Samuel, Kings, and Chronicles are believed to date from this period, being referred to as the "Deuteronomist history."

The process of writing, compiling, and editing continued through the Captivity in Babylon. The books of Moses, the Pentateuch, were assembled either during the Captivity or just after, all being given a final edit in Ezra and Nehemiah's day in the mid-fifth century. They became the official, authorized, and unchanging canon that was the foundation for the religion.

As biblical archaeologist William G. Dever notes, the Pentateuch and Deuteronomic history "were set down in writing in the present form *at least* 500 years after the Exodus and Conquest they purport to describe."[1] (His emphasis.)

Naturally, the writers and editor drew on older sources—songs, poems, books now lost, and important oral traditions—but inevitably, during the process of assembling the canon, the sources were reinterpreted and reworked to match the situation of the day, inconvenient passages being quietly airbrushed out. In effect, they were revising both the religion and their own history.

The various "songs" inserted into the texts as poems—the "Song of the Sea" in Genesis, the "Song of Deborah and Barak" in Judges, and so on—are among the most genuinely ancient passages. This makes sense: as generations of Israelites knew them well, the writer/editors could hardly have felt free to change them.

The big problem for Bible researchers is determining just which parts of the Hebrew Bible are genuinely old, which have been edited and "revised"—and which were entirely invented. And the same goes for the older sources, which themselves had been amended, exaggerated, or had even started out as folklore and tall tales.

BIBLICAL MINIMALISTS

Only so much can be deduced from the texts themselves. To uncover how much of the biblical account can be taken seriously, it should be compared and correlated with the histories of the peoples around the Israelites, and with archaeological discoveries. And here Bible scholars encounter further problems: what *should,* if the Hebrew Bible accounts are correct, have been there in the historical and archaeological record simply turn out to be conspicuous by their absence.

Outside biblical accounts, there is scant evidence for the Israelites' origins. The earliest known historical reference is on the famed Merneptah Stele, erected at Thebes in the fifth year of Pharaoh Merneptah's reign (ca. 1209 BCE), which includes "Israel" in a list of those defeated by the Egyptians, the grammar implying a people or tribe rather than a land.

There are some references to peoples who *may* be the Israelites, but they remain controversial and lack any detail. There are, for example, the "Apiru" or "Habiru" in Canaanite texts from the fourteenth century BCE, which has been related to "Hebrews," and the "Shasu"—described by Dever as "donkey-mounted pastoral nomads"[2]—who appear in Egyptian texts between the fifteenth and thirteenth centuries BCE. One group is called the "Shasu of *Yhw*," which many take to be Yahweh. On the other hand, some think that *Yhw* is a place name. But that's it.

Most glaringly—and to traditionalists shockingly—that includes what was supposed to be the heyday of Israelite civilization, the kingdoms of David and, particularly, Solomon. The latter purportedly presided over a mini-empire, treated as an equal by the great kingdoms around him: according to the Hebrew Bible the pharaoh of Egypt gave his daughter to Solomon in marriage, a rare privilege and a sign of great respect for Solomon's power—marriages then being primarily diplomatic alliances. Yet there is no reference to these allegedly great Israelite kings in any of the neighboring lands' records. Most startlingly, not the slightest trace of Solomon's celebrated Temple has ever been found.

This has led to a great skepticism among historians, seeing its most extreme form in the "biblical minimalists," who take a highly legalistic approach to the Bible's historical claims: unless specific proof of an event, figure, or era can be produced, they simply never happened. (The opposite position is that unless an event can be proved *not* to have happened, then it did. Ironically, in their own way minimalists take the Bible just as literally as fundamentalist Christians and Jews.)

To the minimalists, *everything* in the Bible before about the eighth century BCE (when there is some historical and archaeological support) is invention and myth: there was no Moses, no Exodus, no conquest of the Promised Land, no golden age of David and Solomon—some even believe it was all entirely made up. In fact, there were no Israelites, just Canaanites who created a new past for themselves. As William G. Dever puts it, according to the minimalists, the Hebrew Bible is just a "pious hoax."[3] Which also means the ancient Israelites were also nonexistent.

Sadly, but perhaps inevitably, there is a political dimension to this. The biblical minimalists' theories are seized on by ideological opponents to the modern state of Israel, since if ancient Israel never existed then of course the basis for the Israelis' claim to the land is undermined. Some minimalists are even politically driven to prove that Israel never existed, essentially weaponizing its nonexistence.

Pure bias will never discover the truth. In fact, as we'll see, the archaeology and other historical evidence do support the basic outline of the Hebrew Bible story, albeit still casting doubt on some of the detail. But it sheds quite a different light on the *religion* of the ancient Israelites.

So political and religious prejudice aside, what is the hard evidence for the main story?

THE PROMISED LAND

Despite the drama of the creation and the Flood, the story of the Israelites really begins with a descendant of Noah named Abraham—originally Abram—in the book of Genesis, the first of the five "books of Moses."

Abraham's family hail from "Ur of the Chaldees" (*Ur Kasdim*), believed to be the Sumerian city of Ur, the ruins of which lie close to Nasiriyah in southern Iraq. But when the story really starts he is living in Harran, a major Mesopotamian city whose remains are in southern Anatolia (today's Turkey, near the border with Syria), where his father had emigrated.

God, then called "El," tells Abram to leave Harran and travel to the land of Canaan, which he promises to give Abram's descendants and where they will establish a great nation. Canaan is what is now the Southern Levant—a huge area comprising modern Syria, Lebanon, Jordan, Israel, and Palestine.

Abram obediently sets off with his wife Sarai and his father's household, including his nephew Lot and their families, slaves, and livestock. Although they go straight to Canaan—first to Shechem and then settling in Bethel (both places are important later)—they do much wandering around the region. They spend time in Egypt and have various adventures, including escaping the fate of Sodom and Gomorrah—one of God's more dramatic cautionary tales.

Through later visions, God makes a covenant with Abram, promising his descendants the whole land between Egypt and the river Euphrates—a vast territory. As a sign of this agreement, God gives Abram a new name, Abraham, said to mean "father of many nations," while Sarai becomes Sarah, or "noblewoman." It is never explained why God chose Abraham, or the nature of his side of the bargain, other than to ensure all his male descendants are circumcised.

Abraham and Sarah—as promised by God—against the odds and indeed biological probability, finally have a son together, even though Abraham is 100 and Sarah 90: the boy is Isaac, second of the patriarchs.

Abraham's son Isaac and his wife Rebekah have a child, Jacob. It's he who, by his two wives, the sisters Rachel and Leah, and their respective handmaidens, fathers the twelve sons who become the founders of the tribes of Israel. (He also has a daughter by Leah, Dinah, but she doesn't get a tribe.)

Then—in one of the Bible's more random episodes—Jacob wrestles all night with a man who turns out to be God. After this he is given the name, or nickname, "Israel," said in Genesis to mean "one who has struggled with God." However, modern scholars consider a more likely etymology "El struggles" (the story being an attempt to explain the mistaken etymology). "Israel" is given to Jacob's descendants and ultimately the whole nation, distinguishing them as El's people.

Jacob's son Joseph is his favorite because, although the penultimate of the twelve, he is the firstborn by his preferred wife Rachel. Jacob shows his favoritism by giving Joseph the famous coat of many colors—the "dreamcoat" of the musical—although the exact translation and meaning of the Hebrew phrase is uncertain, other than being a convenient plot device. This makes his brothers and half brothers so jealous they sell him to some passing merchants. They tell their father that he had been eaten by a wild animal, showing Jacob the coat they had stained with blood.

Joseph becomes a slave in Egypt, but thanks to his prophetic skills—not only interpreting dreams but divining with silver bowls, or *scrying*—he rises to the post of vizier, top official to the pharaoh. He takes an Egyptian name and the pharaoh gives him as bride Asenath, daughter of the priest of On, or Heliopolis—by whom he has two sons, Manasseh and Ephraim.

Some years later, during the famous famine, which Joseph has prophetically preempted by organizing a great store of grain, his brothers arrive in Egypt, sent by Jacob to find food. They fail to recognize Joseph, but he finally reveals himself, forgives them, and gets them to bring his elderly father from Canaan—along with all their families—and they are reunited. The whole clan, also honored by the pharaoh out of respect for Joseph, settles in Goshen in the Nile delta.

Shortly before Jacob's death, Joseph takes his two sons Manasseh and Ephraim to meet him, and Jacob/Israel declares they will share in his inheritance as if they were his own sons. This explains why later the tribes said to be descended from them are numbered among the twelve, and why there is no tribe of Joseph. Manasseh and Ephraim are occasionally referred to jointly as the House of Joseph (*benei-yosef,* more accurately "sons of Joseph"), and sometimes as "half tribes."

When the story restarts 400 years later, at the beginning of Exodus, the descendants of Jacob/Israel's sons have multiplied so greatly that a later pharaoh, fearing they might overwhelm Egypt, has enslaved them as workers on building projects.

But a hero is at hand: enter the legendary Moses. Although raised as an Egyptian prince, he is really from the tribe of Levi; as a baby his mother set him adrift in a basket on the Nile after a pharaonic decree that all male Hebrew babies be killed at birth. He was found by the pharaoh's daughter who, for reasons best known to herself, decided to raise him as her own son. Fortunately, an unnamed sister of Moses saw her take the baby from the bulrushes and arranged a wet nurse from the Levites, so Moses grows up knowing his true heritage.

The adult Moses kills a slave master he sees mistreating an Israelite and has to flee the country, traveling to Midian in Arabia on the eastern side of the Red Sea (the western region of modern Saudi Arabia known as the Hejaz). There he marries the daughter of a priest of Midian, whose name, depending on which page it occurs, is Jethro or Reuel or Hobab, and joins his household. (According to Genesis, the Midianites are also descendants of Abraham, from his son Midian, born to his second wife—so they are kind of kin.)

One day while tending the flocks of Jethro/Reuel/Hobab, Moses encounters the burning bush, where God appears, assigning him the mission of freeing his chosen people from bondage in Egypt and leading them to the Promised Land.

At this point in the story there is a major shift: God's name has changed. Previously he was El, but now when Moses asks who he should say has sent him, God declares himself as Yahweh. (More accurately YHWH, the "Tetragrammaton," because the ancient Israelites had no written vowels. It became *Jehovah* in Latin.)

God's important new identity is underlined in his enigmatic answer, *"Ehyeh asher ehyeh"*—"I am who I am" or, as most specialists prefer, "I will be who I will be" (it could even be "I was who I was," Hebrew not being explicit on tenses). Moses is to tell the Israelites that "I am" (*Ehyeh*) has sent him. Thereafter, God is referred to as "I am" (or possibly "I cause to be"), which effectively becomes his name, Yahweh. It is more properly a title used in the absence of a name as such, deriving from a verb meaning "to be," or "to come into being," but exactly what it means remains a mystery. Even the Bible writers had little notion of what *Yahweh* signified. In later tradition *YHWH* became too sacred even to say aloud.

The writers of Genesis and Exodus obviously thought the change of name highly significant, studiously avoiding using "Yahweh" to this point in the story. God explains to Moses that although the patriarchs didn't know him by that name, he *is* the same God who appeared to Abraham, Isaac, and Jacob. But now God is overwhelmingly referred to as Yahweh ("the Lord" in English Bibles), although *El,* translated as "God," is still occasionally used. In the ancient tongue, *Yahweh* may be related to the Hebrew for "Lord"—hence the usual English translation.

Moses—aided by his brother Aaron, who conveniently turns up in Midian (and who inexplicably escaped being murdered as a baby on the orders of pharaoh)—returns to Egypt to negotiate the release of the Hebrews, seemingly a rather big ask. However, with the help of Yahweh's immoderate plagues, eventually he triumphantly leads the Israelites out of Egypt.

Initially the Israelites settle at Mount Sinai, or Horeb, for two years, where Yahweh's religion is properly codified, marking the end of vague promises and platitudes. With his new name, God has become more definite and organized. His message is finally clarified with his momentous meeting with Moses on the mountaintop, where he gives him the Ten Commandments (later expanded to over 600). The great iconic leader is also given the basic obligations of Yahweh-worship—the sacrifices, keeping the Sabbath, the holy festivals, and so on. These take up the whole of Leviticus, the third book of the Bible.

The instruction is not confined to words: Moses is also instructed how to make the fabled Ark of the Covenant. This is the mysterious focus of the religion, a strange and powerful device—even, occasionally, a weapon of mass destruction. And as Steven Spielberg puts it, the Ark is "a radio for talking to God." Yahweh uses it to communicate with Moses and later the priests, the first being Moses's brother Aaron.

We know what the Ark looked like, from the quite detailed

description in the Bible. It's a chest of acacia wood with carrying poles, covered in gold. It holds the stone tablets inscribed with the Ten Commandments and other sacred objects, and on top is the "mercy seat" (*kapporet*) where Yahweh appears to talk to Moses, either to give him instructions or hold the people of Israel to account for their backsliding. Only Moses is allowed into Yahweh's presence. When the people are on the move, the Ark is carried before them—covered with animal skins to conceal it from their gaze. Later, it is paraded at the head of the Israelite army when they go into battle.

The Ark is housed in the Tabernacle, a portable shrine—or even a temple—that can be packed up and carried with relative ease in the form of a huge tent with curtains and gold-covered boards. It is erected inside a sanctuary marked out by a perimeter of woven sheets and wooden poles.

After two years and two months, Yahweh commands Moses to lead the Israelites to the Promised Land of Canaan. But once there most of the people, with the exceptions of Joshua and Caleb, are afraid to invade it (partly because they think it's inhabited by giants). Yahweh condemns them to forty years wandering in the wilderness so that none of the cowardly generation (apart from Joshua and Caleb) will ever live there. Later, Yahweh even bans Moses and Aaron from entering the Promised Land because he considers their gratitude to fall short.

The Israelites duly wander around for forty years, getting into battles and having other adventures, and being fed miraculously with manna and quails. Eventually, as the time comes for them to enter the Promised Land, Moses dies, but not before delivering a long list of rules and regulations that comprises most of Deuteronomy, the last of the "books of Moses." (Aaron had died long before.)

Moses's appointed successor Joshua, from the tribe of Ephraim, then leads the Israelites on the long-awaited conquest of the Promised Land from the Canaanites, starting with the city of Jericho and gleefully slaughtering whole peoples—men, women, children, and often their livestock too—on Yahweh's orders.

Despite Yahweh's repeated promises to clear the land completely of its inhabitants for his chosen people, the Canaanites are not completely expelled. The books of Joshua and Judges acknowledge that some were allowed to live among the tribes, effectively as slaves. Even some of the Canaanite nations survived within the Promised Land—apparently because Yahweh wanted to use them to test the Israelites' steadfastness.

When the job is finally done Joshua divides Canaan between the twelve tribes. More accurately there are thirteen. The priestly tribe of Levi, that of Moses and Aaron, has land allotted to individual Levite families within the territories of the other tribes. But because of the two "half tribes" of Ephraim and Manasseh the land is still divided into twelve.

Joshua's tribe of Ephraim is given the huge honor of custodianship of the Ark of the Covenant, the Tabernacle now being erected permanently at Shiloh (modern Khirbet Seilun in the West Bank) in Ephraim's lands. This is the first major center of the Yahweh religion.

Joshua also has the embalmed body of Joseph, which the Israelites had brought from Egypt with them, buried at Shechem as he had wished. Shechem (in or near modern Nablus in the West Bank) was one of the Israelites' earliest holy sites—the first place Abraham is said to have visited in Canaan, where he set up an altar to God. What has long been believed to be Joseph's tomb is venerated today by Jews and Samaritans, although sadly it seems not to be his tomb at all.

For about two centuries after the conquest, until the establishment of a monarchy, the tribes went their own way as a loose confederation or league trying to clear the remaining pockets of Canaanites out of the land or allying against external threats, particularly from the troublesome Philistines. During those tough times they were led by "judges" (*shoftim*), more accurately "leaders." One was a woman, Deborah.

ENTER THE PROPHETESSES

The story so far has been mostly about men. In fact, women are surprisingly well represented in the Bible, many being depicted in a positive light—or relatively so, given the time and culture. Women play prominent, sometimes pivotal, roles in many individual Bible stories—Delilah in the Samson tale, the prostitute Rahab, who shelters and assists the spies Joshua sends into Jericho, and so on—and of course they feature in the story of Israelite origins as wives and mothers. But not unexpectedly, given the general attitude to women across the ancient world, they rarely enjoy positions of authority.

Indeed, under the monarchy the wives of the kings had no official role (although of course a few influenced their husbands, Lady Macbeth-style). As Athalya Brenner, the Dutch-Israeli pioneer of feminist biblical studies, points out, only Israelite kings' foreign spouses are referred to as "queens"; the native-born are simply wives.[4] However, queen mothers did have an official role at court with some political influence, sometimes being given the title "Lady" (*gebira*). As we will see, queen mothers have an important role in our investigation into the lost goddess.

However, a few nonroyal women also appear to have some kind of status, either in politics or even in the Israelite religion. Yet on the rare occasions they appear, there always seems to be something missing or obscured. They just pop up without explanation or backstory—always included in the case of men—and then often disappear just as abruptly. Almost certainly, the writers—or more likely later editors—are being evasive. There's something about these women they don't want us to know. Perhaps they would have been left out entirely if they had not been so important to the story (which implies that many other women *have* been left out). And they are often found in some of the oldest biblical narratives.

There's Miriam, the prophetess sister of Moses and Aaron. She first appears by name (as "Aaron's sister," with no mention of Moses) after the crossing of the Sea of Reeds. Although often assumed to be older sister who kept watch over the baby Moses in the Nile, the Old Testament never actually says so. Miriam appears in the narrative when, with tambourine in hand, she leads the women in the last part of "The Song of the Sea" in celebration of the Israelites' trouncing of pharaoh's pursuing army.[5] This song is generally accepted as one of the earliest parts of the Bible, a separate text that was incorporated into the Exodus narrative.[6]

(The song describes a great wave caused by Yahweh's "breath"—a sudden storm—that overwhelms the Egyptians, which is more likely to be true than a miraculous parting of the sea.)

Miriam only reappears in the book of Numbers, when she and Aaron challenge Moses on his claim to being God's spokesman (after, in an apparent non sequitur, criticizing him for marrying a Cushite woman, as if the two complaints are linked). Summoning them to the Tabernacle, an angry Yahweh declares that, while he has spoken to Aaron and Miriam through visions and dreams, he speaks face to face only with Moses. For her temerity, Yahweh strikes Miriam (but not Aaron) with a skin disease (likening it to a father spitting in his daughter's face), although it seems the condition only lasts for seven days.[7]

Then, during the wandering in the wilderness when the Israelites stop at Kadesh in the Desert of Zin, without any drama, explanation, or message, Miriam dies. That's it.

The other of the "two great female figures of pre-monarchical Israel"[8] is Deborah, one of the judges, also described as a prophetess. Renowned for her wisdom, her "sphere of influence is the hill country of Ephraim,"[9] where she sits beneath a date palm tree and people come to her for advice and judgment.

The main part of her story, though, is her role in a conflict between the Israelites and the Canaanites, when her counsel proves decisive to the victory. The Israelites were being oppressed by the Canaanite king, Jabin. Deborah relays to Barak, of the tribe of Naphtali, God's command to raise an army to confront him. Barak obeys and—insisting on taking Deborah into battle with him—defeats Jabin's army under its commander Sisera, freeing Israel and ushering in forty years of peace.

Like Miriam, Deborah proclaims a song—the "Song of Deborah and Barak" in praise of God[10]—which, also as with Miriam, is perhaps among the oldest passages of the Hebrew Bible, being near contemporary with the events it describes.[11]

Deborah's story, as we will see, provides key clues to the hidden tradition of the sacred feminine among the Israelites.

In fact, as Brenner observes: "The two great female figures of pre-monarchical Israel, Deborah and Miriam, fit into the same category [as the men discussed] of great leaders. The only sphere that is out of bounds for them at the outset is the priesthood."[12] However, both women have a religious function, being described as "prophetesses"—chosen women to whom Yahweh speaks, and who then relay his words to the people.

These two special women feature early in the story, even before the term *prophet* is applied to any man. Later, of course, the famous prophets with books of the Bible attributed to them are men, although a few prophetesses still occasionally appear.

It also appears that women had some kind of official function in the Tabernacle, the forerunner of the Temple. There are two mentions of "the women who served at the entrance of the tent of meeting," although unlike all the other functionaries they are neither introduced nor explained.

Exodus's description of the making of the Tabernacle paraphernalia includes the fact that the bronze basin and its stand were made "from the mirrors of the ministering women who ministered at the entrance of the tent of meeting."[13] In the book of Samuel, the corrupt and immoral behavior of the sons of the high priest Eli that leads to the loss of the Ark includes sleeping with "the women who were serving at the entrance to the tent of meeting."[14] For once it is the *men* who are condemned for illicit sex, with no suggestion that the women led them astray.

Who these women are and their exact function at the Tabernacle is never explained; perhaps the reader was expected to know. But every other thing about the Tabernacle, its practices and functionaries are described in excruciating detail in Leviticus—twice, in fact: once when Yahweh gives the instruction and again when they are carried out.

We might be tempted to leap to a scurrilous conclusion about women who hang about outside places frequented by men, but the texts never suggest their activities are eyebrow raising. Their role is, however, somewhat controversial. We'll be returning to it later.

Transgressive women do feature prominently in a major theme of the Old Testament, however. From Moses onward, the story is punctuated with accusations of apostasy on the part of the Israelites—turning from the worship of Yahweh to other gods, either the old deities from before Yahweh's time, the revival of Canaanite practices, or the importation (usually by women) of foreign gods from neighboring peoples, for which they are duly punished by Yahweh. One obvious candidate is the famous golden calf made by the Israelites while Moses is up Mount Sinai talking to—or rather listening to—God.

During the wandering in the wilderness, while the Israelites are encamped at Peor, the men are led astray into the worship of the god Baal by the women of the Midianite city of Moab. This leads to what is later known as the "incident of Peor," causing Yahweh to send a plague that kills 24,000 Israelites.[15]

Although Yahweh had decided to destroy them all, his rage is tempered by a touching act of devotion on the part of Phinehas, Aaron's grandson. He runs a spear through an Israelite man and Moabite woman while they are having sex. Realizing from this that some are still faithful to his ways, Yahweh calls off the plague and grants Phinehas the hereditary high priesthood.

During the period of the judges, the Israelites revert to their old ways whenever a judge's back is turned—particularly returning to the worship of Baal, the Canaanite storm and fertility god who was widely venerated before the arrival of the Israelites.

All this serial apostasy is the stock excuse for any setback or defeat during the conquest of the Promised Land and the era of the judges. After all, if a serious downturn of fortune was not the Israelites' fault, it would mean Yahweh broke his promises. And that, of course, was unthinkable.

But did any of this actually happen? Do the biblical minimalists have a point—are these stories just undiluted myth?

IS THE BIBLE HISTORY?

The Exodus is generally dated to the reign of Ramesses the Great, 1279 to 1213–12 BCE, although some go for a pharaoh or two on either side.

In any case, as most scholars today consider the Exodus story complete fiction, trying to correlate it with Egyptian history is for them a pointless exercise.

The basic notion that the Israelites were enslaved in Egypt is not so farfetched. Canaanites and other Semitic peoples certainly settled there, mostly around the eastern Nile delta, the nearest part to Canaan. There was even a dynasty of Canaanite origin in the fourteenth century BCE that ruled the north of Egypt, during a period when the country was split into two kingdoms.

Semitic names appear among both paid and slave workers throughout Egypt's history, beginning long before the putative time of the Hebrew slavery and continuing long afterward. Yet no Egyptian texts or inscriptions so much as hint at a vast mass of slaves or workers leaving the country or being expelled. But the Bible claims there were about 600,000 men, plus women and children, so about 2.5–3 million people in all.[16] One would think someone in Egypt would have noticed them leaving: for one thing, an outflux of such a mammoth body of workers would have had serious social and economic consequences, obviously leaving some mark on Egyptian history. But mark there is none.

So the Exodus, if it happened at all, must have been on a much smaller scale than the biblical account would have us believe.

Another problem with the Bible story is that the books of Exodus and Numbers refer to places and people that simply did not exist at that time. The cities of "Pithom and Rameses" where the Israelites are said to have been forced to work on building projects for the pharaoh were real places—Per-Atum and Per-Ramessu—but those names were not used until the seventh century BCE.[17] Similarly, the Egyptian fortress town of Migdol on the eastern border of the Nile delta, referred to during the Exodus from Egypt, was only built in the seventh century BCE at the earliest.[18]

During the wandering in the wilderness, the book of Numbers makes a great deal of the Kingdom of Edom, but again such a state did not exist until the seventh century BCE. In the thirteenth and twelfth centuries BCE, according to both archaeology and Egyptian texts, it was inhabited only by nomadic peoples. The whole region through which the Israelites are said to have meandered was very sparsely populated at the time.[19]

Great excitement when excavations at Jericho found it had really been destroyed by warfare was tempered when the destruction was dated to around 1500 BCE—about three centuries too early for Joshua's legendary conquest. More damningly, it has been proved to be the work of the Egyptian army. Since then it had been entirely abandoned and uninhabited. The same goes for the second city, Ai, listed in the Israelites' itinerary of invasion.[20]

Of the thirty-one cities said to have been taken by Joshua listed at the end of the book named after him, twenty have been identified, and only two, Bethel and Hazor (the largest in the region at the time), show signs of largescale destruction in the thirteenth century BCE, although it is unclear whether they happened in the same time frame.[21]

Of course, the fact that these accounts date from at least 500 years after the event shows that the writers/editors simply described what was familiar from their own time. None of their readers would have known any better. Neither would the writers themselves: before the modern concept of history, people invariably pictured the past as being like their own day. Seeing the writings in context: the Old Testament was written in an age of titanic clashes between empires—Assyrians, Babylonians, Persians—with vast armies being controlled by tyrants. It is not surprising that the Bible writers would have imagined the era of Moses and, particularly, Joshua in the same way.

So far, the Bible's version of history is looking distinctly shaky. However, as William Dever—a champion of the archaeological approach—has shown, the evidence unearthed from beneath the soil *does* fit the Bible's account, often remarkably. But it is just on a considerably less epic scale.

Hundreds of ancient sites—mostly villages with populations of less than a hundred—have been identified and excavated, showing that in some parts of Israel there was a great increase in population during the twelfth century BCE, the era classified as "Iron Age I." Lawrence E. Stager sums the situation up in *The Oxford History of the Biblical World* (1998): Whereas 88 settlements have been found from the Late Bronze Age, 1500–1200 BCE, housing an estimated population of 50,000, in the same areas 678 were found from Iron Age I, 1200–1000 BCE, over 90 percent of them being new foundations, with a total estimated population of 150,000. Moreover, the newcomers were all of the same "material culture," which was distinct from the Late Bronze Age villages.[22]

However, as Stager explains:

> Most of these new settlements are located in the highlands or the plateaus on both sides of the Jordan River. Settlement is especially dense in the territories of Manasseh and Ephraim in the west and in Gilead and Moab in the east, both "frontiers" having been sparsely settled in the Late Bronze Age. This extraordinary increase in occupation during Iron Age I cannot be explained only by natural population growth of the few Late Bronze Age city-states in the region: there must have been a major influx of people into the highlands in the twelfth and eleventh centuries BCE.[23]

Dever summarizes the situation (his emphasis): "The significant fact in all these figures is that in contrast to other areas of Canaan, the *hill country*—where most of the supposedly Israelite people settled and later developed into a nation-state—witnessed a population explosion in the 12th century B.C.E."[24]

It was nowhere near the same scale nor so fast as the population explosion described in Joshua, but nevertheless it happened. And significantly, it happened in the area that was allocated to the tribes of Ephraim and Manasseh.

In fact, once the hype is removed from the conquest of the Promised Land, it fits the archaeological evidence rather better. Although at the end of Joshua there is a list of the thirty-one defeated kings, as Kenneth

Kitchen, the British historian specializing in the ancient Near East, states: "In fact, the biblical accounts simply have a body of people entering Canaan, destroying only three 'cities,' and killing in conflict the petty rulers of a number more—but without taking all these over. Settling-in took much longer."[25]

The archaeology also shows that in the lead-up to 1000 BCE—in the era of the early kings, Saul and David—the "highland village culture was rapidly being transformed into a 'proto-urban' society that was much more highly centralized."[26] Many of the villages were abandoned, and towns—some with populations of up to 2,000—appeared.

Such a transformation, as Dever points out, leads to exactly what the Bible describes: political centralization, social stratification, a sense of national identity that demands a national history (or myth)—and the creation of a religious orthodoxy that legitimizes the authority of the king, who rules by the will of the god, in this case Yahweh. And it also means taxes, to pay for monumental building projects.

Now we see that many of the biblical minimalists' objections are explained away by the basic human trait of exaggeration, epitomized on a heroic scale in the Old Testament.

Recognizing this factor puts into perspective some of the biblical narrative that attracted the minimalists' particular scorn. David and Solomon, for example, did not rule vast numbers of subjects. They were just chieftains of petty kingdoms, which is why they left little mark on their neighbors' chronicles.

Disappointingly, this penchant for hyperbole extends to the legendary Temple of Solomon and largely explains why no archaeological trace has ever been found. Because of its importance in religious history, we tend to imagine the Temple being gigantic, like one of the more impressive Gothic cathedrals. But according to the dimensions given in the Bible it was only the size of a modest parish church.

So, judging by the archaeology, there does seem to be an authentic, historical core to those early Bible stories, even if it is buried under layers of propaganda, swagger, and even imagination.

But, despite the evidence of an influx of people from outside Canaan in the twelfth century BCE, the one element that most scholars of the Hebrew Bible reject is the story of the Exodus, or any connection with Egypt. The modern consensus is that it is pure fiction.

According to the mainstream view—especially in the absence of any archaeological evidence of Egyptian influence on early Israelite settlements—the Israelites were either native Canaanites or, if they did migrate to the region, came either from the south or east of Canaan, not from Egypt. However, the case is considerably stronger than they would have us believe . . .

BORN OF EGYPT

The most immediate evidence is the name of the Israelites' iconic savior from the wicked pharaoh. *Moses* is an Egyptian name. It means "born of" and was commonly used by pharaohs, suffixed to the name of a god, to indicate their symbolic kinship with the deity, as in Thutmose ("born of Thoth").

Of course, the Exodus story has Moses being raised as an Egyptian prince, which might account for his name. But the tale makes little sense even on its own logic. The Bible's claim that his name was derived from "to draw out" (*moshe*)—as given to him by the pharaoh's daughter because she drew him out of the river—is obvious nonsense. Why would an Egyptian princess give him a Hebrew name anyway? Wasn't keeping his Hebrew blood a secret the whole point?

Clearly, that was invented to explain Moses's name in Hebrew terms—which would make no sense if, as the minimalists maintain, it was complete fiction. Why invent a hero with an Egyptian name and then go through such convolutions to explain that it wasn't really Egyptian? A much more likely scenario is that the later Israelites had traditions about an Egyptian named Moses who played a pivotal role in their history but, because of a deep-rooted hostility to Egypt, were uncomfortable about admitting it. So they came up with a story to explain that, although he was a prince of Egypt, he was really an Israelite.

In fact, the story of baby Moses being cast adrift on the Nile was hardly unique, the same tale being told of the third millennium BCE King Sargon of Akkad, though his birth legend came from long, long after he lived, from the seventh century BCE at the earliest. So it is even possible the Sargon story was inspired by Moses's, not the other way around.

However, British researcher Robert Feather points out that a similar narrative, which certainly predated Moses, was told in Egypt: in order to hide him from the evil god Set—the enemy of Osiris who wants to kill his infant son Horus—Osiris's goddess-wife Isis puts the child in a reed boat floating on the delta marshes.[27]

So probably Moses was an Egyptian born and bred, although he must have formed some kind of bond with the enslaved Hebrews. In fact, he is by no means the only person in the story with an Egyptian name. There are others, and they are all from the elite Levi, Moses's tribe, and members of the Shilohite priesthood that guards the Ark of the Covenant at Shiloh.

Over a century ago it was recognized that Phinehas, the grandson of Aaron and the first high priest, had an Egyptian name, a variation of Panehesy, which could mean "the southerner" or "the Nubian" (*pa-nhsi*). There are several priests and officials with that name recorded in Egypt, so perhaps it was particularly associated with high officials, including religious functionaries.

Phinehas is important: it's him, not Aaron, to whom Yahweh grants the hereditary high priestship, declaring "it shall be to him and to his descendants after him the covenant of a perpetual priesthood."[28] Although Aaron is the first priest, the hereditary line is not actually established through him—Exodus only ever calls him "priest" (*kohen*), never "high priest" (*kohen gadol*).

There is another Phinehas—a descendant of the first one—later in the book of Samuel, who is the brother of Hophni, another Egyptian name. Phinehas and Hophni are Levite priests, sons of the then high priest Eli and the last of the direct line descended from the first Phinehas. Their corrupt ways lead to the Ark being captured by the Philistines, with Eli and both his sons being killed.[29] The high priesthood then passes to a line descended from another of Aaron's sons (until Solomon allegedly returns it to the original line by appointing Zadok).

Another Levite name of Egyptian origin is Merari, which goes back to earlier in the story. His name is believed to derive from the Egyptian *mer,* or "beloved." He is one of Levi's sons, who is only mentioned in passing in Genesis, among those who come—with Jacob and his extended family—to settle in Egypt with Joseph. But his descendants, known as the Merarites, are one of the clans within the priestly tribe of Levi, given specific responsibility for carrying and caring for the Tabernacle, the tent-temple that houses the Ark of the Covenant.

As Mark S. Smith of Princeton Theological Seminary writes, "The various Egyptian names in Shilohite lineage (Moses, Phinehas, Hopni, [*sic*] and Merari) may point to the Egyptian background of the Levitical Shilohite priesthood."[30] This also suggests that the story is based on hard facts; giving Egyptian names to members of the priestly line makes no sense if it is all pure fiction.

We can add another Egyptian name to the list, which—tellingly, perhaps—scholars seem to neglect: Miriam, the sister of Moses and Aaron. If Moses was Egyptian, then she was also. Her name, too, could derive from the Egyptian *mer* (beloved), which often prefixed those of high-status females, meaning "beloved of . . ." a god (in the same way that -*mose* was used as a suffix for boys). One of Ramesses the Great's daughters was Meritamen, "beloved of Amun."

As with Merari, later Jewish tradition associated Miriam's name more with "bitter"—supposedly because she embodies the Israelites' condition at the time of her birth—deriving it from *mar yam,* or "bitter sea." But this is far too contrived, especially when the evidence is very much in favor of the Egyptian *mer.* This raises another, very exciting possibility.

Could it be that the Merarites—caretakers and carriers of the Tabernacle, no less—were really descended from *Miriam?* Was the story of their descent from Levi's son Merari a later invention to avoid any connection with a woman?

The giveaway is that, according to Genesis, Levi named his son Merari before he, along with all his brothers and Jacob, emigrated to Egypt.[31] This makes no sense on the story's own logic and seems contrived to crowbar in a man with the "beloved" name so the Merarites can be traced back to him. (Merari is one of three sons—the other two have Hebrew names.)

All this suggests that the first Levites did not merely have Egyptian names, but that they *were* Egyptian. William F. Albright, the celebrated American biblical scholar, clearly thought so, writing that the Levitic priesthood "perpetuated their Egyptian traditions as late as the eleventh century" (BCE, to the time of Hophni and Phinehas).[32]

However, according to one school of thought Levi was not originally considered a tribe or even an individual. It simply meant "priest," and only later were the Levites retrospectively upgraded to tribe status. There are few Levites in the Exodus account, nowhere near the numbers of the other tribes, which is presumably why they were never given their own territory, just parcels of land within that of other tribes. It was probably a small group, perhaps just a family—obviously including Moses, Aaron, and Miriam.

But how many Israelites really came out of Egypt—and did they include all the twelve tribes?

THE TWO TRIBES

Because of the different way the tribes of Ephraim and Manasseh are treated in the Bible, it was suggested as far back as the 1950s that only they were ever in Egypt.

While the other tribes are traced back to the sons of Jacob/Israel, Ephraim and Manasseh are said to have been descended from two of his *grandsons*—the two sons of Joseph. As already noted, there was no tribe of Joseph (although the term is used occasionally to refer to Ephraim and Manasseh collectively). For this reason, they are occasionally called "half tribes," and sometimes referred to jointly as the "sons of Joseph."

They are the tribes with the most specific connection to Egypt, since they claim descent from Joseph and his Egyptian wife Asenath—daughter of the high-status priest of Heliopolis—and so are not only half Egyptian but the only tribal forefathers to have been born in Egypt.

Some researchers include the tribe of Benjamin in this grouping, as they are descended from Jacob's other son by his favored wife Rachel, making him Joseph's only full brother. This implies that those three tribes were recognized as a related and distinct set. Scholars sometimes refer to the three as the "Rachel group."

In the Genesis account, although Manasseh is the firstborn, when Joseph takes them to his aged father Jacob to be blessed, he bestows the blessing usually reserved for the firstborn on Ephraim instead.[33] When Joseph questions this, Jacob tells him that it is because Ephraim's descendants will have greater glory. As indeed they did, at least before David established the monarchy. It was an Ephraimite, Joshua, who is credited with planning and leading the conquest of the Promised Land. (Although the story, as we have seen, is a massive exaggeration, it still gives Joshua the leading role.) And it was Ephraim that was given the honor of custody of the Ark of the Covenant when the Tabernacle was given a permanent home in Shiloh, in their lands. The "blessing" story probably reflects and was devised to explain retrospectively a change in the relative status of the two tribes at some point in Israelite history.

It would be a mistake to take these tales literally; they are origin myths, but of course they have a real origin to explain. They tell us that the tribes of Ephraim and Manasseh were connected more closely than the others, were considered to have a part-Egyptian heritage, and that when the Israelites first arrived in Canaan they—particularly Ephraim—were the most powerful and important of the tribes.

Because of all these factors, and the logistical difficulties of the conventional Exodus story, some have logically concluded that *only* those tribes came out of Egypt, the other nine already being there. This neatly reconciles the "Canaanites only" school's case with the evidence for a genuine connection with Egypt.

The 1962 edition of *Peake's Commentary on the Bible*—a reference work based on the latest scholarship of the time—explains the then-current interpretation:

> It may be gathered from the Blessing of Jacob that Joseph was origi-
> nally, on first entering the land, a single tribe. The two later lists show
> that this large and powerful group (Jos. 17:14) was later on divided into
> two groups, Manasseh being at first the more important of the two;
> ultimately the position was reversed and Ephraim became the leading
> tribe of the Rachel group, a change which is reflected in the story of
> Jacob's blessing the two sons of Joseph (Gen. 48:12–20). It is to this
> group that the tradition of the sojourn in Egypt belongs, and it was
> this group which came up from Egypt, and, under the leadership of
> Joshua, himself an Ephraimite, entered Canaan on the east and set-
> tled in the central part of Canaan, the "hill-country of Ephraim."[34]

In this scenario, originally only Ephraim and Manasseh had the tra-
dition of the sojourn in Egypt, but over time it was extended to all the other tribes, probably because of Ephraim's dominant position.

By the time the monarchy was established, all the ten northern tribes were sometimes referred to as the House of Joseph, reflecting both Ephraim and Manasseh's dominance and the absorption of the others into the tribes' foundation myth. This extended the legend, with its core of historical truth, to the other tribes as well.

Evidently, in the days before the monarchy was set up under the Judahite David, Ephraim was the most powerful and preeminent of the tribes—a status Ephraim was reluctant to surrender. This led to the breakup of the kingdom. The power struggle between Ephraim and Judah runs through Israelite history, even into New Testament times.

We referred to this theory in *The Masks of Christ* as a means of reconciling the apparently contradictory evidence. As it was solely based on reading between the lines of the biblical accounts, it appeared ultimately unprovable, but since then we came across William G. Dever's 2003 *Who Were the Early Israelites and Where Did They Come From?*, which presents archaeological—and other—evidence that backs up the theory considerably.

Dever notes that the "Joseph cycle" of stories in Genesis—believed to be a separate narrative incorporated into Genesis—has many "distinctly Egyptian" elements, and even follows the conventions of Egyptian literature: "Thus while the Joseph Cycle as it now stands may be largely fiction . . . it can be read as providing an actual Egyptian background for some elements in early Israel, however small."[35]

Even more significant is the archaeology. The new settlements that sprang up in the twelfth century BCE are nearly all in the hill country that was the territory of Ephraim and Manasseh—the location of almost all the sites that fit the culture of "proto-Israelites."[36]

Revisiting the story of the Promised Land's conquest in the light of the theory that only Ephraim and Manasseh came from Egypt makes sense of a curious episode at the climax of the book of Joshua—one that even has supporting evidence from archaeology. It is generally described as the "renewal of the covenant," when the league of the twelve tribes was officially established.

The first phase of the conquest complete, Joshua summons the representatives of all the tribes to Shechem and demands they make a choice: either "put away the gods that your fathers served beyond the River [Euphrates] and in Egypt" and commit themselves totally to Yahweh or continue to worship their old gods and earn his wrath. He declares the Ephraimites' loyalty to Yahweh and the others, naturally, also decide to go with Yahweh. Joshua "reaffirms for them the statutes and laws," recording them all in "the Book of the Law of God." He then sets up a "large stone" as a mark of the event.[37] Those who believe that only Ephraim and Manasseh came out of Egypt think the reference to the gods they served in Egypt is merely a post-Ezra revision.

The episode makes no sense. We are told Joshua has led all twelve tribes in a campaign of conquest in Yahweh's name and with the sign of their covenant with him, the Ark, always carried ahead. And yet Joshua has to give them an ultimatum to stop worshipping their old gods! Bearing in mind the sheer exaggeration in the Old Testament, what happens if we reframe this story? What if Joshua and his tribes arrive from outside the land and carry out a much more modest conquest? Then they bring the other tribes—native Canaanites—together and force them to adopt the worship of the new god they have brought with them. Rather than renewing the covenant, where the native tribes are concerned he is *establishing* it. And in imposing Yahweh worship on the Canaanites, the Israelites are also establishing themselves as overlords.

Peake's Commentary presents its interpretation of the episode:

> Joshua is represented as offering the gathered tribes the choice between the cults which they have hitherto followed, that is, the cults of Mesopotamia (v. 15), or the local cults of Canaan, and the cult of Yahweh which the house of Joseph has brought with them into Canaan. . . . The league then make the choice of Yahweh as the God of the united tribes, and the choice is ratified with due ceremonial at the sanctuary of Shechem.[38]

As biblical scholar Walter Rast observes: "It is generally agreed that Joshua 24 contains old traditions about a covenant ceremony at Shechem to which a great deal of Deuteronomic expression has been added."[39] That is to say, the event—which was too well known to be glossed over—has been reinterpreted in terms of what the religion had become five or six centuries later, subsumed into a larger epic of conquest.

Although there have been digs at Shechem on and off in a piece-meal fashion since the 1930s, it was finally excavated properly in 1973 (by a team that included Dever). What had been believed to be a fortress (*migdol*) turned out to be a Canaanite temple dating from around 1650 BCE. It is described in Judges as "the stronghold of the house [temple] of El-Berith,"[40] although it also says it was previously known as Baal-Berith, confirming the archaeology that it was originally a Canaanite holy place, sacred to their god Baal. After a period of disuse, it began to be used again some time between 1400 and 1300 BCE. Then in the 1100s BCE it was extensively altered to include the erection of a large standing stone, which fits the Joshua account.[41]

THE MAGIC BOX

Despite the blind spot of many academics, the more one delves, the more Egyptian the story becomes. For example, the practice of male circumcision that God decrees as a sign of the covenant was a characteristically Egyptian practice—ironically avoided by Canaanites back then.[42]

The Ark of the Covenant, which the Israelites construct to Yahweh's precise specifications almost immediately after their Exodus, also has its nearest equivalents in Egypt. William F. Albright also noted that the Ark of the Covenant and Tabernacle were "completely foreign" to Canaanite culture.[43] Kenneth Kitchen goes further: "The Egyptian quotient in the Exodus narrative, the Tabernacle, and other features demand an Egyptian background."[44]

So where did Moses get the idea of the Ark? Many researchers—although they tend to be from the alternative community—see the similarity between the Ark in Exodus and the portable chests, carried on poles, found in the tombs of Egyptian pharaohs, most famously Tutankhamun's.

Graham Hancock in *The Sign and the Seal* (1992) also drew attention to the "shrines," or rectangular caskets, that contained Tutankhamun's sarcophagus. They were made of wood plated with gold, like the Ark. Hancock writes that "it was difficult to resist the conclusion that the mind that had conceived the Ark of the Covenant must have been familiar with objects like these."[45] Given Moses's Egyptian origins, it is hard not to agree.

Then there are those mysterious creatures, the pair of cherubim that Yahweh decreed be set on top of the Ark, on the "mercy seat" where he would manifest to talk to Moses. Clearly the cherubim are connected with Yahweh's materialization—the "glory" that appears when he descends into the Tabernacle.

Individual cherubs or pairs of cherubim feature elsewhere in the Hebrew Bible. Two or more are posted by God to guard the Tree of Life in Eden. In less mythological territory, cherubim feature heavily in the Temple of Solomon, which replaced the Tabernacle as the focus of worship. They also appear in Ezekiel's visions—he claims to have seen a brace of living cherubim by the Chebar canal in Babylonia during the Exile.

Tantalizingly, these fantastical creatures are never described anywhere in the Hebrew Bible, presumably because everyone already knew what they looked like. Neither is their exact function spelled out, although they are clearly important.

There are some isolated references in the Psalms and the book of Isaiah to God being "enthroned" on (or above) cherubim. One scholar points out that "enthroned over the cherubim" (*yoseb hakkerubim*) is "the constitutive and distinctive title afforded to YHWH in the cult and theology of the First Temple."[46] Yahweh's association with cherubim was important and in some way—now lost to us—actually defining.

The English word comes from the Hebrew *K'rubh* (or *keruv*), which is both singular and plural, but the exact meaning always comes from the context. Nobody knows what it means, but it is generally accepted to derive from the Akkadian *karibu,* describing an intermediary between humans and gods, usually by relaying invocations to heaven. This is most likely given the cherubim's position on the Ark and in the Temple believed to be Yahweh's house.

Like everything on that magic box, the two cherubim on the Ark are made of gold, with their wings spread out to "overshadow" the mercy seat, looking toward each other.[47] Presumably when God manifests on the seat to talk to Moses he appears under their protective wings.

Nowhere does it specify the cherubim's size, but we know the mercy seat is 2.5 cubits long by 1.5 wide—about 4 feet by 2.5 feet. It also depends on whether they were kneeling (as most people think) or standing. Images of the cherubim are also woven into the Tabernacle veil before the Ark, and also the ten curtains that make up the tent. Cherubim are obviously extremely important.

In fact, they are the only figures—divine, human, or animal—featured in the Ark and Tabernacle (and later the Temple). And as their presence blatantly contravenes the second commandment about not making images, later mythmakers would never have dared to invent them. Clearly, they were genuinely ancient, there from the arrival of the Yahweh cult in Canaan—so authentically dating from Moses's time.

But what were the cherubim? Is it possible to make educated guesses about their appearance? All the Bible tells us is that they had faces and wings. Since they could stand they must have had feet too, but we don't know how many.

The usual academic explanation is that they were winged sphinxes—body of a lion, human head, and eagle's wings. Sphinxes were common to many ancient Near Eastern cultures, usually associated with temples or as the guardian deity of kings. Their image is frequently incorporated into seats of power, often labeled "lion thrones."

Of course, sphinxes are most obviously associated with Egypt, although theirs tended not to have wings. Winged sphinxes were very popular in Phoenician iconography, so scholars usually believe that they inspired the Israelite cherubim. But there's a flaw in their argument: They base this on the presence of cherubim in Solomon's Temple—built by Phoenician craftsmen—but that couldn't have applied to the earlier Ark. (As we have seen, most specialists reject the literal truth of the Exodus story, so to them the antiquity and Egyptian influence on the Ark is irrelevant.)

Another problem with the sphinx idea is that all the comparative examples from outside Israel—the lion thrones, for example—date from the tenth century BCE at the earliest (most are two or three centuries later). Again, this might work around the time of Solomon, but not if the Ark really originated with the Exodus.

Various other suggestions have been made—winged bulls, giant birds—but, as the *Theological Dictionary of the Old Testament* concludes, no one candidate fits all the data.[48]

Faced with this conundrum, some, like William Dever, argue that *cherub* is a generic term for a "mixed creature" made up of parts of different animals and humans (rather like "chimera").[49] But a hybrid doesn't really work; if a cherub's exact form could vary, the biblical instructions about making the images should have been more specific.

The other popular candidates for the cherubim are winged deities—human shaped, nearly always female, with wings instead of arms, in the style usually associated with the great Egyptian goddesses Isis and her sister Nephthys. While such images are found in many ancient Near Eastern cultures, they are clearly inspired by Egypt.

Graham Hancock notes that the shrines in Tutankhamun's tomb, referred to above, were decorated with standing winged goddesses thought to be Isis and Nephthys.[50] They are protecting the shrine.

Raphael Patai, who we will meet again in chapter 2, cites an illustration of an ivory plaque excavated from the Ivory House of King Ahab of Israel, who reigned 873–852 BCE, of two winged female figures, kneeling toward each other and holding lotus flowers. They are strikingly like the Egyptian images of Isis and Nephthys. Patai calls this "the closest illustration found to date of the Cherubim."[51]

Today, the cherubim are usually depicted as sacred female figures, as in *Raiders of the Lost Ark* and other fictional and artistic depictions. But given the Bible's scant detail, ultimately it is impossible to know what they looked like, although we are inclined to the theory about winged goddesses—probably Isis. And even the next best candidates, the sphinxes, also point toward Egypt.

Another aspect of the conundrum is that later in Judaism's history—after the destruction of the Temple by the Babylonians, the loss of the Ark of the Covenant, and the reinvention of the religion by Ezra and his peers—the religious leaders became distinctly evasive about the cherubim. Collectively people remembered that they were important in the early days, but a wall of silence rose around any detail about their appearance or precise function. After all, any association not just with the old enemy Egypt, but with Egyptian *goddesses,* would be beyond the pale.

THE MANY GODS OF ISRAEL

If we consult the Bible as the unvarnished truth, we are in for a big disappointment. Of course, the "history" of the Old Testament is pure propaganda. It is deliberately written to support not a political but a religious agenda (although the two are related): to promote the cult of Yahweh—but mainly, one suspects, its priesthood. As the Bible was written so much later it can never be an accurate description of the Israelites' original beliefs—only of the fifth century BCE writers' own, projected back to the peoples' origins.

It might come as a surprise to most Christians and Jews, but scholars overwhelmingly acknowledge that contrary to the impression in the Hebrew Bible and what generations have been led to believe, the ancient Israelites were *not monotheists.* As the Canadian Egyptologist and archaeologist Donald B. Redford writes, "'Mosaic monotheism,' . . . is a will-o-the-wisp. Most scholars would deny that, in the thirteenth century B.C., the traditional time slot for Moses, the Hebrews had approached anywhere near the exalted plane of 'monotheism.'"[52]

It is not so surprising. Monotheism rarely comes naturally, and in the ancient world (with the possible exception of the heretic Egyptian pharaoh Akhenaten, as we will see) it wasn't only unknown but would have been thought absurd.

The ancient Israelites were in fact *monolaters,* focusing their worship on one god—while acknowledging the existence of others. This practice was very common in the ancient world. Temples and shrines were usually dedicated to one particular god in a pantheon, and towns and villages had a patron deity that was the focus of their rites without excluding the veneration of others. Monolatry—favoring one god over all the others—was an extreme version of this.

In fact—another big surprise—despite the post-Exile rewriting, the

Hebrew Bible doesn't pretend otherwise. It is not written from the perspective that Yahweh is the only God, but the only god the people of Israel should worship. The existence of other gods is not just implicitly, but often *explicitly,* acknowledged throughout the early books, as in the Song of the Sea—one of the oldest passages in the Bible—thanking and praising Yahweh for delivering them from the pursuing Egyptians: "Who is like you, LORD, among the gods?"[53]

Throughout the Hebrew Bible, there are many references to other gods (*elim*). But while sometimes apparently they just concern their images, to the ancient world the images *were* the gods. And often the Bible transparently refers to other deities.

Even Yahweh himself, according to the Israelites' sacred texts, portrayed himself as one god among many. After all, the first commandment is: "You shall have no other gods before [or beside] me"[54]—not that there *are* no other gods.

The Bible opens with the words, "In the beginning God created the heavens and the earth." However, the word for "God" is *Elohim,* which, as the *-im* suffix shows, is *plural*—literally "the gods."[55] In fact, Hebrew does permit a plural noun to be applied to an individual but usually only when he, she, or it is understood to be one of a group. So, the first sentence of the Bible could equally validly be translated as "In the beginning *a* god created the heavens and the earth."

Throughout the creation story, God refers to himself in the plural. When he decides to create the first man, Adam, the literal translation is, "Then the *gods* said, 'Let *us* make man in *our* image.'"[56]

Remarkably, there is no explicit statement of Yahweh as the one and only God—as opposed to being the most superior of a whole host of deities—in any of the historical books of the Hebrew Bible. As Simon Schama points out, Isaiah—based on the writings of a prophet who lived in the eighth century BCE, although heavily reworked 300 years later—is the first book of the Bible "to insist unequivocally not just on the supremacy of YHWH but on the exclusiveness of His reality."[57] It has Yahweh declare, "besides me there is no god."[58]

In the episodes about the Israelites turning to the worship of other gods, the issue isn't even that the deities are false, but that they are not the right one. Paul Sanders of the Protestant Theological Seminary in the Netherlands summarizes (his emphasis): "It has been demonstrated that passages in the Hebrew Bible which were traditionally regarded as monotheistic do not aim at refuting the existence of gods beside YHWH. In the first place it is the *veneration* of other gods which they condemn."[59] Sanders adds: "There are some passages in the Hebrew Bible which . . . seem to imply a remarkable recognition of the religions of other peoples. The existence and power of the gods of these peoples seem to be completely acknowledged."[60]

This explains why the worship of other gods became such a threat—precisely because their existence was acknowledged, and even their worship and propitiation accepted up to a point (at least at first).

The Bible's most frequent charge of apostasy was the worship of Baal, whose worshippers are singled out for special opprobrium. Baal could do just as much as Yahweh; he just was not the god to whom the people's ancestors had committed. The problem was not that he was a false god, but that he was a *rival* god. The people should not worship him because they had made a deal to devote themselves to Yahweh alone. It was breaking the covenant, which would bring down Yahweh's wrath. And from the many cautionary tales of plagues and slaughter, they knew what *that* would mean.

To those conditioned to believe that the Israelites were always Yahweh-worshipping monotheists, it gets worse. It is not just that they acknowledged the gods of other peoples were real, but in the Hebrew Bible itself other deities are associated with the God of the Israelites.

On occasions, God (as El) presides over an assembly of other deities—a common feature of Mesopotamian and Syrian mythology. This heavenly court is sometimes called the "sons of God," clearly referring to lesser, or second-level, deities that are considered El's offspring (just as the gods and goddesses of Greece were thought to have been fathered by Zeus and in turn had their own offspring). John

Day, professor of Old Testament studies at Oxford, observes, "Just as an earthly king is supported by a body of courtiers, so Yahweh has a heavenly court. Originally, these were gods, but as monotheism became absolute, so these were demoted to the status of angels."[61]

In some of the books—for example Job—"sons of God" was changed to "angels" in the Greek translation that became the Christian Old Testament, although it is still "sons of God" in the Hebrew version.

Significantly, "God" in the phrase "sons of God" is only ever El, never Yahweh. The sons of God who intermarry with the daughters of men, producing the "heroes of old,"[62] are only a mystery in monotheistic terms. If instead it is "sons of El" then it's just the same as tales of Greek gods and goddesses, offspring of Zeus, who interbreed with mortal men and women and produce heroes such as Hercules.

Psalm 82 describes God (as El) presiding over the "divine council" to give judgment among the gods:

> *I said: "You are gods,*
> *sons of the Most High, all of you;*
> *Nevertheless, like men you shall die,*
> *and fall like any prince."*[63]

The title "Most High"—*Elyon*—stresses El's status as the highest of the gods, which makes sense in the context of an assembly.

In these passages, God is always El. Although in some of the later texts the prophets also speak of Yahweh presiding over assemblies, by then they are just angels—there's no indication they were originally gods in these passages. The prophet Micaiah sees Yahweh surrounded by the "host of heaven," and Isaiah describes them as seraphim.[64] Clearly the concept of God presiding over a heavenly "court" had been transferred to Yahweh, and now that he has become the one and only God, the rest of the host had to be downgraded.

Which raises the question of the relationship between Yahweh and El.

THE SON OF GOD

As we have seen, there are two names for God in the Hebrew Bible, along with several other titles and epithets. He begins as El ("God") but then reveals his new name of Yahweh to Moses.

El was not unique to the Israelites. As chief god of the Canaanites he had been worshipped long before the Israelites arrived on the scene. Yahweh, however, *is* unique to the Israelites, a name unknown previously and unknown to all other peoples of that era. Meindert Dijkstra of Utrecht University comments: "It is still a puzzle that the name and character of YHWH appeared out of the blue in the ancient Near East."[65]

Because references in the early story associate Yahweh with regions to the south of Canaan, the area of Edom and Mounts Sinai and Seir, it is generally thought that his cult originated there. However, that is simply because the stories of the Israelites' Exodus from Egypt, and their subsequent meanderings through foreign wildernesses, are dismissed.

Wherever it came from, his cult was then taken into the land of the Israelites, being established in highland sites such as Shiloh (in Ephraim) and Bethel (in Benjamin), where it seems to have remained for some time before eventually spreading to the rest of Israel.[66]

Clearly, El was important to the early Israelites—after all, they identified themselves by his name, "Israel." But it is equally clear that the change from El to Yahweh was significant to the writers of the Pentateuch. In Genesis God is only ever "El," but after the revelation of the name Yahweh to Moses, that name predominates for the rest of the Old Testament. God is overwhelmingly "Yahweh," although El is still occasionally used. The contexts, however, are revealing—in his role as creator, or when he is presiding over his heavenly court. When the God of the people of Israel is referred to, he is always Yahweh.

In the early books, Yahweh *never* dwells in heaven, although El does. After the building of Solomon's Temple, that is where Yahweh is thought to live—it is literally his house. (The connection between the Tabernacle and Yahweh's physical presence is more ambiguous.)

The names of biblical characters also highlight this shift. Individuals' names often incorporated the name of their god. In the five books of Moses, personal names including "El" are common, but there is only one—Joshua himself—that honors "Yahweh." (*Joshua* means "Yahweh is salvation.") In fact, "El" personal names predominate until the period of the monarchy, after which they become almost exclusively "Yahweh" names.

This suggests that the shift from El to Yahweh really happened, and the Old Testament stories are based on genuinely ancient traditions: if the fifth-century writers had made them up there would be considerably more "Yahweh" names in the early days.

The consensus is that El and Yahweh were originally separate, and were understood as such by the early Israelites, but that at some point the two were amalgamated into one.[67] Exactly when is unclear, but it seems to have happened by the time of the kingdoms of David and Solomon.[68]

The two separate deities make sense given the intermingling of the two cultures. El was worshipped by the Canaanites before the Israelites arrived, whereas the new arrivals brought the previously unknown Yahweh with them.

A likely explanation of the original relationship between the two is provided by the Song of Moses, another of the very early songs that was incorporated, unchanged, into the Hebrew Bible, this one into Deuteronomy. The original song is thought to date from the eleventh century BCE.[69]

One verse in today's Bible relates how God—the "Most High"— divided the human race into nations "according to the number of the sons of Israel" (*bene yisrael*), which makes little sense. However, it does in the earliest known versions found among the Dead Sea Scrolls: "Sons of God" (*bene elohim*). As Paul Sanders, a specialist in the Song of Moses, notes, this verse "does not cast doubt on the power of gods beside YHWH."[70] Which, as we now know, is surprisingly standard. But there's more . . .

In Canaanite mythology, El was believed to have seventy sons. It is a more than reasonable assumption that the same applied to Israelite lore about El. Significantly, as the Bible tells us repeatedly, the Israelites believed that the human race was made up of seventy nations. If so, there would be one nation per son of God, so El's division of humanity among them makes sense. In this light, the exact wording of the Song of Moses is highly significant:

> *When the Most High [Elyon] gave to the nations*
> *their inheritance,*
> *when he divided mankind,*
> *he fixed the borders of the peoples*
> *according to the number of the sons of God [bene*
> *elohim].*
> *But the LORD's [Yahweh's] portion is his people,*
> *Jacob his allotted heritage.*[71]

Again, *Elyon* emphasizes El as the highest of the gods. We can paraphrase this as: "When El, the highest god, divided the human race among his sons, Yahweh's portion was Jacob (i.e., Israel)." In other words, Yahweh was one of El's *sons,* to whom El allotted the people of Israel (and vice versa).

This certainly explains the special relationship, the one-to-one con-nection between God and people that is the whole basis of the Old Testament and of the Israelite religion and its later developments. It explains the sudden switch from El to Yahweh that happens when the latter reveals himself to Moses—as the god of Moses's people—and why El takes a background role afterward. And it explains why, much later, after the two gods were merged into one, "sons of God" had to be changed to "sons of Israel."

So, their relationship was originally father and son. This would have been how the Yahweh cult presented his worship to their fellow Israelites, slotting him into their pantheon and cosmological beliefs. It was unusual in the ancient world for a people to worship the supreme god directly, and anyway, to worship the lesser gods was also to implicitly venerate him.

In their original holy texts, the Israelites considered El the more remote supreme God—the creator of the world and mankind—and Yahweh of the second rank of deities conceptualized as his sons. Later, as the cult of Yahweh—and its priests—became increasingly important, the accounts were rewritten to make El and Yahweh one and the same. But it was no wholesale revision, just amounting to an occasional tweak. The books still distinguished between their roles and spheres of influence.

Seen in this light, originally Yahweh was the god appointed by El to protect the Israelites, in return for their exclusive worship. El would still be the supreme deity but the day-to-day prayers and sacrifices would have focused on Yahweh. The existence of other gods and goddesses would still be recognized, and rites in their honor or for their favor would be acceptable as long as they were less impressive than Yahweh's. Of course the priesthood would have been dedicated to Yahweh.

But as Yahweh's cult was increasingly identified with centralized royal power, it demanded ever-more exclusivity. Other deities—most obviously Baal—were removed, their worship and worshippers condemned, and the highest, El, became ever more remote. Eventually only the worship of Yahweh was acceptable, and at that point El and Yahweh were merged into one. Monolatry became monotheism. We will see how the story unfolds later.

YAHWEH THE EGYPTIAN

Yahweh's iconography—or rather lack of it—is genuinely strange for the time. It is another shift that happens when El "becomes" Yahweh. In Genesis, El is portrayed strictly anthropomorphically. He walks the Garden of Eden in the "cool of the day," so presumably he suffers from the heat. He makes the first man in his image (or rather, *their* image), which apparently includes their size. He appears to the patriarchs as a man, eating and chatting with them, and even has a wrestling match with Jacob.

Yahweh is different. His exact form is a mystery, not to be revealed to mortals. Although he speaks "face to face" with Moses, that is just a figure of speech, as he will only reveal his back to him on Mount Sinai (although even that is an honor), telling him, "you cannot see my face, for man shall not see me and live."[72]

There is also a sense of evasiveness about his name—the name that isn't really a name. While the practice of addressing a deity by an honorific title (as one would a king) was common in the ancient Near East, their real name would also be known. For example, Baal—the Canaanite god who was Yahweh's great rival—also means "Lord," but his real name of Hadad was no secret.[73] The Israelite god was—almost—unique; no one knew his real name.

Even more strangely, unlike other ancient gods, Yahweh has no iconography, no standard image in pictures or statues. There was certainly a prohibition on representing Yahweh visually in the later period covered by the Hebrew Bible (just as there was on saying his name), although some researchers believe he was originally depicted as a man on a throne.[74] But as that was the Canaanite representation of El, it might be the result of confusion between the two deities.

There is more evidence that Yahweh was represented symbolically as a standing stone or pillar (*massebot*), such as the one erected by Joshua at Shechem. There are several references to stone pillars in holy places before the building of the Jerusalem Temple, but their purpose and function are never explained, although they are clearly religious. Some think that is how the early Israelites represented Yahweh, though it escaped the Bible writers' censorship as by their day this particular example of *aniconism*—depicting a deity as a natural object—had long since ceased to have any meaning. Even if the *massebot* did represent Yahweh, it was still rare not to also use a more specific human—or animal-shaped—image.

Despite certain similarities with Baal—although there are major differences too, as Baal was also a dying-and-rising fertility god—unlike El, Yahweh can never easily be associated with any of the Canaanite gods or indeed the gods of any of the surrounding peoples. So where did he come from?

There is a well-known theory that links the Israelites with Akhenaten, the weird "heretic pharaoh" who established a revolutionary new religion based on the worship of a single god, overthrowing the traditional polytheistic religions of ancient Egypt and setting up what is often described as the world's first monotheistic religion.

Akhenaten ascended the Egyptian throne as Amenhotep IV in the mid-1350s BCE and ruled for seventeen years. Five years into his reign he changed his name to Akhenaten, in honor of the god Aten, establishing his worship as the official religion. He also founded a new city and cult center, Akhetaten, better known today as Amarna—hence Akhenaten's reign being called the "Amarna period."

Aten—meaning "disk"—was originally an aspect of the sun god Ra but Akhenaten, for reasons lost to history, came to consider Aten not only as a separate god but elevated its worship to the exclusion of all others. Breaking with the traditional iconography of the ancient religion, he had Aten depicted solely as the sun disk, with its life-giving rays ending in hands. Aniconically, in other words.

Over the course of his reign Akhenaten pursued a policy—starting gradually but gathering momentum—of eradicating the cults of the other gods (particularly the dominant one of Amun-Ra) and focusing totally on the Aten. The priesthoods of other gods were summarily closed down. None of this was popular, to say the least. The people wanted—perhaps needed—their many gods and goddesses.

After Akhenaten's death, the old cults, particularly that of Amun-Ra, staged a comeback under his young (and controllable) son Tutankhamun: depictions of Akhenaten and the Aten-disk being vandalized in an attempt to eradicate him and his works from history.

When Egyptologists discovered the existence of Akhenaten and his sun religion in the 1890s through excavations at Amarna, the realization that an apparently monotheistic religion had been established so close in time to the origins of the Israelites—Akhenaten must have reigned little more than a century before the Exodus—proved too great a temptation. Suddenly academia was awash with theories linking the ancient Israelites to the heretic pharaoh. The theory still has its champions, such as Robert Feather, author of a series of books on the origins of the Israelite religion among refugee Aten-worshippers fleeing the backlash against Akhenaten, and the influence of Atenism throughout Israelite history, from Moses to the Dead Sea Scrolls.

To the pious Victorians and Edwardians who rediscovered Akhenaten, it was self-evident that monotheism was the pinnacle of civilized religion. After all, it was the backbone of their Christian civilization, which was, of course, to them self-evidently the best the world had ever seen. To them, religious thinking evolved from primitive to civilized, beginning with animism (a "simplistic" belief in nature spirits) and progressing through polytheism to the sophistication of monotheism.

However, that model of progress is increasingly seen as outmoded and just plain wrong, both morally and factually. Modern disciplines such as anthropology no longer see religious thinking in such neatly defined categories.

The once-precise definition of monotheism has become clouded, and the line between it and polytheism blurred. There is monolatry, which looks very like monotheism if seen without any historical context. And religions categorized as polytheistic often regard the different gods and goddesses as manifestations of a single creator-god—for example that of Heliopolis, the religion of *very* ancient Egypt—so could be seen paradoxically as essentially monotheistic.

But was Akhenaten's Aten-worship true monotheism, or was it a form of monolatry? Sadly, no one knows enough about the theology to be sure. A major stumbling block to the theory that Yahweh began as the Aten is that he was never depicted as the sun disk.

The German-born American professor of history of religions Karl Luckert, though, in his 1991 *Egyptian Light and Hebrew Fire*— developing an idea of celebrated German Egyptologist Kurt Sethe— points out the similarities between Yahweh and another Egyptian deity.

Ironically, this was the one whose worship Akhenaten set out to destroy, and that had gone underground during the Amarna years: Amun.

Although Amun had been included in the Egyptian pantheon since the earliest times, his cult was established as the official religion by Ahmoses I, founder of the Eighteenth Dynasty around 1550 BCE, who ruled from Thebes, Amun's cult center for over a thousand years. When it was state sanctioned, Amun was equated with Ra, hence Amun-Ra, and his theology and iconography evolved significantly.

Suppressed during the Akhenaten years, the cult quickly reestablished itself after his death, which is why his son Tutankhaten was renamed Tutankh*amun*. (Akhenaten began his reign as an Amun-worshipper— his original name of Amenhotep meant "Amun is satisfied.")

"Amun" derives from *imn,* meaning "hidden" or "invisible," making it not really a name at all, more an attempt to *conceal* the god's true name and identity. When his worship became the pharaonic cult, this became an important aspect. In one text, in the collection of the Leiden Papyrological Institute, he is called "he who hides his name from the gods."[75]

The Amun cult believed that not only must his name remain secret, but that anyone who did discover it—and, worse, actually utter it—would instantly die. A similar concept lies behind the concept of the Hebrew Tetragrammaton, Yahweh's secret name that must never be spoken.

There is a famous story from the Nineteenth Dynasty (1350–1200 BCE), where the guileful goddess Isis tricks Amun into revealing his true name, becoming the only deity who knows it, although she swears to keep it to herself.[76] (Interestingly, when he tries to distract her by giving her other names, one of them is "Aten.") Clearly, this concept of a god's true name being hidden—and being death to pronounce—is characteristically Egyptian. Yet more evidence that Yahweh originated in Egypt, whether or not Luckert's Amun theory is correct.

Although traditionally depicted similarly to the other gods of Egypt—in human form, crowned with a plumed crown and holding an ankh and scepter—the idea took hold that this was not Amun's *true* form, which was altogether more mysterious: "his form is unknown, that beautiful shimmering (hue of) color which has become a beautiful but secret form."[77]

And so says the Leiden Papyri:

> One is Amon, hiding himself from them, concealing himself from the (other) gods, so that his (very) color is unknown . . . no gods know his true form. His image is not displayed in writings. No one bears witness to him. . . . He is too mysterious that his majesty might be disclosed, he is too great that (man) should ask about him, too powerful that he might be known. Instantly (one) falls in a death of violence at the utterance of his mysterious name, unwittingly or wittingly.[78]

As Luckert summarizes: "The godhead's hiddenness, together with the obscurity of his name and his general compassionate interest in human affairs, at every stratum of human history, is highlighted by a number of characteristics that scholars customarily reserved for Yahweh of the Hebrews."[79]

Although a public cult, there was also great secrecy surrounding Amun's temple rituals. His image was hidden in a concealed part of the temple, off-limits to everyone except the high priest. It was kept in a "closed shrine" when carried aloft in solemn procession.[80] Inevitably this recollects the Holy of Holies in the Tabernacle and Temple, which only the high priest could enter, and the Ark of the Covenant, which also carried sacred objects hidden from the sight of all but the high priest. Even the Ark itself was covered when carried in public.

Akhenaten's famous Hymn to Aten—which many have seen paralleled in Psalm 104—in fact used similar language to the inscriptions on stelae praising Amun, so it is possible *they* were the inspiration for the psalm.

Amun gradually subsumed the attributes and roles of other deities, to the point that some consider his religion effectively monotheistic.[81] And as Luckert points out, as an Egyptian prince, inevitably Moses would have been familiar with the Amun cult and its theology.

But, just as there are striking parallels between the "hidden" deities Amun and Yahweh, there are some glaring differences. Most notably, Amun was associated with water and the breath of life, whereas Yahweh was a god of deserts, fire, and storms. Indeed, Amun was the *calmer* of storms. Luckert suggests that, because of the differing environments of the Nile Valley and the Arabian desert, Amun became associated with another Egyptian deity, Set (or Seth). The combining and recombining of gods was, of course, something of an Egyptian specialty.

Although today Set is often thought of as the ancient Egyptian equivalent of Satan, he was an integral part of their pantheon and his worship was perfectly legitimate. He had his own temples and priesthood, and pharaohs took his name (Seti) just as they did others'. And we know Set was included in the Amun cult's pantheon. To the Egyptians, Set was the god of deserts, storms, and foreigners, which would certainly make the ancient Israelites Set's people in Egyptian eyes. Alternatively, the desert aspects of Yahweh could have been picked up when living among the Midianites—after all, Moses was said to be the son-in-law of their priest.

Luckert's proposal—though, like all theories about Israelite origins, it's ultimately unprovable—is that the Yahweh cult began as a religious innovation by Moses, with his "twofold Hebrew-Egyptian mind."[82] Perhaps it was a melding together of religious beliefs he learned in the desert of Midian with the Amun cult, then in its heyday in Egypt.

It may not be either/or: All these Egyptian gods—and even the Canaanite versions—may have played a part in creating Yahweh. In Ramesside Egypt Set was also identified with Baal, under the composite name Sutekh-Baal. Willliam F. Albright suggested that the cults of Amun-Ra, Aten, and Sutekh-Baal influenced Moses's thinking.[83]

As Luckert emphasizes: "Even though the Exodus religion historically and foremostly represents a reaction against Egyptian civilization, . . . its theological tenets nevertheless come into better view when they are seen as having emerged from that same civilization."[84]

In particular, Luckert sees the Egyptians behind the Hebrew

creation myth, with God using magical words of command (through the agency of his "Spirit," which we'll come to later in this book); it has much more in common with the creation stories of the Egyptian Heliopolitan cult than it does with Canaanite or Semitic myths.

Now we see that whatever the minimalists—and, many not-so-minimalists—allege, there is a genuine Egyptian core to the whole story: Moses, the Ark of the Covenant, the Egyptian names of the priests who are its custodians—and even apparently Yahweh himself.

Behind it all is the fact that the religion of the ancient Israelites was *not* monotheistic. It became so later—and the Hebrew Bible was later rewritten to make it solely about Yahweh, after the discovery of the lost Book of the Law in 621 BCE, initiating a revision that would end with Ezra and Nehemiah nearly two centuries later. The "discovery" is, of course, highly suspicious. It's much more likely that the scroll was the handiwork of later reformers who planted it.

But as Simon Schama puts it (his emphasis): "The truth was that it was the fierce 'Yahweh Alone' book-fixed monotheism that was the novelty. . . . But the Ezra-Nehemiah exclusivism now held co-religionists to a higher stricter standard, and they presented their version of YHWH worship as having *always* been that demanding, even though this was historically not the case."[85]

In other words, it was the "backsliding" condemned throughout the Old Testament that was once the conventional Israelite religion—but history was rewritten. But as John Day comments: "Yahweh was very much the chief god in ancient Israel, and the other gods and goddesses would have been worshipped as part of his pantheon."[86]

"Gods and *goddesses* . . ." Not only was the Old Testament revised to present a "Yahweh-alone" version of events, with the obscuring and erasing of other gods, but some of those abandoned deities were *female* . . .

2

The Divine Consort

In 1967 a remarkable, ground-breaking book by the Hungarian-born American professor of anthropology Raphael Patai was published. *The Hebrew Goddess* presented landmark evidence for female forms of the divine—what is now known as the sacred feminine—in various Judaic traditions. Soberly and factually, it set out to show that, despite the traditional presentation of the Jewish God as unwaveringly, even aggressively, male, the expression of female divinity had always been present—in various forms, some more obvious than others—in Judaism. Appearing in the heyday of the 1960s' counterculture (although Patai himself was conventional enough), *The Hebrew Goddess* synchronistically arrived at the right moment, helping to open the way for Jewish women to find a place in a faith where men had, it seemed, always been the sole voice of authority. Sadly, however, the average female synagogue worshipper remained ignorant of this exciting spiritual potential, as did mainstream Christians and the wider world.

Although concentrating on Judaism from the last centuries BCE to the Middle Ages, Patai's book opened with the status of *goddesses* in ancient Israel and the era of the kingdoms—a startling, often even shocking concept in the '60s, and one that still has the potential to unsettle even now. Since then, however, many of his conclusions and speculations, based on a close reading of the Hebrew Bible and comparisons to other religions, have been vindicated by archaeological and other discoveries. We personally owe him a great debt, for he opened our eyes to what is, of course, to most believers, a complete shake-up of Jewish religious history. But *goddesses—in Judaism?*

One of the first readers of *The Hebrew Goddess* as a student was William Dever, who found it utterly compelling. But as the Harvard establishment united to dismiss Patai's work, Dever was advised not to waste his time on it. Since then Dever has risen to become one of the world's top biblical archaeologists—and his own discoveries have confirmed much of Patai's academic "heresy." Dever writes that Patai's book was "30 years ahead of anything else on our subject," and later, "the new archaeological data that I present . . . only confirm what Patai knew all along about the existence of a Hebrew 'Goddess.'"[1]

This was obviously potentially explosive stuff, but—as frequently happens with radical challenges to the academic Establishment—at the time it sank almost without trace. Few other biblical scholars or archaeologists acknowledged Patai's prescience. He is rarely mentioned, even today.

Yet, as we hope to prove, not only was Patai spot on about the very existence of a Hebrew goddess, but that she also had a thriving, proud priesthood dedicated solely to her worship.

THE JEALOUS GOD

In the Hebrew Bible, when discussing the Israelites' "backsliding" to the worship of other gods, the word *asherah* occurs some forty times, sometimes in conjunction with Baal. Clearly this refers to a deity at the center of some highly dubious cult, at least as far as the writers were concerned. A feminine noun, sometimes it appears to refer to an object, often in the plural, *asherim,* and sometimes seems to be simply a female name, but always it's intimately associated with devotion, even adoration, of a forbidden sort. It's not a huge leap to conclude that *asherah* was a feminine deity, and one who was worshipped by "heretics" in ancient Israel. Of course, the implications are immense, both for the history of Judaism but also the roots of Christianity. And the questions just keep on coming.

Was this Asherah really a Hebrew *goddess?* Was her cult truly, as the Bible makes out, heretical? Or are the books of the Old Testament really covering up some secret revelations about the sacred feminine? And what relationship, if any, did this Asherah have with that most male of gods, Yahweh? Piecing together the evidence, often tiny bit by tiny bit, she emerges as a startlingly important lady.

The first mention of her in the Hebrew Bible is in Exodus, when Yahweh makes his covenant with Moses on Mount Sinai. God commands the Israelites that when he's driven the Canaanites out of the Promised Land, "You shall tear down their altars and break their pillars and cut down their Asherim (for you shall worship no other god, for the LORD, whose name is Jealous, is a jealous God)."[2] Cutting down "Asherahs" implies she was symbolized as objects.

Similar injunctions appear in Deuteronomy, the final laying down of the Law, allegedly by Moses, including one not to "plant any tree as an Asherah beside the altar of the LORD that you shall make."[3] So an Asherah is, or can be, a tree. The fact that such a practice had to be prohibited suggests that setting up an Asherah tree next to altars to Yahweh was a popular tradition. Already a rather different picture is emerging: worship of Asherah trees was obviously much more widespread than the Bible would have us believe—and seemingly lasted for considerably longer.

As we now know that these books were composed much later, following the "discovery"—or rather invention—of the "lost" Book of the Law, or Deuteronomy, in 621 BCE, the warnings must relate to the situation as it was at *that* time. Clearly, Asherah, whoever she was, was a threat to the "Yahweh alone" movement—his influential hardcore devotees—as late as King Josiah's day. As William Dever asks rhetorically (his emphasis), "why would later reforming priests and prophets condemn these things so vociferously *unless they remained popular* in Israelite religion?"[4] Authorities are rarely "vociferous"—or even aggressive—toward a movement unless they're afraid it is a threat to their control of the people.

But why are we only discovering the truth about Asherah worship now? Why has it taken millennia for the Hebrew goddess to be acknowledged?

When the Hebrew Bible was first translated into Greek, Latin, and English the meaning of the word *asherah* was unknown. Because of its association with sacred places and trees, the second-century BCE Greek Septuagint translated *asherim* as "groves," which passed into the Latin Vulgate and then into other translations such as the King James Version—and onward into every Protestant denomination. As far as the average churchgoer was concerned, if they even noticed the relevant passages, they shrugged them off. Who cares about some weird tree fixation from so long ago? And there the matter rested for over 2,000 years.

The puzzle was finally solved in 1929, during excavations of the ancient Canaanite city of Ugarit—modern Ras Shamra—on Syria's Mediterranean coast. In the ruins of the Temples of El and Baal they unearthed hundreds of clay tablets dating from the fourteenth century BCE that depicted their myths. Naturally many of them referred to the Canaanites' supreme god, El, but there was something else, something potentially quite astounding . . . a previously unknown goddess appeared alongside the great god El: Asherah, the supreme female deity of all Canaanite deities.

So far from being literally made of leafy stuff, *asherah* turns out to be that most unexpected of beings, a Canaanite goddess. Her existence certainly explains the Bible's charges of apostasy back in the old days, while there were pockets of Canaanites still around. And it explains why she was paired with Baal, and why the Hebrew Bible repeatedly warns the Israelites off her worship, just as it did with Baal's.

However, as in any detailed historical investigation, it's not quite so simple. As we've seen, before the later reformers rewrote history, the ancient Israelites worshipped several deities. That was quite normal back then. So was Asherah veneration not an aberration after all, but originally an everyday, deeply embedded part of the Israelites' religion? After all, although devoted to Yahweh the people also venerated the supreme god El, and since to the Canaanites Asherah is El's wife, it makes sense that she was also goddess supreme to the Israelites.

In fact, as Patai notes: "In view of the general human, psychologically determined predisposition to believe in and worship goddesses, it would be strange if the Hebrew-Jewish religion, which flourished for centuries in a region of intensive goddess cults, had remained immune to them."[5] Strange indeed—but perhaps not as strange as the later goddess-free Jewish and Christian traditions, although as we will see, the sacred feminine never truly abandoned them.

The way the Hebrew Bible deals with Asherah is telling. First, the invective against her worship was aimed at the people of Judah at the time of the later religious reforms—it was a current problem for the Yahwists, not one from the dim and distant past—so clearly the worship of Asherah, if it had been absorbed from the Canaanites back in the day, had simply not gone away.

More unexpectedly, unlike the Baal cult, which was universally condemned, the veneration of Asherah is handled ambiguously. Although some of the books implicitly condemn her and her rites, usually by association with Baal, the condemnation is never spelled out. The attitude of other books is much more relaxed. The prophets Elijah, Elisha, and Jehu, while stridently against the Baal cult, never so much as mention Asherah. In fact, as Saul M. Olyan, author of *Asherah and the Cult of Yahweh in Israel* (1988) comments: "This is indeed striking. The evidence suggests that no prophet . . . opposed the asherah, except for those subject to the deuteronomistic influence."[6] He argues that the anti-Asherah passages are the most characteristic of the "Deuteronomists"—the hardline "Yahweh alone" faction. For the writers not under heavy Deuteronomistic influence "the cult symbol was not considered illegitimate or non-Yahwistic."[7] No Asherah trees for the Deuteronomists, but for everyone else, as Mark S. Smith observes, "it would appear that the symbol of the Asherah was a general feature of Israelite religion."[8]

Yet history was shamelessly rewritten to have posterity—including all of us—believe the worship of Asherah never even happened. In that, the patriarchs were scandalously successful. Until now.

MOTHER OF THE GODS

Having discovered her existence, details of Asherah are disappointingly thin on the ground. All the Old Testament tells us, from its grimly Deuteronomistic high ground, is that she was a goddess and had some connection with trees.

Even the roots of her main name are uncertain, but another of her names, as given in the Ugarit texts, *Qudsh* or *Qudshu*, means "holy" or "sanctuary." Emotionally and spiritually, of course, this idea of a holy haven fits precisely with the idea of a *mother* goddess, provider of a safe place and a warm embrace in times of trouble. In the Bible she's only ever "Asherah," the name Qudshu never appearing—although, as we will see, it may lurk between the lines, revealing a potentially quite sensational aspect of the Asherah cult in Israel. But what else can we know about this tantalizingly important goddess?

She is consort of the high god El, and as such is "Mother of the Gods." Her other titles include "Lady of the Sea," being particularly venerated in the seaports of Sidon and Tyre. These honorifics encompass all the many faces of a cosmic goddess. Another frequent epithet was "the Lion Lady," her children being her "pride of lions." And lions are not known for their stay-at-home timidity.

Asherah was also there at the beginning of all things, the feminine hand in genesis, known as "the creatress of the gods." She was involved with El in the creation of the first man, rather curiously "not by physical interaction, but by way of a mental process in which the god and the goddess both participated."[9]

Like all ancient deities, Asherah had several aspects and roles.

Most often she was depicted as an elderly lady, a matriarch—the goddess, as modern pagans would say, in her crone phase. She influenced her husband El through her powers of persuasion, petitioning him on behalf of the other gods (though sometimes "depicted as a power-hungry woman who manipulates the heavenly court"[10]). She's effectively co-ruler of the heavenly realm. Significantly, as we will see, this side of Asherah is connected with the role of earthly queen mothers—that is, the mothers of monarchs.

In another of her divine aspects, an obviously younger Asherah was also a fertility goddess, ruling over both sexuality and motherhood. Even when not being referenced for her sexiness, as we see in *Only One God?* edited by Bob Becking and Meindert Dijkstra, she is still associated with the erotic:

> She is said to have given birth to 70 sons and has the characteristics of a *dea nutrix,* that is, a goddess seen as wet-nurse of gods and men. This implies that she not only is an eroticizing goddess of fertility playing an important role in the religion of the vegetation, but also and sometimes foremost a caring and protecting deity. In various texts her breasts and nipples are mentioned, not with a sexual connotation, but as metaphor for her divine care.[11]

Early peoples had none of the recent West's shock or coyness around women's bodies. Canaanite figurines from the fifteenth–twelfth centuries BCE, showing a female form with emphasized breasts and pubic triangle, sometimes riding a lion or horse, have been identified as Asherah. More accurately, they represent her as Qudshu, basically her sexy, rather than matriarchal, mode. Clearly, her all-round inclusivity would naturally appeal to her female worshippers, especially given their difficult, circumscribed lives with little hope of independence or opportunity to have their voices heard—or even for being taken seriously as individuals. Asherah was not only the deity to whom they prayed and sacrificed, but must also, in their quiet hearts, have provided a rare permissible role model. And for most of her reign, what a role model she must have been . . .

Unlike the much later Virgin Mary, she was a *complete* archetype, to whom ordinary women with complicated love lives or messy domestic situations, health concerns, and anxieties, could turn and feel that the goddess would empathize with them. She would not judge them for being "sinful," nor set impossible standards to follow.

Unsurprisingly, the Ugarit texts and Asherah's other names, titles, and iconography, reveal that she was hugely popular across the ancient Near East, from Egypt to Mesopotamia, often being assimilated with other goddesses with similar aspects. In Egypt she was one of many imported Canaanite deities, such as Baal, who were worshipped during the New Kingdom (1550–1070 BCE). There she was called Qudshu or *Qadesh*—her alternative name in the Ugarit texts, meaning "the Holy One"—a fertility goddess associated with sexual ecstasy. Egyptian depictions show her naked, standing astride a lion. Both Egyptian and Canaanite texts associate Asherah, under her name of Qadesh, with the much-beloved goddess Hathor. Traditionally, Hathor—with her strokeable cow's ears—embodied the more obviously nurturing aspect of goddesshood, while Asherah, though also motherly, could be feisty, even militant.

The famous Egyptian artifact known as the Triple Goddess Stone, which was in the collection of the Treasury of Winchester College, England, until it was stolen in the 1960s, shows a figure with the typical iconography of Qudshu but with the inscription "Qudshu-Astarte-Anat," revealing her melding with two other major goddesses.

There are worse goddesses to be linked with than Astarte. The famous alabaster statue now in the Louvre Museum, Paris, depicts a softly voluptuous figure and huge mesmerizing eyes made of semiprecious stones. Apart from her crown in the form of the crescent moon, and some metallic jewelry, she is naked. The overwhelming impression is one of stunning beauty, the exquisite work of art being created by an adoring worshipper. Astarte was very popular in most cultures in the ancient Near East, particularly in seaports, where she was the original model for figureheads on sailing boats. She is mentioned in the Hebrew Bible—nine times, in fact, but under the name Ashteroth.

In view of Karl Luckert's theory that Yahweh was modeled on the Egyptian god Amun, it is intriguing that the latter had a wife, Mut, whose titles also included "Lady of Heaven" and "Mother of the Gods." She too was a lioness deity, the Upper Egyptian counterpart of the famous half-human, half-lioness goddess Sekhmet, divine female embodiment of war, vengeance, and, conversely, healing. Sekhmet was loved and feared in equal measure by her multitude of worshippers. Mut is considered the sister of Sekhmet, as well as Hathor. Mut was obviously seen as the ultimate role model for female empowerment, as her temple at Karnak was the only one run solely by priestesses.

GOD'S OTHER HALF

Asherah's iconography, alternative names, and titles in Canaanite myths help us understand her place in Israelite religion. They take us that telling bit closer to the mysterious "Asherim" in the Bible. An Asherah could be a living tree planted in her sanctuary, perhaps in an indoor shrine or temple. Or it could just be a stylized tree in the shape of a wooden pole. Seemingly, there are a few references to a wooden image of the goddess herself—for example, in the second book of Kings, "the carved image of Asherah."[12]

The Bible frequently associates the Asherah tree with a pillar or standing stone. Interestingly, in early Israel Yahweh himself was represented in aniconic—purely symbolic, not representational—form by a standing stone. But Asherah trees were rarely far away. Saul Olyan explains an unexpected link: "The patriarchal narratives of cult founding at Bethel, Hebron and Beersheba indicate that the sacred tree and the pillar (*masseba*) were legitimate in the Yahwistic cult early on. . . . Even in the texts of the Deuteronomistic History relating the events of the monarchic period, we find evidence that the asherah was associated not with Baal but with the cult of Yahweh."[13]

So Asherah trees stood beside Yahweh pillars. At the very least, they were thought of as particularly close. Significantly, the second commandment's prohibition on making "graven images" also applied to the goddess. No statues of Yahweh were allowed, but neither were statues of Asherah, making her a rare female deity in that era. Unlike the exquisite statue of Astarte, we have disappointingly little visual imagery of the Hebrew goddess.

It is possible to reconstruct Asherah's relationship with Yahweh and his people, though some clues are well hidden and most have to be inferred. We recall the "renewal" of the covenant by Joshua at the holy site of Shechem after the conquest of the Promised Land. If we are right, this was really about the newly arrived tribes asserting their authority over the local people by compelling them to adopt the new god they had brought with them, Yahweh, as their patron. They were *not* insisting that the other tribes *replace* their gods with Yahweh, but that they incorporate him into their religion in a respectfully prominent way.

The event was symbolized by Joshua erecting a pillar close by a terebinth tree—which by implication was considered sacred. As the tree represented Asherah, Joshua's act was neatly symbolic of the installation of Yahweh into the native Canaanite tribes of Israel. The tree was already there; the stone was new. This would explain the later descriptions of pillars and trees set up side by side.

Coming to the realization that Asherah was a bona fide Israelite deity, evidence for her worship rapidly accumulates. There are the "pillar-base" figurines, small terra-cotta female figures with emphasized breasts that have been excavated in large numbers from the 1920s onward, identified as representations of Asherah. Over 2,700 have been found, 400 in Jerusalem alone. Most are from the eighth and seventh centuries BCE, in the period of the monarchies.

They are "pillar-base" because the lower half of the body merges with a column or stand. So although the breasts are emphasized, her hips, genitalia, and legs are not even represented, presumably as they're irrelevant. This Asherah is very much a nursing mother, focusing on fertility and the nurturing of children—and therefore very much centered on the family. Nearly all of these pillar-base statuettes were found in domestic settings, clearly part of the daily devotions of the ordinary folk—as charms, talismans, or votive offerings for family blessings. No similar male statuettes have ever been found.

An earlier genre of figurines, although much fewer and dating from the tenth and ninth centuries BCE, are more obviously sexual. They depict a nude woman with a hair style—or wig—reminiscent of the Egyptian goddess Hathor; unashamedly, Asherah in her Qadesh persona.

But what exactly was Asherah's relationship with Yahweh? As more and more evidence came to light, from deeper analysis of the Hebrew Bible and archaeology, something that would have once been unthinkable became only too clear, as Mark S. Smith points out, "the evidence would suggest that Asherah was a goddess venerated in the Jerusalem temple devoted to Yahweh and was therefore regarded as his consort."[14] That should hardly surprise us. As all deities in the ancient Near East were paired, Yahweh should be no exception. Yet so conditioned are we in the West to think of Yahweh as a stern Father with no companion—and certainly no equal—the revelation that *God had a wife and she was worshipped beside him in the great Jerusalem Temple* still has the power to rock old certainties on their very foundations.

While no one is suggesting that academics actively schemed to prevent this rather important fact about Yahweh becoming widely known, it was effectively kept under wraps by their very reluctance to discuss it. They had no wish to give it the oxygen of publicity. After all, it was *sensational,* and scholars are never happy with seismic revelations. They just can't cope, especially if it means overturning decades, even centuries of accepted wisdom. In fact, the first book proposing that Asherah was Yahweh's consort was published as far back as 1949—W. L. Reed's *The Asherah in the Old Testament*—but who knew?

It was only in the 1980s that God's relationship with Asherah began to be seriously explored—and even then almost exclusively in the rarified world of academe—when key pieces of the jigsaw finally fell into place. The picture has become even clearer in the decades since, but still, who knew?

A BOMBSHELL AND AFTER

A major piece of the puzzle—William Dever calls it a "bombshell"[15]—that made sense of the various symbols attached to Asherah arrived with something of a bang in the 1980s. And it came not from a university researcher but from Ruth Hestrin, curator of the Israel Museum in Jerusalem. Despite her position, because of her nonacademic status Hestrin soon found no one was interested in publishing her hypothesis, let alone taking her seriously. It was an enormously frustrating time. Then she approached Dever, who saw its importance immediately and was instrumental in getting it published in the *Israel Exploration Journal* in 1987. The discovery is now accepted and features prominently in scholarly discussions of Asherah's place in Israelite religion—but scandalously Ruth Hestrin's name is rarely even mentioned.

Hestrin began by observing that Canaanite art frequently shows two wild goats or ibexes, standing on their hind legs and nibbling on the lower branches of a tree. The scene also appears on a ewer, or dedicatory vase, found in the ruins of a temple in the city of Lachish. (Although Lachish became an important city of Judah, the temple and these artifacts are from an earlier time when it was under Canaanite control, before the twelfth century BCE.) The ewer contained a mutton bone and was inscribed "An offering for my Lady Elat." Elat is a feminine form of El.

This is quite something. Clearly, as her name suggests, Elat is El's other half and therefore *equals* the supreme, male being. And it gets better (or worse, depending on your attitude to such matters): Elat is one of *Asherah's* names in the Ugarit texts. Hestrin realized the Canaanites' tree-and-goat image was therefore a symbol of Asherah.

Hestrin also noticed that a goblet found in Lachish bears the image of the two goats but has a pubic triangle in place of the tree, indicating, in Dever's words, that "the pubic triangle—symbol from time immemorial of the source of all human conception, birth, and life—and the tree were interchangeable."[16]

Hestrin also knew that Late Bronze Age Canaanite pendants, made of electrum, showed Asherah in a highly stylized way, reduced simply to her head—with Hathor wig—prominent breasts and vulva. But in direct contrast to today, when reducing a woman's image to just her erogenous areas would be considered highly offensive, in ancient cultures omitting the rest of her body—curves and legs especially—was *desexualizing* her by focusing on her reproductive and nursing roles. The important issue for Hestrin, however, was that these pendants show the stylized tree rising up from the vulva.

Finally, Hestrin found Egyptian wall paintings from the second millennium BCE that depict a tree from which a hand emerges to offer a breast to a nursing child. (One of these showed the pharaoh Thutmose III as a child.)

What Hestrin had put together was a whole complex of imagery from Canaan and Egypt where a stylized tree symbolized fertility and nourishment: life, in other words. And it was a symbol of Asherah as the Great Mother. This explains why she had become a tree in Israelite sanctuaries and temples. But what makes Hestrin's discovery even more relevant is that the same image of the tree with goats also appears in *Israel,* although before her revelation nobody realized it related to Asherah. Now it is recognized, it sheds important light on discoveries at Israelite sites.

Archaeological evidence of the early Israelites' Asherah worship is hard to come by—but if her cult images were made of wood, which would naturally decompose over the years and be lost to history, that's hardly surprising. One significant find, though, is the "Taanach cult stand," now in the Israel Museum.

This was discovered at Taanach—modern Ti'inik on the West

Bank—one of the cities given to the Levites, therefore a Yahweh cult and major administrative center. The stand is from the tenth century BCE and is basically a fancy terra-cotta table or pedestal about three feet tall, for displaying ritual objects. It comprises four very crudely decorated tiers, or registers, each showing a different scene and imagery—some of which clearly relates to Asherah.

The second register down shows the highly stylized tree with the rampant goats nibbling at the leaves that was identified by Ruth Hestrin as Asherah imagery. The bottom register shows a naked woman with Hathor-style hair and pointed breasts flanked by two angry-looking lions, in the Egyptian Qadesh tradition. As the leading American Bible scholar Susan Ackerman comments, this is "a cult object permeated with the imagery of Asherah."[17] Judith M. Hadley in her *Cult of Asherah in Ancient Israel and Judah* (2000) goes further: The Taanach stand "not only indicates that Asherah was worshipped at this Israelite site, but that she was also closely associated with Yahweh and his cult."[18]

The stylized tree in the Israelite and Canaanite images is generally identified as a date palm, found in sandy soil in lower, drier areas, and in the Bible Asherah is also represented by a terebinth tree, found in forests and on hills. She was worshipped up high and down low, all over the land.

Trees—especially in arid parts of the world—with their lush leaves and abundant seasonal fruits are obvious signs of fertility and vibrant new life. The date palm produces bunches of succulent fruit, and the terebinth, although not yielding anything edible, explodes in clusters of vital red blossoms every spring. Relaxing in the welcome shade of a tree after the toil of the hot day would be balm to the soul, an apt reflection of a mother's welcome home from work.

However, the palm-tree-and-goat image is also found on another highly significant archaeological discovery—associated with inscriptions that graphically demonstrate the Israelites' belief about Asherah's relationship with Yahweh.

The first was discovered in 1968 by William Dever in tombs at

Khirbet el-Qom near Hebron in the West Bank, once part of ancient Judah. He published a translation the following year, but it made little impact until much later—well into the 1980s. The inscription, dating from between 750 and 700 BCE, is dedicated to one Uriyahu "the Wealthy" and reads: "Blessed be Uriyahu by YHWH and more than his enemies by his Asherah." The phrase "YHWH and his Asherah" is repeated later in the inscription.[19]

Another significant site is Kuntillet Ajrud, on the border of the Negev and Sinai, and was an eighth-century BCE hilltop way station on a desert trade route. Some, such as Dever, believe the location where the inscriptions were discovered was part of a cult complex, though others disagree.

The inscriptions, which have been dated to 776–750 BCE,[20] were discovered in 1977–78 and published in 1978, but again their significance took a while to sink in. On a wall, there is the inscription: "To Yahweh of Teiman and to his Asherah."[21] Teiman, or Teman, is generally identified as the modern Yemen, although there was another place of that name in Edom, a kingdom immediately to the south of Judah.

The same dedication is repeated on a large storage jar, or *pithos:* "I have blessed you by YHWH of Teman and by his Asherah."[22] This pithos also bears a painted stylized palm tree—the trunk of this one rather phallic. It is flanked by the standing and nibbling goats that Ruth Hestrin identified as a symbol of Asherah, which of course matches the inscription. And it shows that the Israelites were still using the originally Canaanite symbolism in the eighth century BCE.

There are also three rather cartoonlike figures, two standing close together and a third, a seated bare-breasted female playing a lyre, in the distance. All three are highly stylized. Who they represent and how they relate to the inscription has long been a hot topic among academics. Some think either one or both of the standing figures is Bes, the intimidating Egyptian dwarf-god of the underworld. Others argue that they represent Yahweh and Asherah. As for the lyre player, she's been identified as either Asherah or Anat. However, it's all academic—in both senses—as it's frustratingly uncertain that the drawings relate to the inscription anyway, illustrating how historical research can be littered with dead ends.

On another pithos at Kuntillet Ajrud—confirmed by the style of pottery to be both Israelite and eighth century BCE—is written "I have blessed you by YHWH of Samaria and his Asherah."[23]

All these inscriptions yield important snippets of information, taking us tantalizingly closer to Asherah herself. We see that in the eighth century BCE, she and Yahweh were paired, and the phrase "his Asherah" indicates—rather sweetly to modern eyes—that she was considered his official consort. This is quite late in Israel's history, confirming that the condemnation of Asherah worship in the Hebrew Bible is very much a product of the time it was written rather than the era it allegedly describes.

All this points to one big, inescapable conclusion: The Israelites considered Asherah to be Yahweh's wife. This is now accepted by the overwhelming majority of historians of the Hebrew Bible. For example, in *The Story of the Jews* (2013), Simon Schama writes, "it had long been unproblematic in Judaea itself to profess devotion to YHWH as well as the consort commonly believed to be paired with him, Asherah."[24]

BREASTS AND WOMB

In chapter 1 we mentioned the "Blessing of Jacob," a poem incorporated into Genesis where Jacob, on his deathbed, asks for El's blessing in turn for each of his sons. David Noel Freedman, the American scholar and archaeologist who translated the Dead Sea Scrolls, says: "In this poem, I believe that a unique survival of the patriarchal age, or more precisely of the pre-Mosaic period, has been preserved substantially intact."[25]

Among the blessings that Jacob calls upon the "Almighty"— "Shadday," a title of El—to bestow on Joseph and his descendants are "blessings of the breast and of the womb."[26] Because of this striking terminology Freedman concludes:

This must also [like Shadday] be a designation or title for a divine being, one also associated with El the Father God. It is difficult to avoid the conclusion that this is not simply a generic reference to human fertility but rather a designation of the great Mother Goddess, the consort of El who is the archetypal divine father. . . .

The consort of El, while not named here, is a well-known goddess in Canaanite religion and throughout the Near East and the Mediterranean world, and as well in the polemics of the biblical writers. She is Asherah who is the consort of El and later on of Baal, known as creatress of living things, the mother goddess par excellence. It is difficult to imagine such a statement in biblical literature after the establishment of Yahwism as the official religion of Israel, but as a reflection or description of pre-Mosaic patriarchal religion it is probably accurate and realistic.[27]

So, according to Freedman, "Breast and Womb" is a title of Asherah, underlining Ruth Hestrin's deductions from depictions of the goddess, where she is represented solely by her breasts and vulva.

Another possible early reference comes in another deathbed scene when, at the end of Deuteronomy, Moses delivers his "final blessing" to Israel. Although Deuteronomy was written very late, this poem inserted into it—like the other songs and poems in the Hebrew Bible—was genuinely old. The blessing begins:

> *The LORD came from Sinai*
> *and dawned from Seir upon us;*
> *he shone forth from Mount Paran;*
> *he came from the ten thousands of holy ones*
> *with flaming fire at his right hand.*[28]

The "ten thousands of holy ones" makes little sense in this context. The word is *qodesh* in the Hebrew, and Meindert Dijkstra suggests that it should instead be read as "Qudshu," the alternative name of Asherah.

He also proposes that the "flaming fire," *eshdat esh,* is a corruption of *asherah.* Dijkstra's version of these lines is therefore:

> *he came among the myriads of Qudshu*
> *at his right hand his own Asherah.*[29]

If Dijkstra is correct, then this is "possibly the only passage in which Asherah is mentioned as YHWH's spouse or companion under her own name and her title Qodesh/Qudshu. In it, YHWH leads the myriads of Qodesh, which apparently may include gods and men, the heavenly and earthly family of El."[30]

The big difference here, of course, is that Asherah/Qudshu is now *Yahweh's* wife, whereas in the earlier Canaanite myth, Asherah was El's wife/consort. And if our interpretation of the Song of Moses is correct—and Yahweh was originally one of El's sons—then the Israelites once believed that Asherah was Yahweh's mother. However, at some point she became his partner—and equal.

Such a convoluted, not to say incestuous, transfer is not unusual, as ancient gods' relationships were very flexible. For example, as we'll see in the next chapter, Asherah came to be identified with the goddess Anat, originally her daughter in Canaanite mythology.

Exactly when and why Asherah was transferred from El to Yahweh is hard to deduce. Perhaps it was a result of the pairing at sanctuaries of Asherah's symbol of the tree with Yahweh's standing stone, as at Shechem. Presumably as El was pushed further into the background when worship was ever more tightly focused on Yahweh, Asherah—who was adored by the Israelites—remained, being paired with Yahweh. Their pagan logic and indeed their traditions dictated that he had to have a consort.

If Karl Luckert's theory that Yahweh began as the Egyptian Amun is correct, Asherah's shift from mother to wife may have been helped by Amun's wife, Mut, sharing some of Asherah's titles, such as "Mother of the Gods" and "Lady of Heaven." But no one knows for sure how it happened, just that it was well established by the time of the monarchy in Jerusalem, some two or three centuries after Joshua's arrival in Canaan. Then it *continued* throughout Israel's history. This is apparent even from the biblical account. As with the other evidence for polytheism, the monotheistic agenda of the Bible writers is scandalously at odds with the facts.

Some have attempted to explain—and even dismiss—the persistence of the Asherah cult as part of the "folk religion," as distinct from "book religion." The latter was the faith of the royal court and priesthood, the establishment elite of the urban centers, the smart city set. The Hebrew Bible is clearly written from their perspective—after all, they were the ones who could read and write, whose words and deeds were set down for posterity. And the prophets might have been wild-eyed and malodorous eccentrics, but they did have access to the upper echelons, dealing directly with tribal leaders and kings. The likes of Isaiah were close associates of the aristocracy, the upper class—even if their relationship was often rocky.

Book religion was important for another reason: It provided the crossover between the political and economic agendas. It sanctified and justified the king's rule while also protecting the priesthood's livelihood through the system of taxes and offerings. Because they were dealing in the hard world of money and power, the religion itself demanded rules—dogmas to underpin the laws and customs. In the ancient world, book religion was rarely about imposing a single belief on an entire people; those at the center could rarely care less what the common folk believed. As always with the rich and powerful, why would they even bother with the beliefs and practices of humble folk beyond their own gilded circle? The religious regime at the top often remained the exclusive faith of the establishment. It's debatable, for example, if even Akhenaten's iconoclastic new religion had much impact on the ordinary Egyptian.

Folk religion, on the other hand, has never cared about dogma. City slickers' rules don't apply where people live hand-to-mouth from the soil. For the ordinary folk struggling with unimaginably harsh reality, religion wasn't about theology but survival—you invoked the gods to ensure a good harvest, a successful pregnancy, recovery from disease, and so on.

Susan Ackerman, contrasting the ideologies of the "prophetic class" to the peasants', goes further: "The ideology of the people, on the other hand, involved incorporating many different religious practices into their worship. With these diversities, the people hoped, they would propitiate all aspects of divine power."[31]

Folk religion is far more flexible and creative, happily mixing elements of earlier customs and rituals into any new religion that might be imposed on them. It is much more fluid, borrowing from neighboring peoples without—significantly—seeing them as necessarily opposed to their own faith. Traditional ways of appealing to the gods are not dropped, just recycled or repurposed. Even today, for example, Catholics in Latin America incorporate elements of old folk beliefs into their festivals, holy sites, and local forms of worship that would never be sanctioned by the Vatican, while still considering themselves good Catholics. Even more extreme are Voodoo and Hoodoo, where Christian saints rub shoulders on their altars with folk heroes and ancient African deities.

The crossover between Yahwism and the Egyptian religion might seem strange, even distasteful to modern believers, but there are many examples. Hundreds of "Eye of Horus" amulets, imported from Egypt, have been found in Israelite tombs, along with figurines of Bes, the Egyptian dwarf-god who was guardian of the dead, alongside other Egyptian and Phoenician deities.

Elements from older Canaanite practices and other local peoples did find their way into the rites of the ordinary Israelites, explaining the biblical references to the non-Israelite gods—such as Astarte. But when it comes to Asherah, according to Saul Olyan, "It is important to note that we are not speaking only of popular religion here; the asherahs of Samaria, Bethel and Jerusalem were a constituent part of state Yahwism."[32]

Asherah worship was once *official*.

But just how long was Asherah loved and worshipped by the Israelites? We follow her divine footprint throughout the story of Israel . . .

THE MONARCHY

The era of the judges came to an end with a major shift politically and socially—and religiously.

During the tenure of the High Priest Samuel, Yahweh—acceding to the wishes of the people, apparently—appointed a hereditary monarchy, the first anointed king being Saul of the tribe of Benjamin. The hereditary rule soon broke down though, as Yahweh—via Samuel—removed his blessing from Saul for ignoring a command: in a war with the Amalekites, Saul had disobediently spared their king and some of the choicest livestock, instead of slaughtering every last man, woman, child, goat, and sheep as instructed.

Saul was succeeded by David of the tribe of Judah, the shepherd boy who, after famously killing the giant Goliath with a simple slingshot, worked his way up to command Saul's armies. Through conquest—not just against Canaanites but also recalcitrant Israelite tribes—David united the twelve tribes into a single kingdom, Israel, under his rule. The time of the judges was over.

The kaleidoscope effect of Israelite chronology is coming more into focus now. Both the Hebrew Bible's internal dating and history agree that, if there was such a person as David, he would have lived around 1000 BCE.

David's consolidation of power included capturing Jerusalem from the Canaanite Jebusites, which he made his capital—not just of his land, Judah, but the whole nation. David's elevation inevitably brought him into conflict with the tribe that had, since the days of Joshua, been the leader, Ephraim, whose capital was the holy city of Shechem.

As a mark of his capital's new status—not to mention his own standing—David had the Ark of the Covenant brought to Jerusalem, obviously intending to make his city the new center of the religion.

This symbolizes a decisive shift in the balance of power from Ephraim to Judah, and the beginning of a rivalry and enmity between the two tribes that lasted into New Testament times.

Before the construction of the Jerusalem Temple, rituals were held in shrines and sanctuaries throughout Israel, which were outdoors, on hilltops. True, there was also the Tabernacle at Shiloh but apparently that was reserved for the priesthood, and in any case rural people needed local places to practice their religion.

It seems even the great Solomon carried out rituals in the countryside, as the first book of Kings makes clear: "The people were sacrificing at the high places . . . because no house had yet been built for the name of the LORD. Solomon loved the LORD walking in the statutes of David his father, only he sacrificed and made offerings at the high places"—particularly at Gibeon, the "great high place" in the land of Benjamin, just north of Jerusalem.[33]

Solomon decided to build the house—or temple, the same word in Hebrew—"for the name of the LORD." It was also a canny political move, continuing the centralization of power and establishing his authority over the kingdom and its religion. As it was not just a temple but a royal sanctuary, it legitimized Solomon as a king who ruled with Yahweh's express blessing. And it allowed him to impose taxes to fund it—not in his name of course, but Yahweh's. (Who would dare deny God his tithe money?) Solomon also built himself a magnificent palace, also with "Yahweh's" levy.

Solomon also appointed Zadok as high priest, to return the priesthood to the original line, as a branch descended from a younger son of the first priest, Aaron, had since taken it over—but this looks suspiciously like a bit of later editorial flimflam (or perhaps contemporary Solomonic flimflam). There's some evidence that Zadok was really a Canaanite.[34]

Israel was moving away from a predominantly rural, village-based society to a proper state like the more developed nations around it—all of which boasted impressive temples to their gods. Solomon's Temple was also a sign that the nation of Israel had arrived. The Hebrew Bible states that both his temple and palace were designed and built by Phoenicians, supplied by King Hiram of Tyre along with much of the material, as the Israelites themselves had little experience or expertise in monumental masonry. Of course, armies of slaves drawn from various conquered Canaanite peoples actually did the hard graft of building these places. The irony of creating the enemy's vanity projects no doubt struck them rather forcibly.

The Temple took seven years to build, around mid-900 BCE. Despite its iconic status in the minds of posterity—especially among Freemasons—Solomon's Temple was not that impressive, especially by the standards of other great civilizations, such as Egypt and those that came after. It was only about 90 feet long, 30 wide, and 45 high. Its design and layout parallel precisely those of excavated Phoenician temples. Interestingly, Karl Luckert cites strikingly similar temples in Egypt to Amun.[35]

When it was finished, with great ceremony and much sacrificial spilling of sheep and oxen blood, the Ark of the Covenant was installed in the Holy of Holies, the chamber at the end of the Temple that was off-limits to all except the high priest. The Temple became the center of pilgrimage for the Israelites, the only place where offerings could be made to Yahweh—at the very least, a smart move economically, as animal sacrifices had to be purchased on site.

The later books are not very forthcoming about what went on in the Temple during these centuries, at least until Josiah's reforms. What it does say is rather illuminating: It appears that all manner of practices connected with other deities went on, not merely in the precinct outside but within the Temple itself.

For example, the Temple's decoration is revealing. The internal walls were engraved with a motif that incorporated images of cherubim, palm trees, and open flowers. The same motif was carved on the doors that sealed off the inner sanctuary. The trees and flowers—and the bronze pomegranates that abound—are standard symbols of the abundance of nature. Pagan fertility imagery, if you like.

The capitals of two famed bronze pillars guarding the Temple vestibule, Jachin and Boaz—famously significant in the lore of Freemasonry—were decorated with "lily work."[36] However, based on an analysis by Yigal Shiloh of the Hebrew University, Jerusalem, Dever concluded they "depict the drooping fronds of the palm tree's crown." He even suggests that the pillars themselves are stylized palm trees.[37] If so, they are obvious symbols of Asherah—as we might expect. After all, she was Yahweh's consort, and the Temple was his house. It's only natural that his wife should share it with him.

Other exotic figures featured in Yahweh's house. Cherubim formed an integral part of the décor of the Temple of Solomon. There were two huge wooden carvings—overlaid with gold—in the Holy of Holies, and many more on the walls and on the doors leading to the Holy of Holies. But as with the Ark of the Covenant and the Tabernacle, we have few details about the cherubim.

We do know that the pair in the Holy of Holies were impressive: Each was a huge 10 cubits (15 feet) high and with wingspans also of 10 cubits. These cherubim were standing and, unlike the Ark's, faced outward. The outer tip of each cherub's outstretched wing touched one of the walls while the inner tips touched each other. The Ark of the Covenant was placed under them so their wings overshadowed it, protectively.

All the inner walls of both Holy of Holies and the main hall were decorated with a motif combining cherubim, palm trees, and open flowers. The same design was repeated on the gold-covered doors to the inner sanctuary. Cherubim were also represented, along with lions, oxen, and palm trees, on the wheeled bronze bases of the ten basins in the temple. As Patai puts it, "the Solomonic Temple contained a surfeit of Cherubim."[38] One connection is obvious, however, as Othmar Keel, author of *The Symbolism of the Biblical World* (1997) observes: "The Solomonic holy of holies bear a certain resemblance to the chapels of Egyptian deities."[39]

Despite building the Temple to Yahweh, Solomon sacrificed to other gods—mostly because of the influence of his many foreign wives, gifted to him through his diplomatic alliances. (Apparently, he had 700 wives plus 300 concubines, though like most descriptions of Solomon's fabulousness this can be taken with a large pinch of salt.)

As the first book of Kings explains, "For when Solomon was old his wives turned away his heart after other gods, and his heart was not wholly true to the LORD his God."[40] It says they included "Ashtoreth the goddess of the Sidonians," which is generally thought to be a mistake for Asherah, as she was venerated in Sidon. However, as several commentators, including Patai, point out, it is unlikely that Solomon's polytheistic worship only happened when he was old, and is probably the Bible writers' way of reconciling his devotion to multiple gods with his image as the great king who built Yahweh's Temple. Presumably his pagan practices were simply too well known to omit from the official record. (The writers seemed willing to sacrifice Solomon's image as the great wise king— weakly letting his foreign wives lead him into heretical, even blasphemous worship—rather than admit he was always a pagan idolater.)

THE DIVIDED KINGDOM

Under Solomon, the kingdom reached new heights, perhaps hardly surprising given the revenue brought in by the Temple. But it wasn't to last: the regime immediately fell apart under his son Rehoboam. When the tribes assembled for his coronation at Shechem in Ephraim—obviously still considered *the* holy place—the leaders of the other tribes, led by Jeroboam of Ephraim, presented a set of demands. These included a reduction of the taxes that his father had imposed to pay for all his building projects. Clearly, the Ephraimites had no intention of relinquishing their old preeminence lightly.

When Rehoboam not only refused but threatened the tribal leaders with violence, ten of the tribes set up their own kingdom under Jeroboam's leadership. David and Solomon's glorious kingdom fractured into the rival Kingdom of Israel, the ten tribes in the north, and the southern Kingdom of Judah comprising just that tribe and Benjamin, although the two had become virtually indistinguishable through intermarriage.

(To avoid confusion with the other uses of "Israel" in the Bible, particularly the kingdom established by David, historians and scholars term David and Solomon's the "Unified Monarchy" and Jeroboam's breakaway one as the "Northern Kingdom," "Ephraim," or sometimes "Samaria.")

This momentous split happened between 930 and 910 BCE. The Kingdom of Israel's capital—that is, the location of the royal palace—was initially at Shechem but in the 870s it was moved to the city of Samaria.

The only biblical account of the Kingdom of Israel we have is that by its rival Judah, which portrays it as a breakaway regime. However, that is the victor's version: given their relative sizes and the fact that the Kingdom of Israel represented the overwhelming majority of the tribes, as well as its wealth and power—not to mention its name—it's more accurate to say that the Kingdom of Israel threw Judah out. Israel rejected the line of David *and* the Temple as the unique place of worship.

For the next 200 years the two kingdoms were rivals, each claiming to be Yahweh's chosen people. They occasionally fought, but also sometimes made an alliance, as they did with other kingdoms.

As the Hebrew Bible was written after the reforms of the religion that culminated in the 450s BCE, it is basically propaganda for the Kingdom of Judah. It set out to prove that it, not the Kingdom of Israel, was the true representative of the religion of Yahweh. Therefore, during the period of the divided kingdoms Israel had to be the villain, reverting to the old Canaanite religion and importing foreign abominations— which to the Bible writers was pretty much the same thing.

The era of the divided kingdom is also when prophets emerged as a force to be reckoned with. These were fiery preachers who claimed to channel Yahweh's very own words, threatening people and kings alike with unspeakable calamities for not keeping the faith. These prophets were desperate to make everyone aware of what *should* appall them, top of the list being backsliding to worshipping many gods—and one goddess in particular . . .

In Israelite myth and legend, the prophetic tradition harked back to the time of Moses—he is never specifically called a prophet, unlike his sister Miriam, but he is their role model, the Chosen One of God through whom he communicates with the people. However, prophets as a distinct type really emerged later, probably in the time of Samuel, the high priest whom tradition also regarded as a prophet.

The word translated as "prophet," *navi*, literally means "spokesman" for Yahweh. The word is also applied to false prophets, and to the cult officials of Baal and Asherah, where it seems to mean priest. But not just men could be prophets. There are also *neviah*—"prophetesses," although there are only five in the Hebrew Bible: Miriam, Deborah, Huldah, Noadiah—one of Nehemiah's enemies—and an unnamed woman by whom Isaiah has a son. As we will see, there are some telling implications of the women who spoke with God.

It seems that early on *prophet* and *seer*, one who used divinatory techniques, were interchangeable. The first book of Samuel says in an aside that in Israel's past, prophets and seers were one and the same, implying things had changed.[41] Deuteronomy expressly forbids divination, so perhaps that's the reason this aspect was downplayed in the later books. In the context of the ancient world, this was unusual, as most cultures—including the later Greek and Roman empires—employed priests and priestesses who foretold the future through a variety of ways, such as "reading" the intestines of a newly slaughtered animal. It is possible that even Yahweh's allegedly antidivination prophets indulged in similar fortune-telling.

There is a similar ambiguity about the prophets' relationship with the Levite priesthood, which was also supposed to speak for Yahweh. Some high priests, such as Samuel, were considered prophets, but they are the minority. David had prophets Gad and Nathan who seemed to act as his personal advisors on matters of state, religion, and lifestyle, and the text treats them as equal to the high priest—for example both Zadok and Nathan anoint Solomon.

Not only were the prophets/seers in a class by themselves but they belonged to a distinct caste or guild—a sort of holy club. They were the priests, or at least sacred guardians, of shrines such as Shiloh and Bethel.

After the schism the *navi* change. They become itinerant visionaries and miracle workers, often from humble backgrounds, allegedly chosen by Yahweh to harangue and browbeat the nation back to their proper religion. But they were not operating in isolation: the first of the great prophets, Elijah, had disciples, and he anointed Elisha as his successor. The prophets had—or aspired to have—political clout, instigating coups and purges on the rare occasions they managed to persuade a king to heed them.

The prophets officiously regarded themselves as keepers of the covenant, their job being to ensure the Israelites honored their side of the bargain so they would continue to bask in Yahweh's grace and favor. They were focused on Yahweh and loftily unconcerned with the other deities, such as Asherah.

The movement within the prophets that ultimately lead to monotheism and the suppression of Asherah, along with other goddesses, appears to have started in the northern kingdom and took root during the eighth century BCE. But why then? Probably as the result of changes in the fortunes of both kingdoms. The first half of the century saw them on a high; they were at their wealthiest and the pinnacle of their political power. To the priests and prophets, this clearly meant they were in Yahweh's good books. It was a sort of American Dream, as Francis Andersen and David Noel Freedman, specialists in the prophet Hosea, explain:

> According to popular and prevailing theological norms there was a permanent correlation between divine favor and prosperous existence . . . the elect people of God were enjoying the just rewards of their faithful behavior . . . the benefits bestowed upon Israel and Judah, the blessings which rained down on them from a benevolent heaven, were adequate proof not only of divine favor but of Israel's moral merit.[42]

But then in the second half of the century, everything went badly wrong. Both kingdoms suffered from the rise of the mighty Assyrian Empire. The prophets felt vindicated—the Israelites' current misery was obviously due to their backsliding. They were no longer keeping their side of the covenant with Yahweh. So, the prophets became locked in a vicious circle that pushed them ever closer to monotheism: the worse things got, the more attention they had to devote to Yahweh.

Perhaps what drove the prophets toward Yahwism was that in times of crisis it was easier to turn to the most familiar national god, especially as he was hallowed by the traditions of the covenant. It was a sort of "temporary monolatry."[43]

However, in the beginning the prophets were *not* monotheists, acknowledging the existence of other gods and goddesses, including those of other nations. But they became progressively more monolatrist, insisting that the people of Israel give their devotion to Yahweh alone (although they still seem to have included Asherah, perhaps on sufferance). Morton Smith, professor of ancient history at Columbia University, coined the term "Yahweh-alone party" for this prophetic movement.

The first of the "Yahweh-alone" prophets—at least that we know about—was Hosea, who started his ranting career around 750 BCE. As Morton Smith comments, Hosea's prophecies are "our first evidence of the reasons alleged to justify the demand that Israelites worship Yahweh alone."[44]

Tellingly, the next of the prophetic line, Amos—the same generation as Hosea—while extolling the worship of Yahweh, was unconcerned with the worship of other gods. The leading biblical scholar Bernhard Lang wryly downplays the significance of the Yahweh-alone movement: "Amos is indeed a prophet of Yahweh but the Yahweh-alone idea does not find expression in his written legacy. Not every worshipper of Yahweh is simultaneously a supporter of the Yahweh-alone movement, which one should not imagine to be too influential."[45]

After Amos came Isaiah and then, around 700 BCE, Micah, who explicitly stated "For all the peoples walk each in the name of its god, but we will walk in the name of the LORD our God,"[46] revealing that even to him there was nothing special about Yahweh apart from the Israelites' promise to worship him.

The Yahweh-alone movement had occasional success in influencing kings, particularly in Judah, to undertake reforms promoting Yahweh worship and suppressing the other cults. However, they seemed to tolerate Asherah, seeing her as an authentic part of Yahwism.

RISE AND FALL OF THE NORTH

Under Israel's self-appointed king, Jeroboam of Ephraim who instigated the schism, an angry Yahweh, via the prophet Ahijah of Shiloh, threatened to expel them from their land. Why? Because they "made their Asherim."[47] Later in the story, there's a reference to the Asherah that Jeroboam installed at the holy site of Bethel[48]—and it was still there 300 years later.

As Raphael Patai observes: "The fact that of all forms of idolatry only the cult of Asherah was mentioned specifically by Ahijah must mean at least that the one variety of religious worship in which the Israelites engaged more frequently than in any other was the cult of the Goddess Asherah, symbolized and represented by her carved wooden images."[49] And it was essentially, as David Noel Freedman notes, "a restoration of the older faith of the fathers."[50] We would go further: the evidence shows that, principally in the lands of Ephraim and Manasseh, which became the center of the northern kingdom, Asherah worship had *never* stopped. As Frank Moore Cross Jr., the eminent Harvard professor of Hebrew explains: "Apparently, Jeroboam's real sin was in establishing a rival to the central sanctuary in Jerusalem, not in the introduction of a foreign god or a pagan idol."[51]

It seems Yahweh was heavily involved in politics—or at least, it was very convenient to use him as endorsement for one's own agenda. With God on our side . . . Sometimes, though, it wasn't God, but his Goddess.

Kings is peppered with references to the widespread popularity of Asherah and the Asherim. They are often described as being "on every high hill and under every green tree,"[52] a stock phrase that recurs in relation to the Asherah cult, both in Israel and Judah, but does rather highlight their ubiquity.

The seventh king of Israel, Ahab, who reigned in the 860s and 850s BCE, and had the dubious honor of doing "more to provoke the LORD, the God of Israel, than all the kings of Israel who were before him," also "made an Asherah."[53] There's also mention of the "450 prophets of Baal and 400 prophets of Asherah"[54] who were accommodated in his palace in Samaria, but even early Hebrew texts indicate that the "prophets of Asherah" part is a later interpolation.[55]

Ahab's infamous Phoenician wife Jezebel—literally a byword for a scheming painted floozie—is perhaps inevitably blamed for all this, and indeed it does seem she was responsible for reimporting the Baal cult from Phoenicia. (Although known to posterity as "Phoenicia," that was its Greek name. In fact the Phoenicians were, and referred to themselves as, Canaanites.) Even Jezebel's name is linked to this near-demonic foreign god: "Jezebel"—*Jez-e-Bel/Baal*—is thought to have originated in a ritual cry from an annual ceremony where the women ritually sought Baal in his dying-and-rising god aspect.[56] (These sort of mystery plays were common for centuries around the Mediterranean, celebrating the deaths and miraculous resurrection of gods such as the Egyptian Osiris, Tammuz—and even arguably Jesus himself, much later.)

For once, there does seem to have been a real threat level to the Yahweh religion from the Baal cult. Ahab and Jezebel made an attempt at a dynastic alliance with Judah by marrying their daughter, Athaliah, to Judah's King Jehoram. Athaliah, like her mother, was also a devotee of Baal, whose cult she introduced in Jerusalem. After Jehoram died— of a disease of the bowels, so horribly and messily, one assumes—his and Athaliah's son Ahaziah became king of Judah. Jezebel's bloodline triumphed, for a time at least, even if she personally did not.

In the Kingdom of Israel, Ahab's successor—his and Jezebel's son— confusingly another Jehoram, was overthrown in a bloody coup led by his general Jehu at the instigation of the prophet Elisha. Jehu took the opportunity to have the entire extended royal family massacred. As the book of Kings gleefully relates, he had Jezebel thrown from her window by the palace eunuchs and then—with literal overkill—rode his chariot over her. With lubricious gloating, the Bible adds that her broken body was then eaten by dogs. Ahaziah, king of Judah—Jezebel's grandson—who happened to be visiting her, was also killed.

Presumably fearing that Jehu was about to claim the thrones of both Israel and Judah (which would have delighted Elisha), Jezebel's daughter Athaliah seized Jerusalem, and ruled Judah for five or six years—one of only two times that either kingdom was ruled by a woman. Clearly, she was not a lady to cross, having all pretenders to the throne of Judah executed, including members of her own family—although one grandson escaped, which is how the line continued. So *both* royal families were nearly extinguished. During her brief reign, before she was deposed and executed by the supporters of the escapee grandson, Athaliah established the worship of Baal in Jerusalem—presumably in the Temple itself.

It is this period, when Baal successfully threatened the primacy of Yahweh, that probably caused the Yahwists' later paranoia about his cult. They then projected his religious sway over the people back into Israel's past, turning him into a supernatural super-villain from the very beginning.

Meanwhile, in the northern kingdom, presumably egged on by Elisha, the usurper Jehu set about eradicating the Baal cult—but "the Asherah also remained in Samaria."[57] So, despite the somewhat desperate impression the Bible writers try to give, even with its association with Baal, the Asherah cult was *not* considered either foreign or *wrong*. Her role, by the side of Yahweh, seemed unassailable. As Patai comments: "It would appear then that only the Baal was considered by Elijah (and the strict Yahwists in general) as a dangerous rival of Yahweh, while the Goddess Asherah was regarded as his inevitable, necessary, or at any rate tolerable, female counterpart."[58]

Asherah was not solely associated with the bloodthirsty Baal: "Cumulative evidence suggests strongly [she was associated with] the cult of Yahweh. An asherah stood in the Bethel temple (2 Kgs 23:15), and other asherahs were set up at various high places."[59]

So, again despite the impression that the Bible wants to give, the people of the northern kingdom had not neglected Yahweh; they had merely also paid homage to other deities associated with him, principally Asherah—just as the Israelites had always done.

The history of the northern kingdom is more chaotic and bloody than Judah's, with frequent assassinations of kings and military coups. With assassins and plotters lurking in every shadow, several of the kings ruled for just a year or so before being deposed. Eventually, though, the northern land settled down and became the richer of the two kingdoms—not surprising as it was so much more extensive than Judah. It reached its peak in the reign of Jeroboam II (died 748 BCE), who spent lavishly on vanity building projects.

By Jeroboam II's day, however, the world around Israel was undergoing immense change. It was entering the age of the great empires that were to sweep across the region in waves, rising, falling, clashing, and enslaving the smaller kingdoms. The first were the mighty Assyrians, who stormed across the Middle East from their homeland in Mesopotamia, creating the biggest empire ever known. (Being the first army to wield iron weapons, it enjoyed a huge advantage.) Naturally Israel's wealth proved an irresistible attraction.

Israel's King Hoshea successfully bought the Assyrians off for a time but stopped making payments when he made an alliance with Egypt—a mistake he lived to regret. Furious, the Assyrians invaded and after a three-year siege in 721 BCE the capital Samaria fell to their King Sargon II. Hoshea and a large swath of its population—27,000 according to Assyrian records—were carried off into a captivity from which they never returned. Peoples from other parts of the Assyrian Empire—ironically in the light of later history, including Babylon—were brought in to repopulate the cities.

When Samaria fell to Sargon, a record of the capture, known as the "Nimrud prism," relates that besides the 27,280 deported Samarians, the Assyrians also triumphantly took "the gods, in which they trusted, as spoil."[60] This was standard victors' plunder, making it crystal clear to the defeated who was now in charge. But there's that telling plural: the term *gods*—idols—revealing that the Samarians were not exclusively Yahweh worshippers.

All this might seem to confirm the biblical claims about the back-sliding northerners reverting to old Canaanite idolatry or bringing in foreign gods, while Judah—with the focus of Yahweh's religion in Jerusalem—kept on the straight and narrow. However, it's also what the Bible says about the Kingdom of Judah.

THE GODDESS'S GLORY YEARS

Although the Hebrew Bible condemns the Kingdom of Israel for idolatry right from moment of the schism, the Kingdom of Judah fares even worse—also from the start. Under Solomon's son Rehoboam "they also built for themselves high places and pillars and Asherim on every high hill and under every green tree. . . . They [the Judahites] did according to all the abominations of the nations that the LORD drove out before the people of Israel."[61]

Again, there's that stock phrase "on every high hill and under every green tree"—and the association with "abominations." The "high places" are the open-air sanctuaries, and the "pillars," or *massebot,* standing stones. This tradition of outdoor worship is clearly depicted as a *return* to the old Canaanite religion (as the Bible writers see it) across both kingdoms. But they were wrong. It was just a continuation of how things had always been.

Once again the emphasis in Judah is on kings who attempt to end these "abominations" and "return" the nation to the sole worship of Yahweh, but they are very much in the minority. Under most monarchs the Temple worship and the veneration of the Asherim simply continued side by side. In fact, Asherah was openly and unashamedly—even *officially*—venerated *in* the Jerusalem Temple.

Two kings after Rehoboam, Asa of Judah (reigned ca. 910–870 BCE) "removed Maacah his mother from being queen mother because she had made an abominable image for Asherah. And Asa cut down her image and burned it at the brook Kidron."[62] "Abominable image"—translated variously as "obscene object" or "horrid thing"—is really just speculation, as the word *miphletset* is otherwise unknown. It is based, however, on a rather melodramatic verb meaning "to shudder with horror." The shudderingly horrified Asa's iconoclasm was part of a purge of the "detestable idols" throughout the land, which Chronicles states was due to the influence of the prophet Azariah—one of the few we hear of in Judah before the fall of the northern kingdom.[63]

According to Chronicles, Asa's son Jehoshaphat (ca. 870–849 BCE) "took the high places and the Asherim out of Judah"[64]—implying that Asherah worshippers had determinedly restored them. But his grandson, Ahaziah—under the influence of Athaliah, daughter of Ahab and Jezebel—officially returned to the old goddess-adoring ways. His son Joash (reigned ca. 843–797 BCE) blatantly "abandoned the house of the LORD, the God of their fathers, and served the Asherim and the idols."[65]

This situation prevailed over the next four reigns until the first of the great reformers, Hezekiah, who ascended the throne around 715 BCE—over a century after Joash's "abandonment." Immediately on becoming king, Hezekiah "removed the high places and broke the pillars and cut down the Asherah."[66] Presumably even these zealous Yahwists did not actually remove the hilltops, as these passages suggest, just the "abominable" signs of rural Asherah worship.

According to Chronicles, Hezekiah also elevated Passover, commemorating the people's delivery from Egypt, to the status of national festival, announcing from then on it was to be held every year only in Jerusalem. Before this, Passover had probably been celebrated in some form, but on a more intimate, family scale.

Chronicles tells us that Hezekiah made overtures to the Kingdom of Israel—specifically sending letters to the tribes of Ephraim and Manasseh—to come and celebrate the Passover in Jerusalem. Though this invitation was widely mocked, some did turn up. Then things got very ugly. Whipped up into a Yahwist frenzy after the festival, the mob went on a spree of smashing pillars and cutting down Asherim in the "high places" throughout Judah *and* the lands of Ephraim and Manasseh. It was state-sanctioned anti-Asherah rioting, no less, and on a huge scale. But the rioters did not reflect the way the religion was really going.

Despite all this violence, as soon as Hezekiah was out of the way his son Manasseh, who became king in 687 BCE, rushed to commission a "carved image of Asherah," which was duly set up in the Temple.[67] As Dever comments: "Thus Hezekiah's 'reform' was a failure. Why? Obviously because it lacked both popular support and subsequent royal approval. Asherah remained in the temple, at home alongside Yahweh, where many—perhaps even most—Israelites thought she belonged."[68]

King Manasseh's pro-Asherah rule lasted for nearly half a century, but his successor Amon managed only two or three years, as he was assassinated by his palace servants. Amon's heir Josiah was only eight years old when he succeeded his father, but he was to become the great reformer. After the discovery of the "lost" Book of the Law—also described as "the book of the law of Yahweh by the hand of Moses"— and as part of his renewal of the covenant with Yahweh, he had the image of Asherah, along with vessels made for Baal and "the host of heaven" removed from the Temple and triumphantly burnt. But it did take him about a decade to get around to doing so.

The "discovery" of the Book of the Law seems to have originated with the Temple priests, the first time they, rather than a prophet, had taken such an initiative. And it did require the endorsement of a prophet, or rather prophetess, Huldah. Presumably all this was to impress Josiah and win him over to the Yahwists' cause. Perhaps we shouldn't be too hard on his memory; after all, he was the victim of the hoax, not the perpetrator.

Meanwhile, Asherah continued to be honored in the countryside, though we can only deduce this because of yet another cycle of persecution. Besides clearing the Temple of non-Yahweh artifacts, Josiah also went on a savage rampage of shrine-destroying, pillar-smashing, and Asherim-hewing, not just in Judah but also the former lands of the

Kingdom of Israel. He led a campaign that destroyed "all the shrines at the high places" that the kings of Israel had built, slaughtering the priests on their own altars.

The northern kingdom was still Assyrian territory but by then their star was waning; otherwise presumably Josiah would never have dared to behave in this autocratic fashion. He even managed to annex a part of the former Kingdom of Israel, including the holy site of Bethel. Josiah, together with his priestly and prophetic advisers, clearly understood "Israel" to include both the kingdoms, seeing it as his mission not only to reimpose his concept of the Law on all Israelites but also to try to restore the original Kingdom of David—indeed, the whole Promised Land of Moses. When he returned to Jerusalem after destroying the northern sanctuaries and massacring the priests, Josiah held a grand Passover festival to celebrate.

Despite all this, as Susan Ackerman says, "The reform was instead limited in scope, temporary in effect, and clearly failed in its goal of impressing a monolithic description of Yahwism on all of Yahweh's devotees."[69] In any case, clearly the reforms did not protect against Yahweh's wrath. Josiah was killed fighting the Egyptians at the Battle of Megiddo in 609 BCE, and within twenty years Judah had fallen to the Babylonians. This also had a revivifying effect on the worship of Asherah, as Raphael Patai notes: "not even the most thorough and zealous Yahwist reform was able to eradicate the tenacious worship of Asherah."[70]

In one respect, Asherah is very similar to the infamous haystack fires so dreaded by farmers the world over. You think the flames have been extinguished, but deep inside a fire still burns fiercely, breaking out when you least expect it. Despite the repeated attacks on her sacred places and even the slaughter of her priests—and presumably an official ban on her worship—Asherah simply burns brightly deep inside the psyches of the people, waiting to break out into the open once more.

The pillar-base figurines identified with the goddess, found in such profusion throughout Judah, flourished at exactly the period covered by the reforms of Hezekiah and Josiah, so clearly the Yahwist message was not only *not* getting through to the ordinary people, but even caused a backlash, focusing them back on Asherah.

Even if the Jerusalem Temple had been purged of other gods and was now sacred to Yahweh alone, as William Dever explains: "we now know that the old Mother Goddess Asherah—virtually expunged from the texts of the Hebrew Bible, and all but forgotten by rabbinical times—never died out, but enjoyed a vigorous life throughout the Monarchy. This is not really surprising, since most biblical scholars now agree that true monotheism . . . arose only in the period of the Exile and beyond."[71]

One reason for Asherah's longevity was presumably because her worship was deeply rooted both in Jerusalem and among the common folk. In any case, at that time it was generally understood that it was only right and proper that a god should have a consort.

Overall, however, never mind their huffing and puffing—and serial self-importance—the prophets had little impact either at court or among the populace. Despite the impression given in later books the prophets were very much in the minority (hence the title of Bernhard Lang's 1983 study of the rise of monotheism in Israel, *Monotheism and the Prophetic Minority*).

As Niels Peter Lemche of the University of Copenhagen points out in his history of ancient Israel, the prophetic movement's religious reforms had no backing from the ordinary people: "Rather, its origins were most likely to have been situated among a *religious élite* which had been relegated to the outer darkness by official Israel, and which no longer played any significant role as far as the general religious consciousness was concerned."[72] (Italics in original.)

At the time of the reforms of Josiah, inspired by the "discovery" of the Book of the Second Law, the Jerusalem priesthood itself seems to have been won over to the prophets' cause. But even Josiah's crackdown on the other cults—including that of Asherah—had no long-term impact.

All this led to "Deuteronomism"—adherents of the "Second Law"—and the creation of the "Deuteronomistic history," referring to the rewriting and re-editing of the past in the books of the Hebrew Bible.

The extent of this rewriting—the creation of history, not as it was, but as the writers believed passionately it *should have been*—was immense in scope, and breathtakingly bogus. According to Professor Robert Karl Gnuse of Loyola University, New Orleans, it interpreted six hundred years of Israelite history "through a Yahwistic lens," using the book of Deuteronomy as a "manifesto."[73] Suddenly the prophets were the great religious heroes from back in the day, when for the most part the truth was they'd been barely tolerated weirdos ranting on the sidelines.

It was by no means an exhaustive revision of history. The Deuteronomistic historians did not completely obscure the truth. For example, although the significance of the Asherah cult was downplayed, it was *not* explicitly condemned.

Indeed, until the Exile, Deuteronomism was pretty much a failure. Then Jerusalem fell to the Babylonians, and the royal, aristocratic, and priestly elite was carried off into Captivity. During their miserable and disconsolate exile, the prophetic view became more deeply entrenched: after all, hadn't the likes of Isaiah and Jeremiah been vindicated?

It is increasingly obvious that the Hebrew Bible was basically Yahwist propaganda, written by his fanatical followers and upholders of the establishment. At all costs, the only true God must prevail against the backsliding of the Israelites into the adoration of other gods, particularly Asherah. However, rather naively, the picture they paint is the exact opposite of their message. It was the worship of other deities, especially Asherah, alongside Yahweh that was the norm, with occasional attempts by kings, under the influence of the prophets and priesthood, to force them to focus on Yahweh alone. And if sheer longevity is a yardstick, then surely Asherah must win every time.

The male establishment regularly endeavored to whip the people up into a frenzy of remorse for adoring their goddess—and indeed other gods—but in effect all they were doing was trying to bring a nonexistent crisis to a head. At least to the average Israelite, there was no crisis. There was no harm, and to them much good, in continuing to love the sacred feminine while also showing respect for Yahweh.

After all, hadn't everyone known for centuries that they were a couple?

A remarkable statistic cited by Raphael Patai reveals the Asherah cult's true place in Judah. Totting up the numbers of years given in the Hebrew Bible for the reigns under which her worship was alternately practiced or forbidden, he found that "of the 370 years during which the Solomonic Temple stood in Jerusalem, for no less than 236 years (or almost two-thirds of the time) the statue of Asherah was present in the Temple, and her worship was a part of the legitimate religion approved and led by the king, the court, and the priesthood and opposed by only a few prophetic voices crying out against it at relatively long intervals."[74]

However, taking the Bible account at face value, Patai counts the installation of the Asherah image in the Temple from the reign of Rehoboam, Solomon's son. If William Dever is right about the palm tree imagery, particularly of the Jachin and Boaz pillars, as honoring Asherah, then she was present in the Temple from the very beginning. We have to add another thirty years, as the Temple was completed in the eleventh year of Solomon's forty-year reign, making her present *for over 70 percent of the Temple's existence.*

THE PURGE

The description of Josiah's Temple purge—so precise some believe it must be based on the official royal archives—is fascinating, largely because of its insight into the organization of the Asherah cult:

> And the king commanded Hilkiah the high priest and the priests of the second order and the keepers of the threshold to bring out of the temple of the Lord all the vessels made for Baal, for Asherah, and for all the host of heaven. He burned them outside Jerusalem in the fields of the Kidron and carried their ashes to Bethel. . . . And he brought out the Asherah from the house of the Lord, outside Jerusalem, to the brook Kidron, and burned it at the brook Kidron and beat it to dust and cast the dust of it upon the graves of

the common people. And he broke down the houses of the male cult prostitutes who were in the house of the Lord, where the women wove hangings for the Asherah.[75]

Josiah having the ashes of the Asherah scattered over the graves of the "common people" implies that it was they who worshipped her most fervently. It was the ultimate insult.

The last part is especially opaque—the ESV translation above being basically just speculation—as the word translated as "hangings" is *bayit*, which is the same word as "house/temple" in the passage. Its literal meaning is "the women wove houses (or temples) for the Asherah." But who on earth knits houses? Dever suggests that it means "tent-shrines," like the Tabernacle, which is the only sensible explanation. But he stresses that whatever they were, they were being made for Asherah— who was therefore present with Yahweh in his Temple.[76]

However, the glaringly unavoidable elephant in the room here is obviously that little phrase apparently dropped almost as an aside into the above passage: "And he broke down the houses of the male cult prostitutes who were in the house of the LORD . . ."

In fact, a passage we quoted earlier, went on: "they also built for themselves high places and pillars and Asherim on every high hill and under every green tree, and there were also male cult prostitutes in the land. They [the Judahites] did according to all the abominations of the nations that the LORD drove out before the people of Israel."[77]

Male prostitutes? Cult male prostitutes? Cult male prostitutes *in the Temple?* It's surprising what you find in the Bible sometimes. Problematic allusions to house-knitting pales into comparative insignificance. Not surprisingly this has stopped many a commentator in their tracks. What could this possibly refer to?

This opens up the whole vexed subject of sacred prostitution and sex rites in the ancient Israelite religion.

3

Israel's Hidden Priestesses

If Asherah was once officially part of the religion, presumably her cult had priestesses. After all, it must have had representatives to carry out the rituals and organize its ceremonies. Women commonly officiated in the ancient world's goddess cults, although the priesthoods were usually mixed—there is only one temple known to be served exclusively by women, that of Mut, the wife of Amun, in Egypt. Where are Asherah's sacred workers? If her priestesses had roots in her ancient past, one might expect to find hints about her cult hidden in the Bible. And indeed there are.

In fact, the Bible does tell us about Asherah's priests—but only to approve of them being executed. Several scholars have suggested that tantalizing apparent references to "cult prostitutes"—male (*qadesh*) and female (*qadeshah*)—actually refer to Asherah's priesthood and temple workers, deliberately misrepresented by the Bible writers. For example, Deuteronomy decrees that "None of the daughters of Israel will be a cult prostitute, and none of the sons of Israel will be a cult prostitute."[1] Then again, as we saw in chapter 1 the women who "ministered" at the entrance to the Tabernacle appeared to have some official function, albeit vaguely defined.

In her study of women in biblical Israel, *Warrior, Dancer, Seductress, Queen* (1998), Susan Ackerman argues that queen mothers—mothers of the reigning kings—in Canaan and Israel who had "significant responsibilities in managing the economic and political affairs of the

94

king's court" also possessed "an official function within their cultures' religious communities. And this was specifically to devote themselves to the cult of the mother goddess Asherah."[2] These are exceptionally important women, suggesting that at an *official* level worship of the goddess was viewed as even aspirational. The queen mothers were, no doubt, role models not only for the ladies of the court, but by extension all women throughout the land. Perhaps they were even *cool*.

As mentioned earlier, other researchers have seen Asherah in her matriarch mode as reflecting the role of Canaanite queen mothers, who—unlike the wives of Israelite kings—had official functions at court. Then there is that tantalizing tidbit, where King Asa of Judah removed his mother from the palace because of the mysterious nightmare thing she made for Asherah—causing him to "shudder with horror"—suggesting a connection between her role and the cult. Ackerman goes on:

> As the human mother of the king, the queen mother would be perceived as the earthly counterpart of Asherah, the king's heavenly mother. The queen mother might even be considered the human representative of Asherah. Such a correspondence explains why those queen mothers for whom cultic allegiances are described or hinted at in the Bible are depicted as patrons of the goddess Asherah.[3]

If Ackerman is right, the queen mothers would not only have been patrons of the Asherah cult, but they would also preside over her Temple ceremonies just as the kings did with Yahweh worship. However, the queen mothers would not have been officially part of the priesthood.

As with every element of Asherah's story, even the existence of her priesthood has to be teased out from the Bible. Could even Moses's sister, the prophetess Miriam, have been involved? There might have been a connection between the *qadeshah* and the women she led. The sister of Moses, the great iconic figure of Jewish history, could even have been a high priestess of a goddess-worshipping cult—as high ranking as Aaron in her way.

The catch-all term "prophetesses" conceals even more clues. In the pre-monarchy story in the Bible only two women, Miriam and Deborah, are described as prophetesses—even before any men are enshrined as prophet. As eminent Bible scholar and Methodist elder Phyllis A. Bird observes, prophetess is the "most important and best-documented religious office occupied by women in ancient Israel," but that it "stands in an ambiguous relationship to the cultus."[4] Note Bird uses the term "religious office"; as the prophets of David and Solomon's day belonged to a sort of professional guild—another type of priesthood distinct from the hereditary Levites—the prophetesses probably belonged to a similar group.

It is not hard to identify their "club." After all, Deborah sits beneath a date palm to pronounce judgment—and we know who that represented. So are the biblical "prophetesses" really Asherah's priestesses?

EVE'S DAUGHTERS

People today usually assume the Hebrew Bible is always negative about women, being written from a very male perspective, and describing a culture—like all others in the ancient Near East—that was stridently patriarchal. We think of the story of Eve, blamed for misleading her husband Adam, taken in by the trickster serpent and bringing about the "Fall of Man." However, as professor of religion at Texas Christian University Claudia V. Camp points out, although women generically are blamed for seducing Israel's menfolk into the worship of other gods (as with Solomon's wives), named individuals are seldom stereotyped negatively—even in the case of harlots.[5] Even common streetwalkers were not vilified, as with Rahab of Jericho, who plays a pivotal role in its conquest by Joshua.

Of course, the Hebrew Bible does condemn women—such as the poster girl for female evil, Jezebel—but then it also lambasts numerous men. On analysis, the original tales from Israel's history did not portray women as morally much different from men—some were good, some were bad. (Of the Hebrew Bible generally, the German Old Testament scholar Klaus Koch remarked drily: "It is hard to find any document in the literature of the world which presents the history of its own people so unfavorably."[6]) It was only when the stories became a canon in the days of Ezra and after that passages were inserted depicting women generically as natural deceivers and corrupters of innocent, righteous menfolk.

Of course, none of that deflects from the fact that early Israelite society—the tribal-based culture of the period of the judges and the kingdom(s) that followed—was primarily patriarchal. The opportunities for women to actively participate in the community, and even their freedom of movement, were tightly restricted. As first daughters and then wives, they were severely confined within the family sphere, essentially the property of fathers and then husbands. The only exceptions were widows and prostitutes who enjoyed certain relative freedoms. And only wives of kings and female members of priestly families had any access to the places of secular or sacred authority.[7] Men held the power, and the disenfranchised women had to find their own ways of getting things done.

Apart from time-honored husband-counseling, women had no ethical or obvious options. Inevitably they were often compelled to rely on cajoling, manipulation, and even occasionally trickery. But unexpectedly, mostly in the Hebrew Bible women are *not* condemned for their wiles. Instead they are actually *praised* for their skullduggery.

But beyond that, there is compelling evidence, at least before the monarchy, that women could and did have a greater role in the running of society, of an authoritative wisdom tradition that was specifically their domain. We have already seen hints of this in the case of Deborah, and there may be others even in the earliest Israelite myths, albeit concealed under later rewriting.

Our modern reading of the apparently negative Hebrew Bible portrayal of women may be the result of something very unexpected. It's not so much that the stories originated in a male-dominated society, but that they have been interpreted by another male-based culture—*our own*. For example, the traditional Christian interpretation of the Adam and Eve story apparently casts Eve, and by extension all women, in a submissive role. She is stupidly easy to con (by the serpent) and naturally deceptive (talking Adam into eating the forbidden fruit). In Christianity the story was used to justify centuries of condemnation of women as the Devil's creatures, as in the horrendous witch trials. There was even a serious theological debate about whether women had souls.

One might expect that twentieth- and twenty-first-century feminists would automatically tear the tale of Adam and Eve into shreds. One would not always be right. The pioneer of feminist biblical interpretation was Phyllis Trible, who in 1973 published a watershed article, "Depatriarchalizing in Biblical Interpretation," in the *Journal of the American Academy of Religion*. In the traditional interpretation of Eve's story, women are inherently inferior because she was created after, and from Adam because of his need for a "helper." But Trible argued that Genesis really says the first human was sexually undifferentiated, *adam* meaning both "man" and "human being." The "creation" of a woman marked the division of the first entity into male and female. So men and women were created together. And Eve's status as Adam's "helper" (*ezer*) does not automatically imply subordination; Trible points out that the same word is also applied to Yahweh, and he's certainly not subordinate. (It's also the origin of the name Ezra, and he was not exactly known for his submissiveness either.)

In Trible's interpretation, the serpent chose to speak to Eve, rather than Adam, not because she was the more gullible, but because she was more able to comprehend a reasoned argument.

Ultimately, it is impossible to know what the Eden story authors were thinking. But surely Trible's reading is just as valid as the more familiar version. She is not, as some might think, projecting modern values back onto biblical sagas and twisting them to fit a modern feminist agenda. Frankly, as theories go, it works!

(In her 2005 book, *The Secret History of Lucifer*, Lynn takes a middle view: Adam is just as culpable as Eve in the myth of the Fall. He's also a real sneak, loudly blaming Eve when God rebukes them for disobeying him.)

Going even further, some see the presence of a wisdom goddess in Eden. Carol Meyers in her *Discovering Eve: Ancient Israelite Women in Context* (1988) comments:

> The prominent role of the female rather than the male in the wisdom aspects of the Eden tale is a little-noticed feature of the narrative. It is the woman, and not the man, who perceives the desirability of procuring wisdom. . . . This association between the female and the qualities of wisdom may have a mythic background, with the features of a Semitic wisdom goddess underlying the intellectual prominence of the woman of Eden.[8]

Wherever you delve, there are traces—sometimes just hints—of the lost goddess even in the patriarchal books. But there is more specific evidence for a line of women with a very particular function. And it was based on a special kind of wisdom . . .

THE WISE WOMEN

While not necessarily believing that there was a wisdom goddess per se—although acknowledging there may have been an "echo" of goddess influence—Claudia V. Camp discerns a tradition of wise women in ancient Israel. However, we believe they are not mutually exclusive, if these women were representatives of the goddess cult. There are clues: for example, Deborah dispenses her wisdom from beneath a date palm, a flagrant symbol of Asherah.

The pioneer researcher of the Israelite tradition of wise women was the Dutch biblical scholar P. A. H. de Boer, who in the 1950s wrote a paper identifying a persistent strand within Israelite traditions of wisdom linked to counseling the leaders. Surprisingly, however, de Boer argued women too were part of this tradition.[9] And to him, Deborah was the key, the feisty judge who called herself a "mother in Israel"—superficially an odd phrase, as no children are mentioned in the story. Perhaps that's just as well. De Boer explains: "In her song she is the strong woman who utters a war-song, and she behaves like a bellicose leader of the united tribes."[10]

He questioned the prevailing view that "mother in Israel" was simply an honorific: "The context leads to the interpretation—one who determines the future as a counsellor. In complicated situations one goes to the judge, and she proves to be a strong woman able to give the right decisions." So he concludes that "'Mother in Israel' means counsellor of the people."[11] And counselors above all need wisdom.

The term "mother in Israel" also appears in the story of another wise woman associated with warfare. This concerns an Ephraimite man, named Sheba, who had led a rebellion against David's rule. (Another sign of the ongoing enmity between Ephraim and Judah.) Pursued by David's general Joab, Sheba takes refuge in the city of Abel, which is then besieged by Joab. An anonymous "wise woman" from the city contacts him, demanding to know why he seeks "to destroy a city which is a mother in Israel" and is part of "the heritage of the LORD." She then makes the killer offer: If the people give Sheba up he must spare the city. When Joab agrees, the wise woman persuades the townspeople to decapitate Sheba and throw his head over the city wall. Joab duly withdraws. Clearly no stranger to uncompromising, even—by today's standards—barbaric actions, by doing this she saves the city from the ravages of Joab's soldiers.[12]

De Boer noted that the verb for "destroy," *mut,* which literally means "kill" or "execute," is an odd description of a city but works for an individual. He suggested that it originally referred to the wise woman herself, the sentence changing over the years, when the "mother in Israel" term was no longer understood.[13] He also noted that later Rabbinic traditions said the woman, not the city, was the "mother in Israel." If so—and it's the only sensible interpretation—then the wise woman belonged to the same line as Deborah.

The wise woman says Abel was where people flocked for counseling and to settle disputes, which de Boer interprets as a place of oracle. Again, this is reminiscent of Deborah, who gives judgment—counsel, probably through divination—from a specific location, beneath the iconic palm tree in the land of Ephraim. Both are places of oracle where a wise woman gives advice.

Another interesting woman, again associated with a specific town, features in an earlier episode in Samuel: the "wise woman of Tekoa."[14] At David's court, she is involved in a complicated scheme by Joab to bring David's exiled son and heir Absalom back to Jerusalem. This began when David's oldest son Amnon raped his half sister Tamar. In revenge David's favorite son Absalom arranged for Amnon to be murdered when he was drunk at a banquet. Absalom then went into exile. Three years later David longed to call him back but realized he would have to be executed as a murderer. What to do? Who to turn to for advice?

Joab sends to Tekoa for the wise woman—she is anonymous like the woman in the Abel story—who goes to David posing as a mourning widow whose son killed his brother in a fight, and asks him to be merciful to the killer so that her late husband's inheritance can continue. When he agrees, immediately she demands why, if he can do it for her son, he can't do it for his own. Caught in her logical trap, David orders Joab to bring Absalom back to Jerusalem.

Although clearly garbled, the story hinges on the authority of the woman, who operates very similarly to the Wise Woman of Abel. Both confront a figure of authority and use similar rhetoric to coax them to do as they desire. As Claudia Camp observes, the women "appear in situations in which they act in a manner associated with a prophet and a military leader, respectively, while using forms of language associated with the wisdom tradition."[15] And both show immense authority. After all, the Tekoa woman takes King David—no less—to task, and more-or-less compels him to do as she says.

Both issue challenges in the form of questions, the Wise Woman of Abel to Joab: "Why will you swallow up the heritage of the LORD?" while the Wise Woman of Tekoa demands of David: "Why then have you planned such a thing against the people of God?"[16] This confrontational stance would have proved highly dangerous for ordinary women, but wise women seem protected by their very tradition. They were obviously *allowed* to speak their minds, presumably because their pronouncements were believed to come from God. Indeed, both use the phrase "heritage of Yahweh/God," implying that they are its keepers.

Building on P. A. H. de Boer's work, in 1981 Claudia Camp wrote a paper for the *Catholic Bible Quarterly* on the similarities between the wise women of Abel and Tekoa, concluding they were not coincidental but showed the women to enjoy an identical leadership role of some kind. As she says, these particular wise women "are representatives of at least one significant, political role available to women in the years preceding the establishment of the kingship in Israel, a role that continued to exist into the monarchic era, but of which we have no evidence after the time of David."[17] They had real political clout—but apparently because they spoke for Yahweh.

Clearly the wisdom role was that of the "mother in Israel," who protects, liberates, and nurtures her people. But mothers are not necessarily passive; they are not always in cuddly mode. After all, there are few fiercer animals than mothers protecting their young.

However, not only does these academics' view of the wise women clarify their tradition, but we have spotted another possible theme: As we have seen, in the early Canaanite days Asherah was admired for her skill in indirect persuasion—or manipulation—of her husband El. This special sort of wisdom is precisely the type that de Boer and Camp attribute to the wise women.

Asherah is there even in the wise-woman legends, the mothers in Israel. She was counselor of the ruling god, using her powers of persuasion to guide him, while the mothers in Israel did the same for their male rulers. The tradition of the wise woman, protector of her people—both from external threats and the misrule of kings—was almost certainly directly related to Asherah and her cult. Her religion was primarily about holding the people together at the most intensely intimate and powerful level: that of mother and child.

No one knows how far back the wise woman tradition goes. Presumably it included Moses's sister, the prophetess Miriam, perhaps even the role model for the mothers in Israel, just as her brother was for male prophets. Miriam questions Moses's authority like the wise women in Samuel, although in this case she loses—Yahweh chooses to back Moses.

ASHERAH'S PRIESTESSES

But is there any truth in the scurrilous accusations of sex rites in the Asherah cult? This is hugely controversial territory among both theologians and academics. Sex certainly played a part in aspects of many ancient religions, and at many levels.

The ordinary folk among Israel's neighbors had their fertility rituals—often to welcome in springtime and to celebrate the harvest. The eminent twentieth-century American archaeologist and rabbi Nelson Glueck remarks about the other Near Eastern cultures: "The excitement of pagan worship and participation in feasts of sacrificial offerings apparently often led male and female worshipers to join together in feverish consummation of fertility rites."[18]

At a higher level, there was the sacred marriage, or *hieros gamos,* where a priest and priestess united sexually to represent the union of god and goddess, to ensure fertility and abundance for their people. Then there is cult or temple prostitution.

Sacred prostitution sees a priestess literally embody the goddess—it was believed—during sexual rites either with priests or male worshippers. Although rarely described as such, this is where goddess worship becomes distinctly shamanic: For the duration of the act, the priestess is not only channeling the deity, she actually *becomes* the goddess. The sacred prostitute really *is* the sacred feminine. In some societies the male supplicant was not required to pay a fee, so some question the accuracy of the term *prostitution,* preferring for example "sacred sexual rites," and "hierodule," or "sacred servant," instead of "prostitute."

The whole topic of sacred sexuality—male or female prostitution or otherwise—is entirely foreign to most people today. As A. T. Mann and Jane Lyle say in their landmark 1995 book, *Sacred Sexuality,* "In our modern world sexuality is largely condemned by major religions. We are taught that it is dark, degenerate, a primary sin of humanity, to be countered only by suppression and redeemed by celibacy."[19] However, they go on: "We know that most holistic and reverential attitudes towards sexuality were evident in the earliest cultures. In many ways it seems that we have degenerated from an initial state of [psychological and sexual] integration with nature, rather than ascended."[20]

Nancy Qualls-Corbett, in her important 1988 study, *The Sacred Prostitute: Eternal Aspects of the Feminine,* notes that profane prostitutes were not the only sort of women who gave their bodies to men: "The degradation of the profane prostitute—who represents the dark side of feminine sexuality—was profound; she was the very antithesis of the sacred prostitute, whose sexuality revered the goddess."[21]

Qualls-Corbett is referring to the long-held belief that in almost all known goddess-worshipping cultures in the ancient world there existed sacred, or temple prostitutes. These were either full-time priestesses, or the goddess's own worshippers, required to give themselves to male devotees for a limited time. This was intended to be a mystical union in which the sexual ecstasy gave both participants a transcendental insight into the nature of the sacred feminine—but with emphasis on the man's experience. Unlike visits to ordinary streetwalkers, however, the implication here is that they have to experience the divine from the goddess's own handmaidens, for as mere men they could never do it for themselves.

Giving themselves to male worshippers was only part of the temple women's role. Priestesses of Isis in Egypt, for example, were required to be usually celibate, but as Mann and Lyle remark, "the cult also contained erotic elements and more than a hint of sacred prostitution."[22]

Outsiders—perhaps not surprisingly—dismissed such ritual fornication as beyond the pale, completely misunderstanding its roots in celebrating the goddess's own erotic and passionate aspect. The Roman satirist Juvenal (ca. 60–130 CE) snapped that the priestesses of the goddess Isis were "no better than bawds," Isis herself being a favorite deity—or so claimed the critics—among Roman streetwalkers.

But did such blatantly sexual practices really feature in the buttoned-up, increasingly patriarchal religion of ancient Israel? The imagery of prostitution, harlotry, and adultery is used throughout the Hebrew Bible when referring to the worship of other gods. Exodus describes the pagan faithful as prostituting themselves, and the prophet Jeremiah accuses the Judahites of "committing adultery with stone and tree."[23] Puzzling—and painful sounding. But as we have seen, the worship of other gods was at one time an integral part of the Israelite religion, leading some, such as Dever, to see such language as specifically aimed at the fertility cult of Asherah.

The term for the "cult prostitute," *qadeshah,* is very different from a profane prostitute, *zonah.* Rahab of Jericho, for example, who provided a safe house for Joshua's spies, was a zonah. Emphatically, though, it is only used of women; apparently the concept of male prostitution was not part of Israelite society, or if it was, no one mentioned it.

But did Asherah worship really involve female and, astonishingly, male prostitutes? Surely there are few asides in the Old Testament whose implications are quite so jaw-dropping! (And presumably these particular passages are not favorite reading in Bible classes or Sunday sermons.) However, the word literally means only "holy or consecrated one." There is no intrinsic sexual connotation at all. That depends entirely on the context.

What is generally translated as "cult male prostitute" is used six times, either in the singular, *qadesh,* or plural, *qadeshim.* There are four references in the books of Kings, all—tellingly—in relation to idolatrous cults. The first, quoted at the end of the last chapter, is when describing Judah's backsliding under Rehoboam and follows an "every high hill and every green tree" reference specifically relating to Asherah's cult.[24] His grandson King Asa of Judah "put away" the male cult prostitutes, and Asa's son Jehoshaphat "exterminated the remnant of the male cult prostitutes" that was left.[25] The final reference in Kings is that enigma during Josiah's purge, when he breaks down their "houses" in the Temple—again, through the mysterious "weaving women," specifically linked to Asherah.[26] The final mention is in Job, where "the godless in heart" end their lives as male cult prostitutes.[27]

Despite the loaded term "prostitute," there's no specific reference in any of these passages to sexual activity. A more natural translation would be "holy men" or "consecrated men." It's only interpreted as "male cult prostitute" because of the way the feminine form of the word is applied to women. In any case, the notion of a sacred *male* prostitute makes little sense in terms of what sacred prostitution is about.

But were there really any female cult prostitutes? *Qadeshah* appears four times in the Hebrew Bible. The first two are in Genesis, back in the time of the Patriarchs, in the rather odd morality tale of Tamar[28]—who is bizarrely listed as an ancestor of Jesus in the New Testament. Tamar was married to Er, the firstborn son of Judah and grandson of Jacob, who was killed by Yahweh for being "wicked in the sight of the LORD" before they have had any children. The custom in such a case was that a widow marry her late husband's nearest male relative—in this case Judah's second son Onan—and their children would be legally the deceased man's.

However, Onan was opposed to the idea of his children with Tamar not being considered his, so when he slept with her he "would waste the semen on the ground"—for which sin Yahweh killed him, too. (Although thought of as masturbation, the sin of onanism is specifically about "wasted" ejaculation.) Judah now only had one son, Shelah, and was unsurprisingly worried that Yahweh would also destroy him, so although he promised Tamar that she could marry him he did nothing about it.

A peeved Tamar, on hearing that Judah was going to another town to get his sheep sheared, disguised herself as a prostitute—which strangely involved putting a veil *on*—and waited on the road outside the town. When Judah passed by, she agreed to have sex with him in return for a goat. Judah gave her his ring, cord, and staff as tokens of the pledge. At this point in the story, Tamar is described as a zonah, a prostitute or harlot, and the fact that she takes payment—the goat— suggests that is precisely what she is.

Back home, Judah sent a friend with the goat to redeem his pledge, but she was nowhere to be found. But something has changed significantly. Now she is described as a *qadeshah,* translated as "cult prostitute" or "shrine prostitute"—the only time the term or its masculine counterpart is applied to a named person in the Hebrew Bible.

Three months later, when Tamar is pregnant, Judah is about to have her burnt for immorality, but she reveals, by showing the tokens, that he is the father. Judah, declaring that "She is more righteous than I," admits he failed in his duty of marrying her to Shelah.

Frankly, the point of the tale is hard to fathom—perhaps you had to be there—but ultimately that hardly matters. As leading Dutch religious scholar Karel van der Toorn writes: "One of the difficulties with this issue is that the difference between secular and sacred prostitution is not always clear in the texts."[29] It's still unclear why Tamar, once a zonah, is suddenly a qadeshah. Any possible explanation has obviously been omitted. There may be a clue, though, in her otherwise mysterious donning of a veil before she couples with Judah: Veils were traditionally worn by sacred prostitutes to represent the hidden mysteries of the goddess. Also, *tamar* means "palm tree"—the hallowed symbol of Asherah.

Qadeshah appears twice more in the Hebrew Bible, once in the injunction in Deuteronomy forbidding the daughters and sons of Israel from being cult prostitutes, and in a passage in the prophet Hosea's book about the people having "left their God to play the whore" by sacrificing on mountains and hills—where men "go aside with prostitutes and sacrifice with cult prostitutes"—associating but not actually equating the two.[30] And they only sacrifice—presumably animals—with the sacred prostitutes. At least here there's no hint of erotic contact except with the profane sex workers.

Although not always with a direct sexual connotation, in the case of the women the term, at least to the writers, does sometimes imply some association with prostitution, or some sort of sexual activity. Emphatically, though, "cult prostitute" is just the English interpretation. Those reading the Hebrew would literally read "holy ones." It's only the implication, supplied by the context, that links the ladies with paid whoredom.

Some scholars, such as Dever, think the word does refer to functionaries of the Asherah cult, "dedicated" to a service of which the Yahwist reformers disapproved.[31] For Meindert Dijkstra, who rejects the prostitute interpretation, they are "presumably temple staff involved in the cult of the Asherah."[32] He links them with the "women who served at the entrance of the tent of meeting" (the Tabernacle) whom we mused about in chapter 1: "Obviously there were some forms of worship that were considered the special domain of a trained class of women. They may have belonged to the female members of the caste of the *qedesim* [*qadeshim*] who played a major role of care and provision in the worship of the Asherah in the Temple of Jerusalem."[33] Analyzing its contexts, Phyllis A. Bird concludes that the word described the religious function of the women: "I believe we must reconstruct a class of female attendants at the rural shrines representing a form of cultic service on the part of women that may once have had a recognized place in Israelite worship, but was ultimately rejected."[34] She, too, suggests a connection with the "women who served at the entrance of the tent of meeting" and with Miriam leading the women in the Song of the Sea. However, we can take it further.

Asherah was also known, in Canaan and Egypt, as Qadesh, which refers to her more overtly sexual, eroticized role. Qadesh is also derived from "holy" or "consecrated." Therefore, the female and male "sacred prostitutes," *qadeshah* and *qadesh,* could simply refer to the priesthood of her cult, consisting of both men and women. Perhaps it should be something like "Qadeshites," meaning "priestess/priest of Qadesh/ Asherah." (Remember that Miriam was buried in a place called Kadesh—or Qadesh—perhaps another clue.)

As the word relates to Asherah's sexual aspect this would explain the association with prostitution, which the hardline Yahwists would naturally have condemned as simple harlotry. And although it does imply that sexual rites of the kind practiced in other Near Eastern cultures played a part in the Asherah cult, perhaps this *only* took place when her Qadesh aspect was being honored.

What about Dijkstra's and Bird's suggestion of a connection with the "women who served at the entrance to the tent of meeting," mentioned so enigmatically in Exodus and Samuel? We recall that the two priestly sons of the high priest, Hophni and Phinehas, were denounced for having sex with them. While presented as the men's sin (which loses Israel the Ark of the Covenant for a while, and Hophni and Phinehas their lives), surprisingly no blame is attached to the women.

Given the usual moral certainties of the Bible writers, we would expect them to thunder that the women had led the priests astray with their predatory whoredom. Indeed, in cases of sexual immorality, such as adultery, the Law says that both parties must be punished by death—and there is no suggestion of rape. Yet it seems that Hophni and Phinehas' transgression was sleeping with the women, while bizarrely it was acceptable for the women to have had sex with them. Perhaps—ironically—priests were not supposed to have sex with the hierodules, except in rituals.

There is further evidence for this cult-within-a-cult even in the book of Hosea, the first of the Yahweh-alone prophets.

"WIFE OF WHOREDOM"

The prophet Hosea's book is essentially one sustained rant that equates the unfaithfulness of his wife Gomer, whom he denounces as an adulteress and a whore, with the way the people of the Kingdom of Israel treat Yahweh—his abandonment in favor of other gods. Some researchers believe this to be more than a mere metaphor. Theologian Stephen Haar of the Australian Lutheran College points out that Hosea was directed by God to "take a wife of whoredom"—not just a prostitute but one who belongs to the "spirit of whoredom."[35] He proposes it meant taking a wife from the women in the Kingdom of Israel who participated in sacred sex rites. If so, Hosea was literally linking his wife Gomer and the goddess cults.

Haar thinks "wife of whoredom" "most probably alluded to a Canaanite sexual rite," concluding: "Hosea married a 'wife of whoredom' as a symbol of the unceasing 'marriage' love between God and

Israel. This theme, which appears often in the prophetical books, was most probably coined after the myth of the *hieros gamos* between the high god and the mother/love goddess."[36] So Hosea's marriage was—at least originally—a sacred one.

To Haar, the original *hieros gamos* rite is essentially being tamed by making it a symbol of Yahweh's relationship with his chosen people. He does, however, consider these cults foreign, Canaanite practices that had infiltrated the northern kingdom, although there is no suggestion that Gomer is a foreigner (and Hosea would certainly have mentioned it if she was). Instead, we suggest it refers to the Asherah/Qadesh cult—and if so, of course Hosea is acknowledging its existence in the Kingdom of Israel, while condemning it (together with his wife) as not being a true part of Yahwism.

British biblical scholar Martin Scott agrees that Gomer was a "cultic" prostitute, and not just a sex worker or adulteress, seeing it signaled in Hosea's demand that she "put away her whoring from her face, and her adultery from between her breasts."[37] He explains: "it is made clear that she is a cultic prostitute, since she had to remove the objects/marks of her cult from herself."[38] Noting the link between sacred prostitution and Israel's apostasy, he argues that, "What this adoption of the symbolism of marriage between prophet and prostitute does is to try and bring the goddess under the control of Yahwism in a form that does not threaten the relationship of Yahweh and the people."[39] He links this to a process described by feminist theologian Rosemary Radford Ruether in which the Yahwists sought to transform "the Sacred Marriage from a Goddess-King relationship into a patriarchal God-servant wife" one.[40]

We can now see that there was a pronounced sexual aspect to Asherah's cult—not surprising, considering that sacred sex was so much a part of ancient worship. But when her cult was suppressed, did this aspect simply die away? We will be returning to this major point later in the book. But there was another goddess linked with Asherah, also with a strong sexual aspect, whose major characteristic was Kali-like violence . . .

4

Goddesses to Be Reckoned With

Now we know that Asherah worship—even adoration—refused to go away in the psyche of the ancient Israelites, often against heavy opposition. But how did it manage to survive the often seismic ups and downs of their history? And was Asherah always their *only* beloved goddess? Her seldom uncomplicated story is naturally inextricably interwoven with that of her people. But what a dramatic story that was.

Nemesis awaited the Assyrian Empire that had brought down the Kingdom of Israel. It had imploded in the last decades of the seventh century BCE, broken up by a series of internal rebellions. But ironically, this defeat of their old enemies did not spell triumph for the Israelites. A new empire had risen from its ashes in Babylonia in Mesopotamia and the armies of its second king, Nebuchadnezzar II, marched unstoppably into Syria, Phoenicia, and Arabia, either conquering cities or levying heavy tribute to prevent invasion—basically imposing a protection racket on a grand scale.

Then came absolute cataclysm for the Judahites, which left a profound scar on their collective soul; the shock of it still resonates today. In 597 BCE Nebuchadnezzar emphatically captured Jerusalem, overthrowing and imprisoning its king, Jehoiachin, who was taken into captivity in Babylon along with the cream of the Judahite elite. The Babylonian conqueror installed Jehoiachin's uncle Zedekiah as puppet king, and for the next decade Judah staggered on as a vassal state. But when Nebuchadnezzar became locked in war with Egypt, Zedekiah took the golden opportunity to rebel. This, as things turned out, was not a wise move. Nebuchadnezzar turned all his considerable firepower on the Judahites, culminating in the unthinkable: After a three-year siege in 587 BCE their beloved holy city of Jerusalem fell. The shock and trauma were immense.

The city was pillaged, its walls demolished and the great Temple—the house of God and symbol of national pride and honor—lay in smoking ruins. The horrors continued: Zedekiah was blinded, after being forced to watch his sons being executed, and was dragged off to Babylon in a second wave of deportation of royals, officials, and priests. The once-proud Judah became a province, Yehud, of the Babylonian Empire, with a governor appointed by Babylon to do its bidding.

JEREMIAH SPEAKS!

Into this febrile mix, enter a Yahwist prophet called Jeremiah, who—all things considered—had something of a lucky break. When the Babylonians marched into Jerusalem, they found him in prison, where he had been thrown because of his uncompromising stance on the moral status of the establishment. His unfettered rants about Judah and its kings being unworthy of Yahweh since the reign of Josiah had not gone down well. Patience at breaking point, Zedekiah finally had him put away for preaching that the Lord had told him he *wanted* Babylon to take Jerusalem, to teach its rulers and people a lesson. Not surprisingly, this vociferous defeatism seriously undermined the morale of the defending troops, especially as Jeremiah showed no signs of shutting up. (Perhaps his claims of a hotline to Yahweh prevented the authorities from executing him for what was, after all, actually treason.)

However, Jeremiah's attitude made him a potentially useful ally to the Babylonian overlords, who released him and treated him well—after all, he had no problem with them as occupiers of Jerusalem. Rather the opposite, in fact: he declared to anyone who would listen, and presumably even those who wouldn't, that Yahweh fully approved of the Babylonian occupiers. Now a free man, Jeremiah joined the entourage of the Jew whom Nebuchadnezzar appointed governor of his new province of Yehud, Gedaliah, whose new court was at Mizpah in Benjamin's territory. (Jerusalem was too wrecked even to consider as a hub.) Many of the Jews who had fled to neighboring lands returned to Judah after Gedaliah's appointment. Perhaps things weren't going to be so bad under the Babylonians after all . . .

Jeremiah wrote—or rather dictated to his long-suffering scribe Baruch—the book that bears his name, a sort of memoir that, among other things, presents a firsthand, if Yahwist-biased, account of the fall of Jerusalem. This is one of the few books of the Hebrew Bible that really is by its alleged author, although like all the others, it was probably given an editorial tweak in Ezra's day. Some of the predictions about the eventual return from Babylon are just a shade too accurate, especially given the extent of Jeremiah's errors earlier in his career about how events, according to Yahweh, were going to transpire.

According to his own report, Jeremiah, the son of a Benjamite priest, started hearing Yahweh's voice in the thirteenth year of Josiah's reign, so in 626 BCE—before Josiah embarked on his reforms. Jeremiah describes himself as a "youth" at the time. After taking some time to prepare himself, he embarked on his career as a wandering prophet of doom, fanatically haranguing the people—no doubt complete with flying spittle—and dictating letters to kings and other officials. They probably saw him as a complete pest.

Despite Josiah's reforms, Jeremiah thought Judah had done nowhere near enough to avert Yahweh's wrath. After all, the "idolatrous" cults were still blatantly in existence. He trotted out the usual anti-Asherah smears, accusing the Judahites of "committing adultery with stone and tree," evoking her iconic pillar and tree image.[1] He repeats other standard formulae and innuendo: "Yes, on every high hill and under every green tree you bowed down like a whore."[2]

Significantly, Jeremiah initially preached that Yahweh had declared the tribes of the northern kingdom would invade Judah and take Jerusalem. God would forgive the former Kingdom of Israel its transgressions, now purged by the Assyrian conquest, and use it to punish Judah, which was even worse. ("Faithless Israel has shown herself more righteous than treacherous Judah.")[3]

About five years after the Babylonian conquest, Governor Gedaliah was assassinated by one of the Judahite royal princes. Fearing Nebuchadnezzar's reprisals, a substantial number of the courtiers at Mizpah, led by the general Johanan and including royals, officials, and army officers, decamped to Egypt. The pharaoh, Apries, was an ally: he had dispatched soldiers to help Judah defend Jerusalem but had shrewdly called them off, realizing that it would be an act of madness to risk a direct confrontation with the all-conquering Nebuchadnezzar. Jeremiah declared Yahweh had told him they had nothing to fear from the Babylonian king, and that they would all die if they went. This was met with some skepticism, and he relates that they forced him to accompany them. (They might have regretted this. Having Jeremiah as a traveling companion was probably something of an ordeal.)

The refugees settled near Tanis in the Nile delta, where there was already a Jewish community. It was one of several that Jeremiah mentions—there were others at Migdol and Memphis, for example. Clearly immigrants from Judah and Israel had settled in Egypt, although we know nothing about their reasons or when they did so. Undoubtedly some had fled during all those years of military menace from the Assyrians and Babylonians, but probably some had migrated earlier. (One crucially important expatriate community that definitely had, we will meet later.) It was in Egypt that Jeremiah dictated his life story.

THE QUEEN OF HEAVEN

Jeremiah must have been rapturous. He had a whole new audience to harangue, ordering them with all the considerable self-righteousness at his command to heed the dire warning of Jerusalem and mend their wicked ways. Most of the communities were in or around the delta but a particularly significant encounter took place further south. Jeremiah names the place as Pathros, but that hardly narrows it down, as that is just the Egyptian term for the "southern land," Upper Egypt, which covers an extensive area.

After delivering a message from Yahweh, Jeremiah relates (referring to himself in the third person, as was his habit):

> Then all the men who knew that their wives had made offerings to other gods, and all the women who stood by, a great assembly, all the people who lived in Pathros in the land of Egypt, answered Jeremiah: "As for the word that you have spoken to us in the name of the LORD we will not listen to you. But we will do everything that we have vowed, make offerings to the queen of heaven and pour out drink offerings to her, as we did, both we and our fathers, our kings and our officials, in the cities of Judah and in the streets of Jerusalem. For then we had plenty of food, and prospered, and saw no disaster. But since we left off making offerings to the queen of heaven and pouring out drink offerings to her, we have lacked everything and have been consumed by the sword and by famine." And the women said, "When we made offerings to the queen of heaven and poured out drink offerings to her, was it without our husbands' approval that we made cakes for her bearing her image and poured out drink offerings to her?"[4]

Jeremiah responded huffily to these shameless apostates, declaring in terms: "To hell with you then, do what you want. But you'll be sorry!" This is the last passage in the book. What happened to him is unknown, but given his propensity for scattergun insults, it seems unlikely he died peacefully in bed surrounded by a loving family.

The Israelite refugees in Pathros took the diametrically opposite position to Jeremiah: To them it was turning away from the Queen of

Heaven and other gods alongside Yahweh (presumably at the urging of similar prophets) that had caused the calamity. But there's a particularly interesting implication. As recorded by Jeremiah, the ritual cake baking and drink offering was not something the expatriate Jews had simply picked up in a foreign land. It had clearly been the custom of "both we and our fathers, our kings and our officials, in the cities of Judah and in the streets of Jerusalem"—a very long-established tradition, back in Judah. Neither was it just practiced by the common people; it was also a rite shared by the grand folk of the royal court. John Day states: "the text in Jeremiah 44 makes it abundantly clear that the worship of the Queen of Heaven was deep-seated among both the ordinary people and rulers of Judah and Jerusalem and had gone back several generations."[5]

In fact, Jeremiah had mentioned the worship of the Queen of Heaven earlier in his memoir, when he was still preaching in Jerusalem, when Yahweh said to him:

> As for you, do not pray for this people, or lift up a cry or prayer for them, and do not intercede with me, for I will not hear you. Do you not see what they are doing in the cities of Judah and in the streets of Jerusalem? The children gather wood, the fathers kindle fire, and the women knead dough, to make cakes for the queen of heaven. And they pour out drink offerings to other gods, to provoke me to anger.[6]

Judging by this description, the worship of the Queen of Heaven seems to have been most prevalent among the women, although approved of by the men. And given the emphasis on an abundance of food in her rites—the celebration of plenty—this goddess must have possessed a well-known fertility aspect.

The identity of the Queen of Heaven is hotly debated among scholars. Given her prevalence among Israelites, Asherah is an obvious candidate, although there are objections that the offering of cakes is never actually spelled out as part of her worship. (This is true, but then the Hebrew Bible never describes her rites in much detail anyway.)

Some, such as John Day, William Dever, and Susan Ackerman, think the Queen is, or may be, Astarte,[7] who appears in the Hebrew Bible as the scribal distortion Ashtoreth (or plural Ashtaroth). As she was the major goddess of the Phoenicians, whose worship spread around the Mediterranean and Near East, it would be surprising if she had not permeated into the folk religion of the Israelites at some level, where she would naturally have been assimilated to Asherah.

Probably the favorite candidate for "Queen of Heaven," but only marginally, is Astarte's Mesopotamian equivalent Ishtar, goddess of fertility, love, sex, war, power, and much else—after all, that was already one of her own traditional epithets. Her rites also included offering special cakes. A few experts plump for the Canaanite war-goddess Anat (of whom more later), who shares many of the attributes of Ishtar.

However, because of the ancient peoples' fluid attitude to deities—particularly goddesses—attributes were easily assimilated and religious practices often transferred. Indeed, trying to pin a precise identity on the Queen of Heaven can be as frustrating and unrewarding as trying to knit fog. Those with similar characters, attributes, and areas of responsibility become interchangeable. They merge and split. Some whom we think of now as two goddesses began as alternative names for just one. Raphael Patai argues this is a strong possibility that this was true of Astarte and Anat.[8]

In Canaanite mythology, Astarte was sometimes the consort of Baal in place of the war-goddess Anat, and in Egypt, she and Anat were the wives of Set. As we have seen, in Egypt Asherah, in her Qadesh persona, was equated with both Astarte and Anat who in turn had much in common with Ishtar. So, the Queen of Heaven could have been any or all of them. But given Asherah's supremacy in the Yahweh religion, she remains a very credible candidate. The bottom line is that the ancestors of the Judahite community encountered by Jeremiah had been worshipping the Queen for generations.

However, there was one other Hebrew community in southern Egypt who associated *another* goddess with Yahweh, and who was actually known as "Queen of Heaven" in some Egyptian texts.[9] This was a remarkable female archetype called Anat. And this expatriate community yielded yet more clues about not just the place of the sacred feminine in the early Israelite religion but also the role of ordinary women—with surprising results.

THE GODDESS OF ELEPHANTINE

Elephantine is a small island—just 1.25 miles by .3 of a mile (2 kilometers by half a kilometer)—situated in the Nile at the first cataract, near the border with Nubia in the far south of Egypt. The island is part of the modern city of Aswan. Elephantine was the Greek translation of the Egyptian *Yeb,* or "place of elephants." As no elephants had ever been spotted there, this remains something of a puzzle. Some think the island looks like swimming elephants.

This tiny island has some fascinating secrets to reveal. From the late nineteenth century, ancient papyri that had been found on Elephantine began surfacing on the Egyptian antiquities market that—to the enormous surprise of historians and archaeologists—belonged to a *Hebrew* community. More papyri were found on Elephantine itself when excavations began in 1901.

It transpired that the community had grown up around a garrison of Hebrew mercenaries stationed there by the Egyptians—and later Persians—in case of trouble on the border. (Israelites were highly regarded as soldiers in the ancient world.)

As the community is customarily referred to as "Jewish" or "Judean" it is naturally assumed its inhabitants had some connection with Jerusalem. In fact, the settlement may owe its origins to the rival Kingdom of Israel or a time even further back in Israelite history. Some academics, such as Bezalel Porten of the Hebrew University of Jerusalem (the go-to scholar on all matters Elephantine), caution that a more neutral term such as "Hebrews" would be more apt, especially as that's what the ancient Israelites called themselves in relation to other peoples.

Eventually a large collection of documents was assembled, covering all aspects of the Elephantine community's daily life, including legal contracts for business, marriages and divorces, and official and personal letters. Although a few are in Egyptian and Greek, they are mostly in Aramaic, a language related to Hebrew, originally spoken by people in western Syria but adopted widely in the region—including in Israel and Judah—after the rise of the Assyrian Empire in the tenth century BCE. Aramaic was the language of bureaucrats and merchants.

Most of these documents date from about 500 BCE to the end of the settlement just over a century later, although a few are from two or three hundred years earlier. However, the community had certainly been around for some time before then—the question is just how long.

To put the period in perspective, it was one of enormous upheaval, being shortly after the return of the Judahites from the Babylonian Captivity, and during Nehemiah and Ezra's reinvention of the religion. In Egypt, it was when (525–404 BCE) the Persian Empire controlled the country after it was invaded by Cyrus II—the liberator of the Jews in Babylon—although records of his conquest state that the Elephantine Hebrew community was already there when he arrived.

The documents enabled researchers to build up fascinating detail about the community's everyday life—which is rare, as archaeologists can usually only deal in what has literally been left in stone. After all, due to the climate, any similar documents in Israel would have perished long before, whereas hot, dry Egypt kept papyri well preserved. Consequently, we know much more about everyday life on Elephantine than we ever did about Jerusalem in that era. And what we discover is extremely telling.

One unexpected detail to emerge was the status of women—perhaps even more unusual for a macho garrison town. Their lives, it appears, were very similar to those of their Egyptian sisters, then the most liberal and egalitarian in the known world. Among many other Elephantine records of women owning property in their own right, there is a legal document concerning the transfer of house ownership from father to daughter—who, moreover, he had by an Egyptian slave girl he married after purchasing her freedom. And women could (and did) institute divorce, which would have been absolute anathema to the Deuteronomists—and, it must be said, to other cultures such as the ancient Greeks and Romans, whose records on women's rights were also unimpressive to say the least. But had the Elephantine Hebrews simply adopted Egyptian ways, or did their community date from before the Law had been "discovered"? Revelations about the Elephantine community were to turn assumptions about the Hebrew religion itself upside down.

It has always been believed there was only ever one Temple permissible in the whole world, the great focal point of the religion—and it had to be in Jerusalem. But in 1907 a dig led by the German archaeologist Otto Rubensohn found three documents relating to a Hebrew *temple* on Elephantine.

There it was, an Israelite Temple—on Elephantine Island. The evidence is unassailable, right there in legal documents relating to the sale of property *adjacent to the temple,* which even enabled Bezalel Porten, in the early 1960s, to reconstruct its dimensions. Even more bizarrely—or apparently so—it was situated next to a shrine to the Egyptian Ram-headed god Khnum, god of the source of the Nile.

After the revelation of the existence of a temple, the ruin of the edifice itself was finally discovered, again by German archaeologists, in 1967. The whole sanctuary was about 130 by 80 feet (40 meters by 24 meters), and the temple itself 40 feet long by 20 wide (12 meters by 6 meters). Not exactly massive but substantial enough.

Yet before the papyri were discovered the existence of the temple was completely unsuspected—there's not a word about it anywhere in history. (Perhaps there are the remains of other temples hidden out there. After all, any evidential records, without the preservative benefit of the Egyptian climate, might just have rotted away.)

The Elephantine Temple was dedicated to Yahu, or rather YHW, the Aramaic form of Yahweh. Yahu is also invoked in contracts, greetings, and blessings in letters, in the forms YHW or YHH. Significantly, this is not the Tetragrammaton (YHWH) that was regarded as the sacred name of God in the mainstream religion, and as it never appears in the Elephantine papyri, this suggests that their version dated back further than the Deuteronomist religion.

The surprises just keep coming. It transpires that even Elephantine was not the only temple outside of Jerusalem. Despite Deuteronomy's injunction that there could only be one temple where sacrifices could be made to Yahweh, there were others—some even built after Jerusalem's. For example, in the 1960s one explicitly described as a "Temple of Yahweh" in inscriptions, was discovered in a fortress complex at Arad in Judah (so also connected with soldiering). Dating from the eighth century BCE—a couple of centuries after the Jerusalem Temple—it had the same layout as Solomon's, including a "Holy of Holies" behind a curtain. Excavations showed that Yahweh was venerated there in the form of a standing stone.[10]

Clearly, it was not actually forbidden to set up temples to worship Yahweh other than in Jerusalem. However, Elephantine's major significance is that animal sacrifices were offered to him there, which *was* supposed to be exclusive to Jerusalem. Therefore, it must have been in operation since before the relevant law in Deuteronomy. We can only be sure that the rule about sacrifice applied from the "discovery" of Deuteronomy in 621 BCE, but even so it establishes that the Elephantine Temple was at least older than that, although the origins and dating of the Elephantine community have been immensely controversial. Nothing in the papyri indicates when it was first settled or when the temple was built. The documents relating to the temple, which are from the period when the community was at its peak, all date from after about 500 BCE.

Most scholars, conservatively, place the founding of the community at around 650 BCE, so between the falls of the Kingdom of Israel and Judah, although some think the founders may have come from the Kingdom of Israel before that, or perhaps they were fleeing the Assyrians in the 720s BCE.

Other clues in the papyri show marked differences in the religious practices at Elephantine. None of the writings, incidentally, are sacred texts: the only religious ones refer to the administration of the temple, so sadly only tell us about its beliefs and rituals indirectly.

There are some clues in the "Passover Letter," written in 419 or 418 BCE by one Hananiah—an official in Jerusalem—to the religious head of the Elephantine community, setting out the correct way to observe Passover: the dates, duration, dietary rules, activities to be avoided and so on.[11] If this kind of instruction was necessary, obviously the community there had no idea about the officially approved practices. It's unknown whether Hananiah sent his letter on the initiative of Jerusalem or whether the Elephantine priests themselves had asked for guidance, but we should remember that this was a time, in the wake of Nehemiah and Ezra's reforms, when Jerusalem was keen to standardize the whole religion—wherever it might be practiced.

It seems the community already routinely celebrated Passover before receiving the letter, but in their own way. It seemed to have had no fixed date, for example. (Maybe they thought it wasn't too diplomatic to draw attention to a festival that celebrated their people's delivery from the wicked Egyptians, while actually living in Egypt.)

Hananiah's Yahwist zeal had a serious effect on community relations. When he visited Elephantine in person, his words or deeds disastrously provoked the priests of Khnum. After the tolerance between the Hebrews and the pagans, Hananiah single-handedly provoked the near destruction of the temple by Egyptian troops at the instigation of Khnum's high priest in 410 BCE. It was rebuilt—although abandoned fifty or sixty years later when the whole community, Egyptian and Hebrew, was moved out.

One of the first scholars to address the issue of the age of this settlement, E. C. L. MacLaurin of the University of Sydney, in a paper in the *Journal of Near Eastern Studies* in 1968, concluded that it had been founded *much* earlier. One of his major reasons was that the Elephantine priests treated Jerusalem and Samaria, the religious centers of the two kingdoms, as essentially the same, which he argues could only be the case if they had left before the division.[12] As the schism took place between 930 and 910 BCE, that's a seriously long time back.

In fact, MacLaurin concluded that the Elephantine community was established even before the Exodus, by Hebrews who had never left Egypt. This is partly based on their use of the "Yahu" form of Yahweh, predating the Tetragrammaton, which MacLaurin took to be established at Sinai just after the Exodus. But as no one knows how long after the event the account in the book of Exodus was written, MacLaurin's conclusions are obviously open to dispute.

However, one of the observations on which MacLaurin built his argument is more credible: "The deities worshipped at Yeb [Elephantine] belonged to a markedly ancient group."[13] Yes, *deities* plural—and *once again the Hebrew pantheon also included a goddess . . .*

The Elephantine community paired Yahweh with a female deity—which was probably enough to give Hananiah apoplexy. But this time the representative of the sacred feminine is not Asherah, but another Canaanite goddess named Anat, or Anath. The papyri mention "Anat-Yahu," meaning "Anat of Yahu," aligning her with Asherah in the sweet-sounding "Yahweh and his Asherah" inscriptions described in the last chapter. John Day firmly summarizes the situation: "It therefore seems indubitable that the goddess Anat, in the form of Anat-Yahu, did function as Yahweh's wife amongst the Jews at Elephantine in the fifth century BCE."[14] But, as we will see, although Asherah could seem like a sweet mother or even Grandma figure, *sweet* is not the most apt word to describe the goddess Anat.

The Elephantine records also refer to a deity called "Anat-Bethel." *Bethel* means "House of God" and often refers to a standing stone, which as we have seen, represented Yahweh.[15] Therefore "Anat-Bethel" is another term for "Anat-Yahu." It seems significant that Bethel was also a sacred site in Ephraim—and one associated with the prophetess Deborah. This is another sign that the "Jewish" community at Elephantine really originated in the northern kingdom.

It used to be assumed that the Elephantine community was made up of "heretical Jews" who, being isolated from the main stream of the religion had adopted ideas from the surrounding pagans. We admit that was pretty much our own stance when we wrote *The Templar Revelation* back in the mid-1990s. However, as more evidence flooded in about the survival of polytheism, particularly goddess worship, in the religion of Israel and Judah, it's become clear that the Elephantine community was *not* an aberration. The only unexpected revelation is that they paired Yahweh with Anat instead of Asherah.

The union of Yahweh and Anat points to a much older origin for the community and temple, at least before the fall of the northern kingdom in 721 BCE. There are no clues in either the Hebrew Bible or archaeology that Anat had played any part in Israelite worship at least since the establishment of the monarchy (around 1000 BCE). There are, however, indications she was known from a much earlier time in Israelite history. But first, who exactly was this strangely powerful Anat?

THE FEARSOME TWOSOME

Anat was another Canaanite goddess who stars in the Ugarit texts, in which she is the daughter of Asherah—but a very different sort of lady.

Put simply, Anat is very, very scary. Although a goddess of love—or rather lust—she also ruled over death, appropriate for a formidable warrior goddess, and highly apt as the object of worship by the mercenaries of Elephantine. Anat positively delighted in gore and guts. One of the Ugarit texts describes her wading "up to her skirts" in the blood of the warriors she cuts down.

Patai explains her uncompromisingly dark side: "In Ugaritic mythology, Anath is the by far most important female figure, the goddess of love and war, virginal and yet wanton, amorous and yet given to uncontrollable outbursts of rage and appalling acts of cruelty."[16] *Wanton* is by no means extreme enough to describe her activities. She coupled with almost anything with a pulse. As Patai puts it discreetly, "she loved gods, men, and animals."[17]

In the Ugarit texts, Anat was the consort of Baal (as occasionally was Astarte). Theirs was, as might be imagined, a passionate and highly charged erotic relationship. One text has them having sex seventy-seven times in a row, Baal sometimes taking the form of a bull, presumably for variety. When not actually fornicating, she and Baal fight side by side—divine comrades in arms, an utterly fearsome twosome.

Difficult to comprehend, she's an endless paradox. One of her titles is "Maiden Anat," but she is also depicted as "copulating with him [Baal] endlessly."[18] A Ugaritic poem celebrates her glorying in gore:

> *Under her, like balls, heads,*
> *Above her, like locusts, hand[s],*
> *Like hoppers, heaps of warrior-hands.*
> *She fixed heads to her back,*
> *Fastened hands to her waist . . .*
>
> *Her innards swell with laughter,*
> *Her heart fills with joy,*
> *The innards of Anat well with triumph.*
> *Knee-deep she gleans in warrior blood,*
> *Neck-deep in the gore of soldiers,*
> *Until she is sated with fighting in the house,*
> *With battling amidst the tables.*[19]

Anat intimidated and visited violence not just on hapless humans, but also her fellow deities—even the supreme god El. In one tale from Ugarit, she threatens that if he doesn't agree to a request of Baal's:

> *I will [strike] your head;*
> *I will make your grey hair run with blood,*
> *the grey hair of your beard with gore!*[20]

Man, woman, or god, you didn't mess with Anat.

In one myth, even poor Asherah trembles with fear when she sees Anat and Baal approaching. In another story, the nightmare duo decides to make war on death itself, by taking on the god of the underworld, Mot. But for once they've overreached themselves: Mot defeats Baal in combat and carries him off to the underworld as his slave. Baal is, at least symbolically, dead, taking on the characteristics of a dying-and-rising fertility god. Annual Canaanite mystery plays, as we saw when discussing Jezebel, dramatized this aspect of Baal, with the women acting out the bereft Anat's search for him.

Anat easily assimilated the familiar role of the mourning goddess, weeping for her lost lover—but with a characteristic twist. She goes through the rituals of mourning, weeping and gashing her skin—ceremonial self-harming. So far, so traditional. But once that's done she pulls herself together, buckles on her weapons and descends to the underworld. There she fights and kills Mot, dismembering his body and scattering the pieces over the fields, thereby freeing Baal besides fertilizing the land.[21] (Usually, of course, it's the dead god, rather than the god of death, whose dismembered parts are strewn.)

Anat was sometimes identified with her mother Asherah, particularly in her Qadesh aspect—which makes sense—as on the Triple Goddess Stone, referred to earlier. Anat was another goddess who, like Asherah, was known as the "Lion Lady."

Anat was known throughout the ancient Near East, her attributes making her instantly familiar to other goddess-worshipping cultures. She had much in common with Ishtar, the favored candidate for the cake-loving Queen of Heaven encountered by Jeremiah; Patai says "one must regard her as heir and kin" of Ishtar.[22] In Egypt, where Baal was equated with Set as Sutekh-Baal, Anat and Astarte were said to be Set's wives.

Anat's status as a most unusual female role model is underlined by several scholars, including her aspect as "destroyer."[23] Elsewhere she is portrayed as "a female, yet she pursues male activities such as hunting and warfare and rejects the feminine roles of wife and mother."[24] William F. Albright describes Anat rather curiously: "Anath the Victorious, a man-like woman, dressed as a man but girded as a woman."[25]

So far what have we gleaned about Anat? She pursues traditionally male activities such as warfare, and even dresses like a man. In modern terms, Anat is either one of the first female superheroes—a warrior queen with supernatural powers, who takes on human men and beats them at their own game—or neatly fits the mold of the classic supervillain, depending on whose side you're on. In her amorality and ferocity she is likened to surely one of the most fearsome of all goddesses known to history—the many-armed Indian deity Kali or Durga, often depicted with men's heads dangling from her waist. Albright adds, "In fact, the respective figures are in some ways so similar that coincidence can scarcely be the only explanations."[26]

Even without the heavy suggestions of an Indian connection—which must remain speculative as there is no known direct link—Anat was certainly no cozy maternal figure wherever she was worshipped. Sometimes she wasn't even recognizably female, certainly not in that time and place: for example, Egyptian depictions usually show her brandishing a spear and shield, an activity usually exclusive to men. Indeed, one twelfth-century BCE text specifically describes her as the pharaoh Ramesses III's shield. And to honor the goddess, Ramesses II named his daughter Bint-Anat, "daughter of Anat," proving just how popular she was in Egypt at the time.

Some of Anat's aggressive battle imagery parallels that of Sekhmet, the warrior lion-goddess daughter of Ra mentioned above, who led the pharaohs in battle, and who also relished wading in her enemies' blood and guts. Her signature myth tells how, when Ra sent her to battle his enemies, Sekhmet became so transported with her blood lust that her rampage threatened to destroy all humankind. She only desisted from the frenzied carnage when Ra dyed a pool of beer red, which she stopped to drink thinking it was blood, becoming so drunk she passed out. Humankind survived.

Bizarrely for a lioness, Sekhmet is often portrayed with a mane, perhaps to underline her ferocious nature. For all their relative egalitarianism, the ancient Egyptians subscribed to traditional concepts of what constituted masculine and feminine, even insisting that their—very few—ruling queens don false ceremonial beards.

(Perhaps curiously, given such a gore-soaked background, Sekhmet is greatly revered—even literally worshipped—by modern occultists and New Agers. They tend to see her more as a protective and empowering force for good, though they're usually very careful to warn against invoking her for vengeance. That would not be wise. On a trip to Egypt in the late 1990s, we were told of how fanatical Islamists had recently defaced statues of Sekhmet in the desert, only for the terrified locals to hear her prowling about at night, roaring. Perhaps it was just their imagination. Or perhaps not . . .)

Given the remarkable fluidity of aspects shared by gods in the ancient world, it should be no surprise that Sekhmet was a form of Hathor (or in academic-speak she's "Mythically identified as a hypostatic manifestation of Hathor"[27]), especially in her destructive aspect. In the Egyptian "bloodbath and beer" story officially known as "The Deliverance of Mankind from Destruction," Ra gives Hathor the job of killing his enemies, and she takes the form of Sekhmet to carry it out.

In view of Karl Luckert's theory that Yahweh was Amun, then it may be telling that some of Sekhmet's characteristics were assimilated by Mut, Amun's wife. It was in Mut's temple at Thebes that the annual festival was held commemorating Sekhmet being turned aside from slaughter by a pool of beer. (During this ceremony her priestesses were *required* to get helplessly drunk—which would, of course, be unthinkable in modern synagogues or churches. Although even the concept of completely sober *priestesses* is enough to give most congregations apoplexy.)

Across the ancient world gods and goddesses were fully expected to be shape-shifters—as even a cursory glance at almost any of the Greek myths reveals. But there was usually a sound reason, as with Hathor assuming the form of Sekhmet, basically to do her dirty work. This might come as a surprise to those today who admire Hathor—with her beautiful cow's ears and wide, open face—as one of the gentler members of the Egyptian pantheon. But it is well to remember that the ancients did not think like us. To them the gods were utterly amoral: gentle one minute and blind with destructive fury the next, even if they had to morph into something more obviously ferocious to do it.

Hathor, though more often associated with "the sun, heavens, trees, dancing, music, royalty, fertility, death, inebriety and joyous revelry" is recognized to have a darker, ferocious side: "In addition to fertility and childbirth, she patronizes love and sex, earning the epithet 'mistress of the vulva' . . . Hathor's martial character is portrayed by her epithet 'Lady of Terror', who is joyful in battle and full of fury for the enemies of Re."[28]

With the ancient goddesses' kaleidoscopic natures—ever shifting and changing their image—even Anat/Anath has a more artistic side. As Meindert Dijkstra explains: "The goddess Anath is known in Ugarit and Egypt as a goddess of war, who [also] plays the zither and sings of love and war" besides, of course, leading "kings and Pharaohs in warring adventures."[29] He links her musical aspect to the lyre player in the picture on one of the Kuntillet Ajrud storage jars associated with the "Yahweh and his Asherah" inscription.

And being a complete role model—embodying as she does *all* female potential—and despite her reluctance to give birth, Anat remains a powerful fertility goddess. This sense of maternal protection extended beyond mere humanity.

PROTECTRESS OF THE ANIMALS

In a paper in the *Journal of Near Eastern Studies* in 1992, Peggy L. Day of the University of Winnipeg uncovered a side of Anat's fertility aspect that had escaped her male colleagues, fixated as they were on Anat's sex life. This is her role as "Mistress of the animals" (*potnia theron,* a term taken from Homer), a well-known function of Greek goddesses such as Artemis. Anat was also said specifically to be the protectress of animals. Only female scholars seem to have noticed this side of her, although—as ever—it would be a mistake to apply twenty-first-century sensibilities here.

As Peggy Day explains: "this veritable obsession with 'fertility,' as it has been vaguely and derogatively defined, has served to obscure an important facet of the goddess Anat. . . . This is the role of 'mistress of animals' (*potnia theron*), which has both a predatory and protective aspect."[30]

The predatory aspect is that of huntress, the protective that of carer for the herds. Traditionally among country folk the world over, these two aspects have not been seen as contradictory but complementary, in the same way a modern farmer cares for the health and wellbeing of livestock destined for the slaughterhouse (although vegans would violently disagree). Peggy Day cites various Ugarit myths depicting Anat in both these aspects, which have been largely ignored in favor of the those that emphasize her bloodlust and sexual excesses.

The mistress of the animals is a common theme in Greek and other art and iconography, where the goddess is shown flanked by, and sometimes holding, game animals or birds (the animals—such as deer and wild goats—are never domestic).

This prompted Day to radically revisit the conventional interpretation of an image from the necropolis at Ugarit. Dating from the thirteenth century BCE, it's the lid of an ivory box (or *pyxis*) of the Mycenaean style: "On it is depicted a goddess atop a mountain, flanked on each side by a goat that is nibbling the vegetation that the goddess offers in her upraised hands. . . . The style . . . identifies the carving as a depiction of the *potnia theron*, 'mistress of animals.'"[31] However, as it was a locally made copy of the Mycenaean theme (rather than imported *objet*), Day argues that it "depicts a mistress of animals indigenous to second-millennium Ugarit. I submit that Anat fits this description admirably."[32]

The tree-with-goats symbolism already discussed in relation to Asherah is clearly a more abstract representation of the mistress of the animals, the goddess represented by her aniconic tree image. As Peggy Day has identified Anat as the original Canaanite mistress of the animals—and especially if she is right in her interpretation of the Ugarit ivory image—this supports the idea that *the "Asherah" tree symbol originally belonged to Anat.*

This transfer of imagery suggests it could have been Anat who was originally paired with Yahweh—something of an explosive relationship, one might think—but this role was later transferred to Asherah.

Presumably, that was why the military Hebrews on Elephantine coupled her, of all fire-cracking goddesses, with Yahweh.

THE HEBREWS' ANAT

There are no direct references to Anat in the Hebrew Bible, not unnaturally leading many scholars to dispute that the ancient Israelites ever had any place for her, putting the Elephantine references as down to "local Aramean or Phoenician influence," for example.[33]

However, Anat is mentioned "albeit quite obliquely"[34] in the Hebrew Bible's account of the older days. Her name appears in place names, such as Beth-Anath—House or Temple of Anat—and Anathoth. These could, of course, be Canaanite names that were simply continued by the Israelites. For example, Judges states that Beth-Anath, which was allocated to the tribe of Naphtali (and was later part of Galilee), was still inhabited by Canaanites who provide their slave labor.[35]

More telling is the adoption of her name by individuals, showing there was a conscious decision to honor the goddess, no doubt hoping to absorb some of her power. The Hebrew Bible only includes a couple of examples, but the one that leaps out is Shamgar ben Anat—Shamgar, son of Anat.

Shamgar was the third of the judges, but more importantly heroically saved Israel from the Philistines, killing 600 of them personally with an *oxgoad*—a cattle-prod stick.[36] As a great warrior, the title or nickname "Son of Anat" is remarkably apt.

In fact, "Son of Anat" was an honorific occasionally chosen, or bestowed upon, Canaanite soldiers, acknowledging their prowess and dedicating them to the warrior goddess. Arrowheads have been found bearing inscriptions such as "Son of Anat" and "Servant of the Lion Lady." But here we have an Israelite warrior, no less, dedicating himself to her.

Shamgar is also invoked in the Song of Deborah, the judge who succeeded him:

In the days of Shamgar, son of Anath,
in the days of Jael, the highways were abandoned,
and travelers kept to the byways.
The villagers ceased in Israel;
they ceased to be until I arose;
I, Deborah, arose as a mother in Israel.
When new gods were chosen,
then war was in the gates.[37]

As we mentioned previously, the Song of Deborah is especially important, as it is recognized as one of the oldest parts of the Bible, dating from the late twelfth century BCE and composed around the same time as the events it describes.[38] And in the context of this investigation, Deborah's song is also key because of what it reveals about the real role of Israelite women.

An often-unacknowledged feminine energy and strength often surfaces in very surprising ways. Despite modern assumptions that ancient Israelite women were always mere chattels and housebound drudges "there was formerly a role reserved for women in the rituals observed for preparation for war, the handling of defeat and celebrations of victory."[39]

One of their roles was the performance of victory songs and dances, such as Miriam's after the defeat of the pursuing Egyptian army, and of course the Song of Deborah. The important role of Miriam and Deborah—both "official" prophetesses—as ritual victory performers, highlights their status, if only as leaders of the women. They also wrote the scripts, as Athalya Brenner explains: "The fact that women did compose victory poems with which they greeted returning military heroes or armies is beyond dispute."[40]

Dijkstra argues that the women who led the victory song and dance—Miriam, Deborah, and the women who come to meet Saul and David when they return from a victorious battle against the Philistines, "with tamborines, and songs of joy, and musical instruments"[41]—represented the goddess of war. All this dancing, parading, and music was later labeled "harlot behavior," in the same way that unorthodox religious practices were righteously dismissed as prostitution.[42]

As well as celebrating the victories, women in the ancient Near East also accompanied the men to the battlefield, where they inspired them by singing war songs—basically acting as cheerleaders, but of course for the deadliest kind of game.

Dijkstra cites examples from ancient Arabia where the women carried an "empty, decorated sedan"—a thronelike chair—into battle.[43] In earlier times the most beautiful girl of the tribe was paraded into battle on the sedan to encourage the men—presumably by making it clear what they could look forward to if they won, soldiers being soldiers. Although Dijkstra thinks she represented the goddess of war, it's possible that both interpretations are just as valid. However, carrying an empty seat into battle inevitably recalls the Ark of the Covenant, similarly borne ahead of the Israelite army.

WOMAN OF FIRE

The story of Deborah, the prophet and judge, goes further, implying Israelite women might well have had a more hands-on function in war itself.

Deborah sits in Ephraim between Ramah and Bethel beneath the familiar symbol of Asherah, "the [date] palm of Deborah" where people come to her for counsel and advice. Given the early association between prophet and seer, they probably really visited her for divination, rather like those who flocked to the Oracle at Delphi in ancient Greece. After all, who wouldn't want to know if their unfaithful lover will return, or if their tent-making business will make money, or if their awaited child will be the all-important male heir?

Deborah is introduced as "a prophetess, the wife of Lappidoth," *eset lappidot*,[44] the only mention of her husband. However, Hebrew uses the same word for "wife" and "woman," and *lappidoth* literally means "torches," so the phrase could equally well be translated as "woman of torches" or "woman of fire"—much more appropriate in the context. (One of the most laughable academic interpretations of this title is that she made candles for her husband!) The titles imply a link with the more ferocious goddesses such as Anat—and even the Egyptian Sekhmet, one of whose titles is "Lady of Flame."

Deborah was a prophet when the Israelites were oppressed by the Canaanite King Jabin's General Sisera. In a tellingly authoritative move, she *"summoned"* Barak of the tribe of Naphtali, demanding to know why he failed to obey Yahweh's command to lead an army against Sisera, even though Yahweh has promised him victory. Presumably it was Deborah herself who delivered God's command.

Barak says he will only lead his men into battle if Deborah accompanies him. She agrees, but, obviously in seer mode, adds: "Nevertheless, the road on which you are going will not lead to your glory, for the LORD will sell Sisera into the hand of a woman."[45]

The battle duly takes place at the river Kishon near Mount Tabor. Every man in Sisera's army is killed, although he manages to escape on foot, taking shelter in the tent of Jael, the wife of Heber the Kenite. Exhausted, Sisera asks for water and rest, and Jael gives him milk and a place to lie down, but as he is innocently sleeping she hammers a tent peg into his head. (Surely proving she's more of a *femme fatale* than Jezebel, being literally *fatale*.) When Barak passes by in pursuit of Sisera she shows him the corpse.

Susan Ackerman believes there is a deep link between Deborah and Anat:

> Nevertheless, while Deborah may want for Anat's unrestrained belligerence, she does appear Anat-like in her role as a female military champion, a woman who, through her endeavors on behalf of Israel in its battle against Sisera, takes decisive and powerful action within the battlefield arena. . . . Thus, while Deborah is surely not just Canaanite Anat in Israelite guise, it is still the case that Deborah's characterization in Judges 5 seems to have been powerfully influenced by the sorts of militaristic attributes associated with Anat in Canaanite myth.[46]

But what else does the Jael-and-Shamgar pairing reveal? According to Benjamin Mazar, the leading Israeli archaeologist, it might indicate that she "fulfilled, alongside Shamgar the son of Anath, the role of the charismatic figure upon whom the spirit of the Lord had descended, and who acted out of inner compulsion in time of supreme test, in her rally to the aid of the people, as did Deborah beside Barak."[47]

Judges fails to mention exactly when Shamgar wielded his oxgoad, other than that it was before Deborah emerged as the next judge after twenty years of oppression. This is no indication of Jael's age when she killed Sisera, but it is possible in her younger days she had counseled Shamgar. Or even fought alongside him. But Jael being paired with a warrior dedicated to Anat points up her own potential link to the great war goddess.

As the scraps of evidence are fitted together, it's increasingly clear that we are not being told the full story of Deborah. And the same goes for the killing of Sisera by Jael. For whatever reason, the story is so important it is told twice, once in the narrative and then again in the Song of Deborah immediately afterward. But in the Song some of the details are significantly different.

In the narrative—clearly a later composition, from the Exile or later—it is told straightforwardly enough: Sisera goes to the tent, is given a bed, and is killed by Jael as he sleeps. In the Song's older version, however, it abounds with both erotic and sacred imagery.

Although various scholars have noted it, Susan Ackerman summarizes it neatly in her *Warrior, Dancer, Seductress, Queen,* noting that first, the tent to which Sisera flees is that of Heber the Kenite. The tale makes much of the fact that the Kenites were descended from Moses's father-in-law Hobab. The latter was a Midianite priest, suggesting that Heber was from a priestly line, and that his wife was from a priestly family. According to the usual interpretation, the tent is pitched at "the oak in Zaanannim," Elon Bezaanaim—*elon* attached to place names always refers to a holy tree. (It is actually "terebinth," not oak, which makes it even more intriguing.) The tent has therefore been pitched on sacred ground, suggesting that Sisera sees it as a place of sanctuary.[48]

Presumably, Jael herself is also important. Mazar summarizes: "It may be concluded that Sisera fled from the battle to the tent of Jael not only to seed the peace which reigned between Jabin king of Hazor and the family of Heber the Kenite, but also because of the special exalted position of Jael, and because her dwelling place, Elon Bezaanaim, was recognized as a sanctified spot and a place of refuge where protection was given even to an enemy. As for Sisera's murder at a sanctified spot, in violation of all rules of hospitality, it may be explained only as the fulfilment of a divine command by a charismatic woman."[49]

The ESV's translation of Sisera's death in Deborah's Song seems pretty straightforward:

> *Most blessed of women be Jael,*
> *the wife of Heber the Kenite,*
> *of tent-dwelling women most blessed.*
> *He asked for water and she gave him milk;*
> *she brought him curds in a noble's bowl.*
> *She sent her hand to the tent peg*
> *and her right hand to the workmen's mallet;*
> > *she struck Sisera;*
> *Between her feet*
> *he sank, he fell, he lay still; between her feet*
> *he sank, he fell; where he sank,*
> *there he fell—dead.*[50]

But there is a highly charged subtext, which is only too easy to miss, buried as it is in the linguistics, once again . . .

Susan Niditch, associate professor of religion at Amherst College, makes a convincing case for the hidden meaning in her essay "Eroticism and Death in the Tale of Jael" (1989). When Jael goes to kill the sleeping Sisera with the tent peg, the verb *bolat*, translated as "went softly" in the ESV and "secretly" by Niditch, is often used of a woman coming to her lover. It "evokes mystery, even romance."[51]

Themes of sex and violence, death and seduction are particularly strong in the Song of Deborah verse that describes the killing of Sisera. Niditch writes of "the visceral sexual quality of the imagery."[52] Her translation goes as follows:

> *Between her legs he knelt, he fell, he lay*
> *Between her legs he knelt, he fell*
> *Where he knelt, there he fell, despoiled.*[53]

"Like the hand, *yad*, the *raglayim*, 'legs' or 'feet,' are used in Scripture as euphemisms for male or female [sexual] organs."[54] And of the word "to lie"—*shakhav (skb)*—Niditch writes: "The vast majority of biblical uses of *skb* in a sexual context refer to illegitimate relations in rape, incest, ritual impurity, adultery, and so forth."[55]

Also, the word translated as "dead" in the ESV, *shadad,* means "destroyed," "ruined," or "despoiled"—all shot through with highly charged eroticism. *Shadad* also describes the condition to which a prostitute falls, as in Jeremiah, for example.[56] "Double meanings of violent death and sexuality emerge in every line."[57]

Niditch compares Jael to ancient Near Eastern war goddesses: "like such figures she is heroic and liminal, a warrior and seducer, alluring and dangerous, nurturing and bloodthirsty."[58] While not specifically mentioning Anat she obviously has a very similar goddess in mind.

Apart from its sacred and erotic undertones, the imagery and language are of violent rape—unexpectedly with the male Sisera as victim. This is reinforced by the next verse of the Song of Deborah, where Sisera's mother, anxiously waiting for him to return and anticipating he will bring the spoils of victory, includes among them "a womb or two for every man"[59]—meaning women from the defeated people to rape, as soldiers then expected as their due. Instead, Sisera himself suffers a similar fate at the hands of a woman.

It is also a very feminine perspective, suggesting the Song was the work of a woman, therefore almost certainly Deborah herself.

It emerges as a powerful—and clever—piece of writing.

As Stephen G. Dempster explains, writing in the *Westminster Theological Journal:*

> The almost inordinate, massive, warlike, feminine presence, obvious in even the most perfunctory reading of both prose and poetic accounts of Israel's deliverance here, is a unique phenomenon in the literature of Israel. It is Deborah who calls Israel to battle, who begins the roll call of the troops from the various tribes, who leads the attack, who sings at the enemies' defeat; and another woman, Jael, applies the *coup de grace* to the enemy by smashing a nail through Sisera's skull. In contrast, the masculine element is downplayed if not actually denigrated. The prose account highlights judge Barak's weakness and his failure to snatch even some of the glory of Israel's victory by at least killing the captain of the Canaanite forces. On this day the glory belongs only to Yahweh and His feminine servants, Deborah and Jael.[60]

So once stripped back to the secrets of the linguistics, the curious story of Jael contains both sacred and sexual undertones, which presumably were more obvious in the original version. There was something ritualistic in the killing of Sisera, something that was the special province of women. We should also recall that in the Song of Deborah, Jael is implicitly paired with Shamgar, son of Anat. ("In the days of Shamgar, son of Anath / in the days of Jael . . .") Jael's role is strikingly similar to Anat's in Canaanite myth, both being "erotic assassins."[61]

These tales from the earliest centuries of Israel's history—even before King David established the monarchy—are clearly missing something about the role of women in warfare. Deborah and Jael are, according to Ackerman, "noteworthy for the actions they take within the traditionally male domain of battle, and Deborah is also described as a religious functionary (a prophet) and as one of Israel's political leaders (a judge)."[62]

The missing something relates in some way to the goddess Anat, a key player in the Israelites' war-making, both as an inspiration to the male warriors and through women such as Deborah, who counseled the generals and helped instill some backbone into the men. There appears to have been a strong ritual element to all this. (Even more unexpectedly, there is a version of this backbone-instilling role for women—or at least *a* woman—in the annals of early Christianity, as we will see.)

But, although there are hints in the Bible accounts, sadly it is no longer possible to reconstruct that aspect in any detail. Either the writers in the sixth and fifth centuries BCE had little or no understanding of the stories because by their day things had changed and the past remained obscure, or they did know—but had no desire to understand.

The story of the goddess continues, however.

ELEPHANTINE REVISITED

Having unraveled some of the tangled hints and clues about female power in ancient Israel, it is possible to understand rather more about the Elephantine Island community.

Although the early Israelite warriors venerated Anat, seemingly her worship had been erased during the period of the kingdoms, both united and divided—so after 1000 BCE. The Elephantine community pairing her with Yahweh therefore suggests that their memories went back a very long way.

It would be only natural for a colony of mercenaries to pair Yahweh with Anat. But had they displaced Asherah as his consort? It was possible; after all, in Egypt, in her Qadesh aspect Asherah had become intertwined in people's minds with her daughter Anat, as the Triple Goddess Stone shows.

Or was it the other way around? Perhaps in the early days, *Anat had been Yahweh's wife,* and it was in Judah and Israel that the role was transferred to Asherah, while the Elephantine Hebrews retained the original couple. Surely that makes more sense. During the period when the Israelites still saw El as the top god, and therefore presumably Asherah as his consort, they must have thought Yahweh also had a wife.

If, as we believe, Yahweh was originally conceptualized as El and Asherah's son, who had been allotted the people of Israel as his nation, it would have been more understandable to pair him with one of their daughters, rather than his mother. Anat was an appropriate consort during the early days when the Israelites found themselves constantly at war with the Canaanites around and within the Promised Land. The judge and warrior-hero Shamgar, son of Anat, demonstrates that.

But how, and why, did Anat become Asherah? Perhaps the evolution was inevitable. As the monarchy became relatively settled, and Yahweh himself became comparatively a little less fierce, it was no longer so appropriate to have a ferocious war goddess as his mate. And the demise of Anat may also have been connected with the eclipse of the roles of women such as Deborah and the other "mothers in Israel." The sword-wielding, animal-fornicating Anat was no longer a suitable role model for the daughters of Israel, while at the same time the motherly and nurturing Asherah became more fitting, specifically to inspire women to accept their place as wives and mothers. And of course, there was another probable reason for Anat falling out of favor: Among the Canaanites she was the wife of Baal, *the* great threat to the worship of Yahweh.

This is all speculation, naturally. The fluidity with which the ancients mixed and matched their god forms meant that a transition from mother to daughter, or vice versa, was easy. But however it happened, there is no doubt that the Hebrews of Elephantine retained a very early form of the religion—and it emphatically cherished a goddess in its heart.

But their love affair with the old ways was not to last. In the fifth century BCE, the period of the papyri and messages sent by Hananiah of Jerusalem concerning the new regime, the Elephantine community was continuing the original monolatry, while in Jerusalem this was hardening into monotheism. Clearly, Hananiah had been appalled by their religious intransigence—even outright heresy. From then on, they were to worship as laid down by Jerusalem. It was no longer acceptable to bestow most of one's favor on one god while acknowledging, and even revering others. There was only one God, and he alone was to be worshipped.

Despite the serial attempts to eradicate her from the hearts and minds of the ordinary Israelites—particularly the women—the sacred feminine never disappeared completely, finding new ways to hide in the soul of the people, flowing through their desires like wine through water. Having been such an integral part of the religion for so many centuries, and being so cherished by generations of devotees—particularly women—it seems unlikely that everything and everyone connected with the cult would just fizzle into thin air forever. She must have gone underground. In fact, she did. It is even possible to trace her secret journey.

Samaria especially was promising territory to harbor the goddess. It had been spared the bitterness of the Babylonian exile that hardened the Jerusalem exiles into monotheists. Also, Nehemiah and his successors had no authority there—it was a separate Persian province, with its own governor.

There are other possibilities for the secret, or semisecret continuation of the Asherah cult. Even the incorrigible Jeremiah acknowledges that his relentless haranguing made not the slightest difference to expatriate worshippers of the Queen of Heaven in southern Egypt in the 580s BCE, so her religion clearly continued after he washed his hands of them. What happened to her?

Then there are those intriguing Elephantine Hebrews, who were still celebrating Anat alongside Yahweh in the 410s. Over half a century later the community was moved out with the end of Persian rule. So where did *they* go?

It's hard to imagine any of these groups giving up on the goddess and converting wholeheartedly to the new patriarchy—even if the *realpolitik* demanded they pay it lip service. The deep need that people—women *and* men—have for the sacred feminine also makes it highly improbable that the goddess would just be unceremoniously dropped and forgotten.

5

Sophia's Secrets

Historical detection is a painstaking business, as readers will have realized by now. Sometimes among the mass of data, huge facts, with perhaps even bigger implications, will emerge—though like an archaeologist it requires much scrabbling through layers of irrelevant material to find them. Locating the *relevant* material is only the start. Fitting it all together into one coherent picture can be tough, especially if there's been a real effort by interested parties over the millennia to prevent the complete picture from ever being known. You don't have to be a card-carrying conspiracy theorist to notice cover-ups and omissions aimed at preventing posterity from basically *getting it*. And perhaps there are few greater conspiracies to cover up than the Old Testament writers' cannily obscured evidence of the great Israelite goddesses—not only their existence, but also their sheer longevity.

Despite the impression the Bible gives, until the Exile, Deuteronomism—the Yahweh-alone movement—was pretty much a failure. Then Jerusalem fell to the Babylonians, and the royal, aristocratic, and priestly elite were exiled. During their miserable and disconsolate banishment, the prophetic view became more deeply entrenched: After all, hadn't the likes of Isaiah and Jeremiah been vindicated?

Then came the monotheistic breakthrough. Its first expression was in the section added to the end of the book of Isaiah—at least half a century after he wrote it—known as Second Isaiah (or Deutero-Isaiah).[1]

This is when the Old Testament becomes completely monotheistic, with Jeremiah and Second Isaiah—in the words of biblical scholar at the University of Toronto John L. McLaughlin—satirizing "the lifeless, powerless idols and draw[ing] the conclusion that the gods they represent are not only powerless, but actually nonexistent."[2] Second Isaiah took the radically new monotheism to previously unthinkable heights. One of his novel concepts is Yahweh as creator of the world and director of all human history. Before that he was only a local god, concerned solely with the nation of Israel.

It's probably no coincidence that this religious upheaval happened in Babylon, where Zoroastrianism, a monotheistic religion—the faith of the Magi—centered on the supreme deity Ahura Mazda, held sway at the Babylonian court. The exiled Judahites might not have borrowed the idea from Ahura Mazda directly, perhaps if anything being indignant about his influence. They may simply have wanted to assert Yahweh's superiority in the race for top god.[3]

The Judahites were theologically—not to mention psychologically—ready for such a radical step after all the ground Hosea and his successors had prepared. Even so, the revolutionary new conceptualization of Yahweh failed to find traction immediately, not becoming "the dominant belief at that moment."[4] This only happened after the Babylonian Captivity—and even then it took a while.

THE INVENTION OF MONOTHEISM

It's important to realize that the scale of the destruction and depopulation of Judah is often exaggerated. While the city of Jerusalem itself was abandoned and in ruins, most other towns and villages remained untouched. From archaeological and other evidence, it's thought that only about 25 percent of the population was transported to Babylon. But the exiles did comprise the elite and educated—the officials, generals, priests and scribes, and craftsmen with useful skills—and it's their stories that are told in the Bible, not the ordinary folks'. Hence the impression today that the entire population was carried off to Babylon—down to the last goat.

The remaining 75 percent—farmers and peasants—remained in Judah. No doubt they found it tough, although the Babylonians redistributed the land among those who were left behind to lessen the hardship.[5]

As for their religion, Susan Ackerman observes in her study of the popular religion in Judah during the period of the Captivity, *Under Every Green Tree* (1992), "Among those who remained behind in Judah, the religion did not change."[6] She adds: "relatively few went to Babylon to be influenced by the program of cultic purification undertaken there. Sheer numbers, then, would be on the side of popular religion. Moreover, our evidence indicates that the various sixth-century cults we have described thrived not on the society's fringes, but in its heart, among all groups and across all classes."[7]

When the exiles were allowed to return to Judah—or rather the new Persian province of Yehud—in the 530s BCE, they were at odds, not just religiously but also politically, with those who had remained behind. The people who emerged from Babylon—mostly descendants of the original deportees—regarded themselves as the true upholders of the religion, besides including many aristocrats displaced from their former estates, which they wanted back. The next century saw this elite struggle to reassert its secular and religious authority. Naturally, the returned landowning nobility failed to get it all their own way. There was conflict with the countryfolk who had not been exiled, and who thought of the land as theirs—after all, they had farmed it with the sweat of their brows for over fifty years.

Another source of political tension was the relationship with the city of Samaria, capital of the former Kingdom of Israel, "a center of provincial power that could challenge Jerusalem, but also the home of worshipers of Yahweh."[8] The Samarians, like those in Judah who had not been exiled, bore little of the bitterness that had effectively hardened Yahweh-worship into monotheism.

Very little information survives about events between the consecration of the Second Temple in 516 BCE and the middle of the next century, when Nehemiah and Ezra emerged as the champions of the landowning and religious elite, taking Jerusalem firmly in their grip. It really took Nehemiah and Ezra to complete the journey to monotheism, with a root and branch shake-up of the religion, including the compilation of the sacred texts that became the Hebrew Bible and the Christian Old Testament.

The conflict between the families of the returned exiles and those who had remained in Judah continued over the course of decades. There's no doubt whose side Nehemiah and Ezra were on: their reforms were as much about reestablishing the position and preeminence of the families they believed had the best claim to the land.[9] As ever, they favored the upper classes.

Nehemiah's own account begins during his service as cupbearer—an important official position—to the Persian King Artaxerxes I at his court. He tells how he was visited by a delegation from Judah, representing the families of those who had returned from exile some eighty years before, imploring him to do something about the ruined and desolate Jerusalem. With Nehemiah on their side, they obtained permission from Artaxerxes to organize the whole-scale renovation of Jerusalem, and later to get him appointed as governor. He went along with the delegation's agenda, only undertaking the rebuilding specifically for those who could prove their descent from the people listed in the "book of genealogy" compiled at the time of the return from Exile. It was to be a home fit for the Exile heroes.

Nehemiah experienced sustained opposition to his regeneration program, which even included a couple of foiled assassination plots. His opponents included a prophetess, Noadiah ("and the rest of the prophets who wanted to make me afraid").[10] Unfortunately, he fails to explain her motivation for opposing him, though her inclusion shows that women could still have a role in the religion even at that late date. Sadly, and even more sadly inevitably, that was not to last—largely due to Nehemiah himself.

After completing the rebuilding of the great city walls, Nehemiah organized an assembly of the families in the square before the Water Gate on the first day of the Feast of Booths (Sukkoth), where Ezra read them the Book of the Law of Moses, Deuteronomy. As he insisted on declaiming the entire thing, this marathon reading must have been something of an ordeal even for the most devout.

On the last day of the festival the people, all dressed in penitent sackcloth, gathered to hear the priests relate the whole story of the Israelites from Abraham onward (beginning "You are the LORD, you alone")[11]—essentially a precis of the historical books of the Old Testament—thereby fixing the official history of the people of Israel. The priests formally confessed the sins of the masses, believed to be the cause of all their problems. More momentously, it was also the time a new covenant with Yahweh was drawn up and publicly signed and sealed. Presumably the people had to take the priests' word that he agreed to his side of the deal.

It was then that the Jerusalem authorities standardized the religion by agreeing on an officially sanctioned canon of sacred texts. They also established a common cycle of festivals marking special moments in the people's history, such as Passover, and sought to impose the same standards across all Jewish communities, in Judah and elsewhere—as we saw in the case of Hananiah's letters to the Elephantine community. This approach was completely new. While most of the previous Hebrew Bible had been concerned with the religious practices of the elite, now *all* the children of Israel were included in the covenant with Yahweh. This had its disadvantages, especially for goddess worshippers.

This apparent inclusivity had an ironic effect—particularly on the worship of Asherah and other gods. They had always been considered intermediaries between the people and Yahweh, who had to be worshipped through the Temple priests. But Asherah could be invoked anywhere—especially in the countryside, bypassing the Temple priesthood. In the past, as the priests were only concerned with their status at court and in the Temple, the independent worship of the rural folk was pretty much beneath their notice. But with the imposition of this more totalitarian regime, ways of reaching Yahweh other than through the official priesthood could no longer be permitted. It was yet another reason for closing down the cults.

Later tradition—both Jewish and Christian—has it that the Nehemiah-Ezra regime marked the final defeat of the instinct for idolatry against which the religion had contended from the beginning. In fact, it was the *invention* of monotheism, with the will of the masses being overturned and the elite priesthood and prophets triumphing. It was only then that Asherah worship was finally suppressed—and history was blatantly rewritten to pretend it had *never* been a part of the orthodox religion.

The transition must have been terrible. Monotheism must have come hard to most of the people. The notion not just of appealing to one god alone, but that there *was* only one god to appeal to in the first place would have been downright nonsensical to most of them—especially as all hint of the sacred feminine had been removed. They must have felt hollowed out spiritually, psychologically abandoned—and deeply, deeply scarred. Even today, Jewish and Christian women and men are unconsciously suffering from that long-ago tyrannical imposition of monotheism and the demotion of the goddess virtually overnight to the status of nonperson. Removing the other gods and the goddess encompassed so much more than vandalizing a few idols. To most ordinary Israelites it meant many of the key aspects of the divine had simply been erased, including of course the eternal mother, creating a very unhealthy imbalance in the national psyche. The loss of the pantheon of deities caused real confusion—and real suffering.

Another consequence of the reforms was the disappearance of the "Asherah" figurines that were so prevalent in former times. Ephraim Stern, the Israeli archaeologist, explains that not a single one has been found after the Exile: "the Jewish exiles who returned from Babylon to the land of their ancestors no longer tolerated cultic figurines."[12]

ALIEN WOMEN

A major result of this religious and social transformation was a definition of Jewish identity, including what it was *against,* as Simon Schama notes: "Ezra's motivation was precisely to weed out heterodoxy, to make Jerusalem the sole Temple for pilgrim festivals and sacrifices, and to place in the hands of the Temple priests the judgment over those who could, and those who could not, be admitted to this reborn, recovenanted nation."[13]

Unsurprisingly, Ezra continued the tradition of blaming the people's lack of faith for their calamities—and of blaming *that* on the women, in particular the "foreign" wives that many Jews had taken during the Captivity and since the return. Ezra's book ends with a naming and shaming list of Jews, including priests, who had married foreign women but had agreed to divorce them. For the sin of loving foreign women they had to offer a ram as a Temple sacrifice in penance. That seems quite low key, but we are not told what happened to the women themselves.

The new religious masters were being disingenuous, to say the least. After all, hadn't some of their greatest heroes—such as Joseph, Moses, and Solomon—married foreigners? Some foreign women had even become national heroines, such as Jael and Rahab. According to Claudia Camp, this radical new move was nothing less than "Ezra's attempt at social engineering."[14]

In fact, the biblical "foreign" does not necessarily carry our modern meaning. The ancient world defined ethnicity differently. Today we see it mainly as genetic inheritance expressed in physical characteristics, primarily skin color. This was not true across the ancient world generally, including among the Israelites. They did not have, for example, the concept of mixed race. Children of a wife from another nation were simply considered Israelites. The ancients defined an individual as belonging to or being apart from a people or nation more in cultural terms—including how they practiced their religion.

There are two words translated in the Bible as "foreign," *nokhri—* which Ezra uses—and *zur,* with both similar and varied meanings.

Camp explains: "They can refer to persons of foreign nationality, to persons who are outside one's own family household, to persons who are not members of the priestly caste, and to deities or practices that fall outside the covenant relationship with Yhwh."[15] All these usages appear in the Hebrew Bible. The words basically mean "someone who isn't part of the group I'm talking about." Or, to put it another way, "not one of us." All cultural, moral, and religious outsiders are "foreigners," though "alien" is probably the best literal translation. (We caution against too much over-excitement: God only married an alien in the least extraterrestrial sense.)

Ezra's rant was not just about foreign women—and foreign religion—but those deemed alien to the new monotheistic version of Yahwism, including native Judahites and Samarians. This had a major effect on the lives of ordinary women in Judahite society generally, as Simon Schama describes: "Women, trapped in the Jezebel paranoia of the Deuteronomist writers, are repeatedly cast as demons of temptation."[16]

Susan Ackerman, speaking of the worship of the Queen of Heaven, makes an important point about the effect of the reaction of the dominant men to the "women's" religion: "Since it is the winners who write history, the importance of this women's cult in the history of the religion of Israel has been obscured by our sources. The ultimate 'winners' in the religion of early sixth-century Judah, the Deuteronomistic historians, the priest-prophet Ezekiel, and the prophet Jeremiah, were men. The biblical texts these men wrote malign non-Deuteronomistic, non-priestly, and non-prophetic religion, and in the case of the cult of the Queen of Heaven they malign the religion of women."[17]

But it was not solely the "religion of women" that was maligned, but women as a whole. And not just the religion of Yahweh that was masculinized, but Judaic society generally. Well, *almost* masculinized.

LADY WISDOM

The sacred feminine was not entirely absent from the canon of books created in the wake of Nehemiah and Ezra's reforms.

There is that anomaly in the Hebrew Bible that is the Song of Songs—the weird erotic love poem with little obvious connection with the Yahweh religion. Its strangest aspect was that it was included in the canon at all. In the early centuries CE there was a dispute over whether it should remain, but its inclusion was defended by the leading sage Rabbi Akiva (ca. 50–135 CE) who declared, "all the Scriptures are holy, but the Song of Songs is the Holy of Holies."[18]

The book is attributed to Solomon—which is debatable and unprovable. Several scholars think it belonged to a fertility cult, dating from before the Exile. Marvin H. Pope, in his 1977 study of the Song, concluded that at least parts of it go back to Canaanite times, citing parallels in the Ugaritic texts. Rosemary Radford Ruether makes an interesting suggestion: "The Song of Songs probably has its roots in Canaanite psalms of the love between Anath and Baal."[19]

Sadly, with so little information about the writer's real message, that will have to remain an enigma.

The sacred feminine did survive more overtly, but it came at a price. She was permitted to continue—but apparently only as a metaphor. Suddenly she is a poetic fancy, as the figure of Wisdom, Hebrew *chokmah* (or *hokmah*), in the book of Proverbs, the nearest thing to a goddess permitted in the new state-approved books.

The word *chokmah* in its general sense appears throughout the Hebrew Bible. It means "wisdom," but the Hebrew also covers general ability and skill/craftsmanship. For example, it is used of Hiram of Tyre, the "son of the widow" who cast the bronze ornamentation for Solomon's Temple, and of those who made Aaron's priestly garments. It also included skill in waging war. And of course, it usually describes individuals famed for their wisdom, such as Solomon. However, in the book of Proverbs wisdom is explicitly personified as a woman, often called Lady Wisdom or Woman Wisdom.

Proverbs gives general advice and guidance on how to live a virtuous and correct life, extolling the merits of wisdom over folly. It's a compilation of wisdom texts from various periods of Israel's history, divided into sections, some attributed to Solomon. One section is based on an Egyptian wisdom text, "The Onomasticon of Amenope," from about 1100 BCE.

With such exotic sources, unsurprisingly the book is "not characteristically Israelite"[20]—in fact Israel is only mentioned once, in the opening attribution to Solomon, son of David, king of Israel. However, Yahweh is very much center stage.

Lady Wisdom appears in the introductory section, which sets the scene. From references to styles of architecture it is thought the "earliest stratum" of this section is from around the time of Solomon.[21] However, the version we have is much more recent—opinions differ on the date of the final draft, but it was certainly after the Exile.

Even usually cool-headed academics find the big question riveting: Why was Wisdom portrayed as a flesh-and-blood woman? Is it just a poetic metaphor for a manifestation of an aspect of God? Or could Lady Wisdom even be a goddess? If so, this would be evidence that the beloved sacred feminine was refusing to go away, even under so much patriarchal pressure, but continuing just out of sight—even in the official texts. There are certainly well-established candidates.

While some have seen the influence of foreign goddesses such as the Egyptian Maat, others look closer to home—including Bernhard Lang, as the subtitle of his *Wisdom and the Book of Proverbs: A Hebrew Goddess Redefined* (1986) makes clear. He writes emphatically in *Dictionary of Deities and Demons in the Bible* (1999):

Wisdom, sometimes in scholarly literature referred to as "Lady Wisdom" or "Woman Wisdom," is the name of a biblical goddess. . . . Although modern interpreters have often treated her as a literary personification, it can be argued that what later came to be considered a mere figure of speech started its career as a "real" deity. Wisdom, in Heb[rew] *hokma* . . . and in G[ree]k *sophia*, is the goddess of knowledge, shrewdness (both implied in the semantic range of *hokma*), statecraft, and the scribal profession.[22]

Given the "wise woman" tradition we uncovered in chapter 3, it is possible that Proverbs was based on one of its texts. But if so, it was heavily repurposed.

Although the flagrant, even official worship of Asherah apparently ceased when the Judahites returned from exile, she remains the obvious homegrown candidate for the figure of Wisdom in Proverbs. However, she might not be a direct descendant of Asherah, Anat, or the Queen of Heaven. She might have been "a literary compensation for the eradication of the worship of those goddesses."[23]

El himself was always regarded as the supreme source of wisdom, but as we know Asherah was known for a particular type. This manifests when she counsels El and persuades him with great psychological cunning to change his course of action—as in the promotion of gods such as Baal to positions of power. Asherah was manipulative, certainly, but arguably in a good way. Her skill at persuasion was considered a form of wisdom.[24] There are even hints of an association between Wisdom and Asherah in Proverbs itself, as in calling Wisdom "a tree of life to those who lay hold of her."[25]

WISDOM AND CREATION

As mentioned previously, in Canaanite mythology Asherah was considered co-creator of the cosmos with El. And Proverbs hints that Wisdom too had a role in creation with Yahweh:

> *The LORD by wisdom founded the earth;*
> *by understanding he established the heavens;*
> *by his knowledge the deeps broke open,*
> *and the clouds drop down the dew.*[26]

(By now Yahweh was explicitly the creator. As he was the only God he had to be.)

Roland E. Murphy, American professor of Old Testament studies and Catholic priest, writes, "Wisdom not only had a role in creating,

. . . but she is in effect the divine activity of God at work."[27] She either shares in the task of creation, or she is the entity/force through which God creates the cosmos. But sadly—even inevitably—later verses introduce an ambiguity that reduces her direct involvement in the work of creation. Undoubtedly this was deliberate.

After her big build-up in the opening chapters, Lady Wisdom herself appears in chapter 8, standing at a crossroads beside a town gate and crying out to the men who pass by, declaring the virtues of following her ways. However, she suddenly veers off unexpectedly:

> *The LORD possessed me at the beginning of his work,*
> *the first of his acts of old.*
> *Ages ago I was set up,*
> *at the first before the beginning of the earth.*
> *When there were no depths I was brought forth,*
> *when there were no springs abounding with water.*
> *Before the mountains had been shaped,*
> *before the hills, I was brought forth,*
> *before he had made the earth with its fields,*
> *or the first of the dust of the world.*[28]

Again, a major point is hidden in the linguistics. The word in the first line translated as "possessed," *qanah,* can also mean "acquired, established, conceived, formed, or created by God."[29] "Created" makes most sense, as this was the "first of his acts" before creating the world. But the alternative "acquired" or "possessed," would mean that *the goddess already existed at the time of creation and was therefore co-eternal with God.* Either way this is a huge revelation: She is co-eternal with God—or at least the very first thing he brought into being.

After elaborating on her presence during the various stages of creation—when Yahweh established the heavens, assigned the sea's limits, and marked out the earth's foundations—Wisdom declares (in the ESV translation):

then I was beside him, like a master workman [amon],
and I was daily his delight,
rejoicing before him always,
rejoicing in his inhabited world
and delighting in the children of man.[30]

Ancient Hebrew being a particularly frustrating language—largely because of its missing vowels—there's more than enough room here for researchers to speculate. *Amon* presents a particular problem for translators—as this is the only time it is ever used in any ancient Hebrew source. By comparison with similar words, *amon* could mean, as here, "master craftsman," but it could equally well mean "confidante"—or even "little child"!

Bernhard Lang and Roland Murphy both think that "child" is most likely given the context.[31] Murphy also points out that the word translated as "rejoicing," *sachaq,* more accurately means "playing." So what does that mean for our understanding of Lady Wisdom? She's certainly childlike, brimful with joyous innocence, summoning up the image of perhaps even Tinkerbell-like dancing and darting about. There's nothing stuffy or pretentious about her. She's effervescent and perhaps even mischievous.

Wisdom is God's child, who plays before him in the world he has created. More dramatically, perhaps God even created the world *for* her, specifically for her to play in. If Lang and Murphy are right, then although Wisdom has no role in creation as such she was Yahweh's first creation who was present—playing exuberantly—while he did all the rest.

Perhaps the original, older version of the opening chapters of Proverbs described Wisdom's co-creator role as very like Asherah's in Canaanite myth, but this was watered down during the post-Ezra rewrites. Echoes do remain, however.

Some believe that the writers deliberately played up the ambiguity between "child" and "master craftsman" to show that Wisdom was both Yahweh's favorite child *and* his co-creator.[32] Lang observes: "It is not without significance *where* the divine child plays. Her playground is the earth, the place inhabited by men and women. . . . There is, perhaps, a hint of her mediating position between the Creator and humankind— a role quite befitting a minor goddess who happens to be the Creator's daughter."[33]

In demoting Wisdom to a "minor goddess" it is not hard to spot the writer's ulterior motive: while seemingly elevating the sacred feminine, in fact she is being tamed.

THE TAMING OF THE GODDESS: THE STRANGE WOMAN

But is Lady Wisdom really a watered-down manifestation of the goddess in the new, hardcore patriarchy? There is goddess imagery in the female character of Wisdom, but it seems transmuted into something not quite right. Was she—as Lang's "minor goddess" suggests—an attempt to *subvert* the worship of the goddess?

But subverted how? In Proverbs, Wisdom is contrasted with another female figure, "woman Folly" or "Lady Folly," *kesilut*, the "wicked twin" of Lady Wisdom. Claudia Camp, in her study of this figure and her relationship to Wisdom, *Wise, Strange and Holy* (2000), calls her Wisdom's "multifaceted negative counterpart."[34]

Lady Folly appears in the chapter immediately before Lady Wisdom makes her debut. She's an adulteress who, going out on the prowl "dressed as a prostitute" while her husband is away and after offering sacrifices in payment of an unexplained vow, meets and seduces a youth. There's an implicit comparison with Wisdom, who stands at a town gate, which—judging by the Tamar story—was the preferred spot for prostitutes to ply their trade, and where she calls out to passing men. But she parodies their usual business. Her message is about the value of wisdom—it's worth more than silver, gold, or jewels—everything that prostitutes demand. (Although one suspects the men weren't too happy being offered wisdom rather than the woman's usual services.)

The adulteress is described as *zur ishshah,* "forbidden woman," but again, literally "strange woman." Also, although customarily translated as "adulteress" *nokhri* actually means "foreigner" or "alien."[35] (The adultery is implied by her deceiving her husband.) *Nokhri* is translated as "foreign" in Ezra's rants about wives who are "not one of us." The Strange Woman is in the same category. Camp observes: "In the context of the emerging canon, Woman as Sexual Stranger is inexorably linked to Woman as Ethnic Stranger and to Israel as Estranged Wife."[36]

Surely, though, the two women symbolize much more than straightforward wisdom and folly—or even deadly erotic invitations. What else could the Strange Woman represent, besides sexual seduction? Obviously, this sort of behavior links her to the religious backsliding Israelites elsewhere in the Hebrew Bible, in keeping with the usual theme of the prophets. The imagery of the Strange Woman reflects their pet rants about foreign—or strange—sex equaling foreign religion.

"Strange sex" was presumably a synonym for goddess worshippers' sexual fertility rites, believed to taint the lives of respectable Jews. Marriage between Asherah followers and the Deuteronomists was clearly something of an obsession among the writers of Proverbs, with the whole idea of strange sex conjuring up pictures of pagan idolatry—and perhaps colorful, even wild marital practices. Strange sex is seen as synonymous with Asherah worship, a spiritual toxin causing fear and anxiety among the patriarchy, an implicit threat to religious "purity."

A superficial reading of the Strange Woman's dealings with the youth suggests another sort of ritual—and a startling one at that. On meeting him, the Strange Woman says:

> *I had to offer sacrifices*
> *and today I have paid my vows;*
> *so now I have come out to meet you,*
> *to seek you eagerly, and I have found you.*[37]

She is implicitly linking her sacrificial offering to sex with the youth, as if at the culmination of a ritual. Alarmingly, the implication is that the youth himself is a sacrifice, as he follows her "as an ox goes to the slaughter . . . he does not know that it will cost him his life."[38]

Fortunately, such a bloody-thirsty finale to the seduction is not to be taken literally. These women were not intent on murdering the men they took to bed. It's the writer's fevered imagining of the Asherah cult's activities—the Yahwist prophets' version of what those nasty, decadent "foreign" women were all about.

In any case, probably the subtext here is that when the youth submits to sex with an Asherah priestess, he is *metaphorically* losing his life as a devout Yahwist. Perhaps this also refers to how he would be treated after his tryst by the righteous community: possibly shunned as if taboo, or even actually dead.

Here Wisdom is being contrasted with the Strange Woman/Lady Folly, who embodies all the negative aspects, from the Yahwists' perspective, of the worship of the Asherah and other cults—throwing a very different light on Lady Wisdom herself. While she shares some of Asherah's characteristics, her role in Proverbs is to lead people to Yahweh:

> *For whoever finds me finds life*
> *and obtains favor from the LORD . . .* [39]
>
> *The fear of the LORD is the beginning of Wisdom,*
> *and the knowledge of the Holy One is insight.*[40]

Through the contrast between the Ladies Wisdom and Folly, "The issue is now life and death, fidelity to the Lord or infidelity."[41] Infidelity to Yahweh is equated with death, as we saw with the youth who sleeps with a "foreign" woman.

The goddess underwent her own slow transmutation, as it became impossible to worship her openly. Her reinvention as *chokmah* in Israelite wisdom literature proves the eradication of Asherah could only go so far. The people craved a goddess still, and she had to be present in their religious imagery *somehow*. But the "Yahweh-aloneists" re-created a goddess as a mere symbol, whereas once she had reigned supreme as a full-blooded female archetype. The new quasi-goddess exists as a mere hint or breath between the lines of biblical texts. Now the sacred feminine figure is firmly under Yahweh's thumb. We are a very long way from Anat, and even far from the days when Asherah ruled both beside Yahweh in the Temple and on hilltops all over the countryside.

Besides, if *amon* really means "child," not "master craftsman," then the goddess figure has moved from wife to daughter, from more-or-less equal partner to dependent inferior.

The message of Proverbs is faithfulness to Yahweh, as well as obedience to rulers—the cream of society, the Judahite elite. Wisdom declares that it is through her that kings reign, rulers make laws, and princes and nobles govern.[42] So to follow Wisdom is to support the status quo.

It could hardly be more patriarchal. As Claudia V. Camp points out, "the dominance of the sexual imagery used to construct Proverb's Strange Woman reflects a significant concern for male control of the household, . . . essentially a secular, patriarchal issue."[43] Lang comments wryly: "Understood as a deity strictly subordinated to Yahweh and having neither shrine nor receiving ritual respects, Lady Wisdom would not endanger monotheism."[44] For "monotheism," read "the menfolk."

Asherah has been split into two, her independent, sexual side becoming the evil Strange Woman, whom Proverbs warns the people—or rather men—of Israel against, while her aspects that the Yahwists approve of, and that support the religious and secular orthodoxy, have been personified in Lady Wisdom.

The Strange Woman represents Asherah in her Qadesh mode—here condemned and cast out—while her more acceptable aspect as wife and mother is embodied in Lady Wisdom. In Proverbs, Wisdom is described variously as mother, sister, bride, and "wife of your youth," all safe, domestic terms. There's no room for a "Lady of Flame," a sword-wielding Anat or fiery Sekhmet now. Hearth and home are the limits for women and girls, and their role model—so diminished she barely exists—is subservient and quiescent.

In other words, Lady Wisdom is a highly sanitized, essentially toothless version of Asherah. In her cold-blooded creation, she was the Old Testament version of the Blessed Virgin Mary, though Lady Wisdom never had the same effect on the faithful.

Lady Wisdom was clearly a cynical tool of the post-Ezra campaign to eradicate the goddess—a sop to the need for the sacred feminine, reinventing her as a supporter for the new One God and the patriarchal status quo. But her role was not entirely negative. Just by existing Lady Wisdom allowed the goddess to retain a place in Judaism, even if she was by then a shadowy presence lurking uneasily between the lines of the patriarchal texts. And her almost subliminal influence continued to be felt; Lady Wisdom was to become the foundation for much more positive attitudes to the feminine in later Jewish traditions, including the Kabbalah. She was a small cutting from a discarded parent plant that was eventually to blossom in its own right.

Apart from her pallid representation as Wisdom, most researchers believe the Asherah cult disappeared after the return from Exile and the reforms of Nehemiah and Ezra, as the new monotheistic religion was consolidated both doctrinally and organizationally.

No goddess—especially not a Lion Lady—was simply going to lie down and die. But given the hard line of the new Temple authorities, if the worship of the Hebrew goddess did survive it would have to find ingenious new ways of surviving the purge. And of course it did.

ALEXANDRIA THE GREAT

One of history's most famous little-men-with-sky-high-ambitions had a part to play in the story of the Jewish goddess, although he never knew it. The Greek Alexander the Great—who although not as tiny as history has painted him, certainly did not possess the stature then required to provoke instant awe in his peoples—wanted to conquer the entire world. When he thought he had done just that, he sobbed uncontrollably, as there was nowhere left to make his mark. Among his acquisitions along the way was—in 333–332 BCE—the Persian Empire, which included the provinces of Judah and Samaria. Alexander's rapaciousness turned out to bestow some benefits. Despite being the foreign invaders, he and his successors made the Greek lifestyle highly aspirational wherever they stamped their presence. The Israelites also fell under the Greek spell—though there were to be other influences on their thinking—and it was during this era that the Jewish goddess was significantly redefined, and sometimes, although marginalized, given a sort of grudging half-life. At least her new guise, subtle though it was, would keep the sacred feminine alive—sometimes only just. But in all her people's travails, she never lost the sparkle of her energy, and they never entirely lost their love for her.

After adding the Persians to his portfolio, Alexander went on to conquer Egypt, where he was regarded as a liberator from Persian rule—and declared the "son of Amun" in gratitude by the Egyptians. (Incidentally, this marked the last days of the Elephantine community, as the garrison was withdrawn in the general upheaval of the transition from Persian to Greek rule. Sadly, all clues about the new location of the Yahu and Anat worshippers went with them.)

By his death at the age of thirty-two, Alexander had amassed an empire that straddled 3,000 miles, from the Adriatic Sea to the Punjab in India, earning him the reputation of most influential and most successful leader in history. As nation after nation fell, it seemed that the stars themselves aligned for him, but as is so often the way with apparently unstoppable triumph, ultimately the gods had other ideas. Alexander met his doom, perhaps from alcohol poisoning, perhaps from assassin's poisoning or even, less dramatically, malaria. Unsurprisingly, after his death his generals hastily divided up the conquered lands, crowning themselves kings. Judah and Samaria were part of the territory ruled from Egypt by the dynasty descended from Alexander's General Ptolemy—the family that was to include the famous Queen Cleopatra.

The Ptolemys were not destined to be great stayers, due to the inevitable power struggles between the Greekified—or "Hellenized," from *Hellenes* meaning "Greeks"—dynasties. In 200 BCE Palestine was taken from the Ptolemies by the Seleucid Empire, founded by another of Alexander's generals, which had expanded from its original territory in Babylon to overrun a vast swathe of the Middle East from Afghanistan to Turkey. Yet again, Judah and Samaria found themselves with a new master. (And with a new name: it's in the Greek era that the Samarians officially become Samaritans, from the Greek *samareitis*.)

Judah and Samaria experienced an enormous transformation through their absorption into the Greek world, as did all the lands conquered by Alexander. The result was wall-to-wall Hellenization. In all the conquered lands Greek culture became the next big thing—architecture, art, lifestyle, literature, philosophy, and, of course, language. Anything Greek was seriously cool, everywhere.

Despite what we might think of such proud people, the Jews and Samaritans embraced Hellenistic culture as enthusiastically as all the other nations. (At least the elite did—presumably the peasantry just shrugged and got on with the basic business of keeping alive as they always had.) The cream of society adopted Greek lifestyles, built in the Greek style, wrote in Greek and took Greek names.

This was when the organization of the Jewish—and Samaritan—religion developed by leaps and bounds. The first synagogues were created as a mix of prayer house and local community center, though perhaps it's ironic that *synagogue,* meaning "assembly," comes from a Greek word. Having a network of such meeting places proved to be an important conduit for standardizing and controlling the religion, similar to the spread of parish churches by the Christian Church in later centuries. Both Judah and Samaria soon boasted intricate networks of these new synagogues.

But while the Jewish faith was being reinforced, it is also difficult to overestimate the effect of Hellenization on the peoples conquered by Alexander and his generals. Apart from much else, it led to a fluid exchange of ideas between nations, as theologians and philosophers from different religions and schools were brought together in major population centers. Some of these ideas proved central to the history of Judaism, and once again it is to Egypt that we turn.

The great intellectual hub of Ptolemaic Egypt was the city of Alexandria, built by Alexander the Great—and of course named for him—on the Nile delta's Mediterranean coast almost immediately after he had taken Egypt. Based around the small town of Rhakotis, the new port was the sleek new Greek gateway to Egypt, and became the capital of the Ptolemaic dynasty.

With crazy rapidity, within just a generation Alexandria was the largest city in the entire world, dazzling with its sophistication. Over the next century it was home to some of the most legendary buildings in history—the great lighthouse of Pharos, the famous Library, the magnificent temple to the god Serapis, to name just a few. And Alexandria also became an intensely prolific ideas center. Anyone who was set on becoming anyone in the extended Greek world made their way there, desperate to make their names in the buzzing new hub.

Like everyone else with personal and intellectual ambitions, Jews and Samaritans flocked to Alexandria, where their expatriate enclaves expanded so exponentially they were soon larger than the population of Jerusalem. Some sources claim Jews made up a third of Alexandria's population, numbering nearly 200,000. They had their own council of elders, and the Great Synagogue of Alexandria was an architectural marvel.

The city was very significant to Jews. It was, for example, where the Hebrew Bible, the Septuagint, was translated into Greek. According to legend, a group of seventy Jewish scholars asked the second of the Ptolemaic kings to authorize a translation for the library, hence the title, which means "seventy." This massive, ambitious project began in the mid-third century BCE and continued over the next hundred years.

Rainer Albertz and Bob Becking, editors of *Yahweh after the Exile* (2003), summarize the impact of the Greek occupiers on the standardization of the Jewish religion: Prior to the Exile, "The Hebrew Bible as well as the archaeological and epigraphic evidence reveals a multitude of Yahwisms, which include an an-iconic, monotheistic form as well as forms in which the veneration of a goddess as the consort of the main deity was construed as acceptable. The Hellenistic period shows clear traces of emerging Judaism." The Judaism of this Hellenistic period was becoming increasingly monotheistic, and "the traditions of the past—on their way to becoming a sacred book—were seen as formative for the ethical code."[45]

As usual, though, we need to bear in mind that this refers to the *established* religion, which certainly did not include everybody who professed to practice Judaism. There remained many variations. Albertz and Becking's "multitude of Yahwisms" continued, although as they had to survive beneath the officials' radar they can only be glimpsed occasionally in the slipstream of history.

Sometimes unorthodox and borderline heretical ideas do appear in acceptably mainstream writings, occasionally glimpsed even in the scriptures. A major example is the way that the figure of Wisdom was developed in the Hellenistic period, becoming a full-fledged goddess in all but name.

SOPHIA

As we have seen, Asherah was effectively sanitized as Lady Wisdom in the book of Proverbs, by morphing her into a metaphor, and transforming her into a bridge through which to reach Yahweh. She is divested of her erotic Qadesh aspect, now being demonized as the Strange Woman. In fact, she is divested of most of her aspects and has almost lost her soul.

However, new imaginings of the Wisdom lore reestablished the independent Chokmah, together with certain of Asherah's traditional associations, some dating back to Canaanite beliefs about her relationship with El. New and explicit connections were made between Wisdom and the goddesses of other nations, especially the most famous Egyptian goddess. The Canadian professor of religion

John S. Kloppenborg wrote in the *Harvard Theological Review* in 1982: "In recent years the thesis of a dialogue between [Jewish] sapiential circles (both Palestinian and Alexandrian) and the cult of Isis has commended itself to a number of critics."[46]

This was new: there's no sign of similar Isis influence in the earlier book of Proverbs. But Jewish thinkers in the new Hellenistic environment were happy to borrow elements of her cult, consciously conflating her with Lady Wisdom—showing that they saw Wisdom herself in very similar terms.

It wasn't a case of Jewish religious intellectuals deciding to absorb Isis into Judaism because they liked the look of her. They recognized the *existing* connections between the Israelite and Egyptian goddesses and sought to explore them further. After all, there was no need to import the sacred feminine into Judaism; they simply used Isis as a novel expression of what they already had. Even so, this new conflation was disingenuously presented as part of the "official" version of the Yahweh cult, which is why the writings survived. But as the writers did their utmost to include the goddess in some form, they must have had access to information about Asherah's original place in their religion. And now they were trying to bring her back. As much as they dared.

Her journey had taken another turn. From her pathetically pallid reflection in Proverbs, Wisdom segued back into a thinly disguised Asherah. These writings also laid the foundation for new expressions of the sacred feminine that were to flower in Judaism—and even in Christianity, many generations later. As Raphael Patai observes: "the female deities of the early, monarchic period did not subsequently disappear but underwent transformations and succeeded in their changed forms to retain much of their old sway over religious sentiments."[47]

Now, thanks to the Greeks, the Jewish goddess was intimately associated with Isis—no mean reflection of her own image. And if you were to have a new divine sister, you could do far worse than Isis. Apart from her many other qualities, she was always the epitome of godly style.

(And given twenty-first-century enthusiasm for her among occultists and the New Age community, she obviously still is.)

Perhaps Isis's enduring appeal is partly explained by her iconography, the sheer glamor and romance that envelops her image like a cloud of exotic perfume. She is goddess of magic, which cloaks her with an aura all by itself. But in any case, arguably no other ancient goddess has the same allure as Isis, which is so immediate it must, somehow, be archetypal.

Typically, she is portrayed as a beautiful young woman, slender, long-backed, high-breasted, firm-buttocked, with the long black hair so immediately associated with Egypt. Part of the success of her image today has undoubtedly come down to us from 1960s' Hollywood, with Elizabeth Taylor's now iconic look as Cleopatra. For once, Hollywood had done its homework. The real life Graeco-Egyptian queen deliberately styled herself as Isis, perhaps to echo—or even boldly satirize—the Caesars' penchant for declaring themselves gods to be worshipped. Isis's fine features and characteristic headdress are also, perhaps strangely, rather similar to the world-famous gold mask of the boy-king Tutankhamun—so familiar that almost anyone would recognize it with just one glance. So, with such powerful visual associations, Isis lurks in the subconscious minds of vast numbers of people even in the twenty-first century, though they might not know her name. Yet even by the time the Jews absorbed her into their own manifestation of the sacred feminine, she already had a long history.

Isis was a very ancient goddess, though beliefs about her had naturally evolved over the millennia. She appears in the Pyramid Texts, the oldest dating from around 2400 BCE, as part of the famous brother-sister tetrad with Osiris, Set, and Nephthys. She had a starring role in the cycle of myths, especially those about the birth of her son, the falcon-headed god Horus. However, she had no role or functions of her own until she was identified with Hathor during the New Kingdom (roughly 1500–1000 BCE).

As the eminent German Egyptologist Jan Assmann explains, listing her superpowers:

Isis-Hathor becomes an all-including deity: the mistress of heaven, the solar eye; the lady of the year and the inundation; the mistress of erotic love and of husbandry, motherhood and female fertility; the personification of pharaonic kingship who elects and initiates the legitimate heir; the chief magician who overcomes all dangers that menace the solar course, the life of the patient (especially the child), and even the fatal blows of death.[48]

In later times—from about the seventh century BCE onward—Isis evolved even more by being merged with Neith, the creator-goddess. It was then she took on a cosmogenic or creatrix aspect. As Assmann gushes:

[Isis] transcends even the border of sex and assumes the character of a male-female primaeval deity beyond creation and differentiation. . . . [S]he inherits the characteristics of the 'cosmic god' . . . who is One and All, hidden and manifest, transcendent and immanent, who created the world by transforming him/herself into the world and who preserves the world and each individual being by his/her will, planning and order.[49]

As Isis's cosmic role and function as creatrix, especially combined with her personal relationship with her devotees is very reminiscent of Asherah, Jewish philosophers found Isis seductively easy to assimilate into their own belief system.

Isis's popularity increased in the Hellenistic period, and carried through into Roman times, becoming one of the most beloved deities among all classes. It was at this time that texts—*aretalogies*—in which she proclaims her abilities and qualities, and the spheres over which she presides, were composed and inscribed on stelae. Isis's aretalogies had a huge influence on the Jewish Wisdom documents.

As both the two main texts to repatriate Wisdom unsurprisingly hailed from Alexandria they were written in Greek—the new common language. So she appears as *Sophia* rather than *Chokmah*. Both resonate with the personification of Wisdom in Proverbs, but expand on it. (Yahweh and God become respectively, in these texts, *Kyrios,* "Lord," and *Theos,* God.)

Although neither book invented the new ideas about Wisdom, they incorporated current thinking in Jewish circles in Alexandria, and probably elsewhere. These texts were as radical as possible, though to an extent they were still sanitized. But given that memories of the Hebrew Goddess—as the Queen of Heaven, Yahu's Anat, the Asherah cult, and its sexier Qadesh side—must still have been swirling around, these books provide a tantalizing glimpse of the goddess's survival.

The first of these two key documents is known as the Wisdom of Solomon, but as it had no connection with the legendary king, scholars call it the book of Wisdom. Included in the Hebrew and Catholic—but not the Protestant—canons, it was written in Greek in Alexandria in the second or first century BCE by an unknown author.

In chapters 7 to 9, "Solomon" praises Sophia's qualities and attributes. Although drawing on Proverbs and Isaiah these chapters also blatantly borrow concepts from the aretalogies of Isis, homing in on her as personal savior, her connection with kingship, and cosmological function.[50]

Sophia, too, is a personal savior—from physical danger, not spiritual temptations—but as this is found nowhere in Proverbs, "the similarity with Isis is here inescapable."[51] It does, however, also chime with the Jews' devotion to the Queen of Heaven in southern Egypt and Jerusalem encountered by the determinedly appalled Jeremiah.

In the Wisdom of Solomon, Sophia is "the artisan of all things,"[52] echoing her role as creator in Proverbs. She is "God's chief agent."[53] However, unlike Proverbs' Lady Wisdom, here Sophia continues to be active in creation, having dominion over the world as "the divine power, active in history."[54] She is also responsible for maintaining the cosmos in good order. Such is her creative function that in later passages even the distinction between Sophia and *God* becomes very blurred.[55]

The book of Wisdom remarkably describes Sophia as both the

beloved and spouse of God—clearly recalling Asherah's relationship with Yahweh.[56] Roland Murphy is explicit, saying: "there is a remarkable love affair between God and Wisdom. She lives with God . . . in a loving marriage relationship."[57]

In the same passage, Sophia is also described as Solomon's wife[58]—particularly interesting given that his wives are supposed to have seduced him into idolatry. But the triad of God-Sophia-Solomon is not as straightforwardly Jewish as it would seem, as it clearly parallels that of Ra-Osiris, Isis, and the pharaoh in Egyptian thinking.[59] Indeed, Sophia's characteristics have a distinct correlation with those of Isis.[60] Even so, none of this came exclusively from Egypt. Most of the book of Wisdom is drawn squarely from Israelite sources.

The second of these central texts during the Alexandrian period is the book of Ben Sira, also known as Ecclesiasticus and in Greek, Ben Sirach. It comprises the teachings of Joshua, or Jesus, ben Sira "of Jerusalem," although it seems to have been written in Alexandria. There's a Hebrew version and a Greek translation, the latter with a prologue explaining it was translated by Joshua ben Sira's grandson, around 115 BCE. Ben Sira's original was obviously a couple of generations earlier, so probably written in the 170s BCE, making it roughly contemporary with the Wisdom of Solomon—though it is impossible to say which came first.

Although the book of Ben Sira was never included in the Hebrew canon it was obviously popular—many ancient copies have been discovered, including among the Dead Sea Scrolls. Again, it's accepted in the Catholic Old Testament but not the Protestant edition.

Most of the book is conventional enough, comprising advice on personal morality and ethics. It addresses a young man, listing ways of conducting himself properly—being kind and fair, honoring parents, not making enemies, helping the poor, not being greedy or arrogant, and generally doing good. There are warnings about adultery—and even just lusting after women other than one's wife—but, unlike in Proverbs, men who get carried away by their desire, and especially those who cheat on their wives, are roundly condemned. It's not the women who get all the blame for leading the men astray.

Toward the end of the book, in what was presumably once a separate text, Sophia—as in Proverbs—speaks for herself, and then the tone changes dramatically. Although again there are general similarities with the virtues and miraculous deeds of Isis, Sophia's words are very reminiscent of an invocation to the great Egyptian goddess found among the hoard of papyri discovered in 1902 in the ruins of the city of Oxyrhynchus (modern el-Bahnasa).[61] The papyrus dates from the early second century CE, but the form of the invocation had clearly been used for a while.

Despite the obvious link to Isis, there are also clear references to the ancient Asherah cult. Sophia says that she was "exalted" in the form of various trees—a cedar in Lebanon, a cypress on Mount Zion, a palm tree in Kadesh, and a rose bush in Jericho. Tellingly, she also declares, "I have extended my branches like a terebinth tree."[62] Note that Sophia manifested as a *palm tree,* a symbol of Asherah, in Kadesh of all places— which was where Moses's sister the great prophetess Miriam was buried.

Perhaps to modern eyes, the whole idea of Wisdom is lacking any real excitement. It might seem a passive, not particularly exciting virtue, usually associated with old age. You can be wise and—let's be honest— really rather dull, confining your activities to doling out advice, only some of which will ever even be listened to, and not necessarily acted upon. But none of that applies to Sophia. She's not only dynamic, but actually essential in the great scheme of things—and always was.

The point is repeated throughout Ben Sira's book that Sophia was created before all other things ("the first-born before all creatures"; "From the beginning, and before the world, I was created").[63] While not the agent of creation as she is in the book of Wisdom, Sophia is "pictured as a member of God's heavenly council."[64] In fact she is the most prominent, being given "priority among God's entourage."[65]

Another development in Ben Sira's book that would have a great influence over later Jewish concepts of the sacred feminine is Sophia's identification with the presence of Yahweh. This awe-inspiring manifestation went before the people of Israel as a pillar of cloud and fire during their wandering in the wilderness and settled on the Tabernacle when Yahweh spoke to Moses. It represents yet another stage in Sophia's evolution as a separate entity from Yahweh.

Delving deeply into the Wisdom tradition, Sophia is soon revealed as an increasingly important divine figure. Bearing no relation to an old grandmother spouting homilies from a rocking chair, she is an active and essential part, not only of creation itself but also the covenant with Israel. The Tabernacle—and by implication the Ark of the Covenant—is said to be hers: "And the One who created me rested in my tabernacle. And he said to me: 'Let your dwelling place be with Jacob, and let your inheritance be with Israel, for you shall take root among my elect.'"[66]

Momentously, here it is *Sophia,* not Yahweh, who is given Israel as her inheritance.

These concepts of Wisdom were profoundly influential. One eminent philosopher who fell under their spell was Philo of Alexandria (ca. 20 BCE–50 CE), a leading light of the expatriate Jewish society. Philo happily borrowed certain concepts from Greek philosophy, but only to enable him to present Jewish theology to a Hellenistic audience (including Hellenized Jews) in terms they would understand. In fact, most of his theology came from already deeply embedded Israelite traditions.

Sophia looms large in Philo's teaching, as Helmer Ringgren explains in his classic 1947 study *Word and Wisdom:* "Here we find Sophia as a cosmic principle, a pre-existent being, the mother and nurse of everything. She is the model from which the visible world was copied. But she is also a creative power, 'the mother Wisdom, through whom everything has come into existence.'"[67]

To Philo the supreme deity had both male and female aspects, represented by the two cherubim in the Temple of Jerusalem. It is ironic that the concept of a dual-gendered God seems to be actually hallowed by age, when to many Jews and Christians today it seems dangerously new and subversive, even blasphemous. Yet it chimes perfectly with the emphasis in most ancient religions on the need for perfect balance, for both male and female deities that encompass *all* possible aspects of godhood—and, indeed, all aspects of the humanity made in their image. The most supreme irony, of course, is that it is the concept of one, male God that would be dangerously subversive, even blasphemous, to the ancients.

As in the book of Wisdom, Philo speaks of God as the husband of Sophia, clearly harking back to the divine couple of the Asherah cult. And by making both the male and female aspects of God partners in creation he is invoking a concept that went all the way back to pre-Israelite, Canaanite beliefs about Asherah as proud co-creator with El.

Another example of common terminology between Philo and the earlier book of Wisdom is the identification of Sophia with God's Word, or Logos. Philo equates Sophia/Wisdom inextricably with the Logos, although sometimes she is its source and sometimes the Logos is her source, though to Philo and his circle the two concepts are identical, with "Sophia" being its expression in Jewish terms, and the Logos in Greek.

If Sophia is essentially the Logos, then—according to Philo—she has unimaginable power. He describes the latter as the "image of God" and, even more astonishingly, *the "Second God."*[68] We are now stepping way, way beyond our usual notions of Jewish theology. Not only is there room for a second deity, alongside Yahweh, but even at this stage of the Jewish religion this other god is *female*.

The Logos was to resurface in the famous opening lines of the Gospel of John, where the Word is equated with Jesus. As we will see, the goddess was also present in the first years of the Christian religion, though the male-dominated Church did its utmost to eradicate her—with *almost* complete success.

SHEKINAH AND THE HOLY SPIRIT

These reimaginings of Wisdom/Sophia as an entity independent of God were to evolve in significant ways. Besides the Logos, there were other manifestations, powerful in their own ways, including the Holy Spirit.

The word *spirit* (*ruach* or *ruah*) is found throughout the Hebrew Bible, and covers the same range of meanings as it does in English: Essence, energy, a state of mind—as in the "spirit of neighborliness"— and mind itself, like the French *esprit*. It also refers to disembodied entities, both discarnate humans and supernatural beings, and the mysterious force that animates all living things. As it was thought to be what endows humans with knowledge and skill—Joshua is "full of the spirit of wisdom"[69]—it was related to *chokmah* in a general sense.

Ruach also means "breath," reflecting the widespread idea among the ancients that the act of breathing is intimately linked to the invisible spirit that inhabits and animates the physical body—and that can fly free, being finally liberated at death. In that sense, *ruach* is also "an embodied soul, a vital principle which manages life and its functions in man through the respiration."[70]

God, too, has a "Spirit" right from the beginning, as the second verse of Genesis has the Spirit of God "hovering over the face of the waters"[71] when the earth is still formless, before even light is created. So understandably, the Spirit came to be identified with Wisdom, the being who was with God before anything else was created.

Although powerful in its own way, God's Spirit tends to be low-profile throughout the Hebrew Bible, being treated simply as one of his attributes. But as Wisdom became personified in the books we discussed above, so too did God's Spirit—*pneuma* in Greek, with the same range of meanings as *ruach*. The Spirit is no longer merely one of God's characteristics: it's an independent being whom both the book of Ben Sira and the Wisdom of Solomon refer to as "Holy Spirit."

Both pivotal books equate God's Holy Spirit with Sophia. Ben Sira says that God "created wisdom through the Holy Spirit,"[72] while to the book of Wisdom Sophia *is* the Spirit, being described as "a breath of the virtue [or power] of God."[73] Spirit and Wisdom have the same functions. In the book of Wisdom, Solomon asks God, "who will know your mind, unless you give wisdom and send your holy spirit from on high?"[74]

And, of course, the Holy Spirit was to feature prominently in the New Testament gospels, and then in the dogma of the Christian religion, usually referred to as the—somewhat mysterious—third member of the Trinity. (It was even more mysterious when referred to as the "Holy Ghost," which caused generations of children to shiver and look under the bed. These days that particular name has largely been dropped, probably because it sounds too reminiscent of Halloween.) But in this egregious Christian reworking something of supreme significance was lost, and the emptiness left behind continues to this day.

Simultaneously with the elaboration of the Holy Spirit in the rabbinic literature, it was being equated with another female entity originally considered a part of God but who came to have her own, independent life: the Shekinah. This comes from an idea in Ben Sira that was developed by Philo of Alexandria, of the *presence* of God as a separate entity. The name derives from *shakhan,* meaning "to inhabit" or "dwell within."

The word used in the Hebrew Bible for the Tabernacle, *mishkan*—literally "dwelling place"—derives from the same verb, showing that Yahweh was thought to be physically present inside it. Exodus is ambiguous—or rather contradictory—about whether Yahweh was thought to dwell permanently in the Tabernacle or if he just visited to give instructions to Moses. But it was there that Sophia had a starring role.

The Shekinah, Sophia/Chokmah, and the Holy Spirit were interchangeable terms for the same divine female, although they emphasized different qualities. And she was derived ultimately from Asherah and probably Anat. Once again, although cloaked and clothed differently, the Jewish goddess lived on.

SAMARIA

Apart from the Jews in Israel and Egypt there was another sizeable Israelite community in those days in the former northern kingdom of

Samaria. Few people seem even to notice them. Yet we believe they were incredibly important, holding the keys to great mystical and religious mysteries. So what was *their* interpretation of the religion? Just how important were the much-hated Samaritans?

The situation in Samaria is complex and confused, especially because so little historical information about then-current events was allowed to survive. And most of what we have is written by their enemies—never a recipe for objective reporting. The Jews only portrayed what was negative about their northern cousins. Ben Sira, for example—not exactly holding back—called them "foolish people,"[75] while another contemporary text calls Shechem a "city of imbeciles."[76] The later chronicler Josephus was outspoken in his depiction of them as a scurrilous and untrustworthy bunch. And of course Jesus's parable of the Good Samaritan only worked because his audience thought there could be no such thing.

The impression the Bible gives is that Samaria was an inconsequential, perhaps tiny, area peopled with the scum of the earth—apart perhaps from that single uniquely good one. Yet Samaria was the larger and more prosperous of the two lands. And presumably, like every other community that ever was, it enjoyed its fair share of useful and kind citizens besides the inevitable villains.

Even the history of the Samaritans was obscured and rewritten by their enemies. The book of Kings claimed that when the Kingdom of Israel fell to the Assyrians the entire population had been deported and replaced with peoples imported from other parts of the Assyrian Empire, making everyone who lived there at the time Kings was written—at around the return of the Judahites from Exile—of non-Israelite descent.

However, Kings' account is blatantly riddled with inconsistencies and implausibilities. It says that the new arrivals brought their own cults with them, which they practiced in the outdoor sanctuaries that the backsliding northerners had conveniently provided for them. But then it has their descendants adopting the worship of Yahweh alongside their gods, so that by the time Kings was written Samaria had reverted to being riddled with cults that sacrificed jointly to Yahweh and other deities. Obviously in their zeal to make the Samarians "not one of us," the writers sought to transform them into both foreigners *and* apostates—even if they had to tie themselves in knots to do it.

Even parts of Kings' own account contradict its message. When it describes Josiah's assault on the sanctuaries in the northern kingdom—then still Assyrian territory—it has him conversing with the locals in Hebrew, and they are suspiciously familiar with the Israelite traditions and legends about sacred sites such as Bethel. Yet there are supposed to be no remaining native inhabitants.

The other history book, Chronicles, says nothing about the complete repopulation of Samaria. Nor do any of the prophets who wrote after the fall of Samaria, who clearly regard the northern population as predominantly Israelite.

There's no doubt that the Assyrians did deport a large number of Israelites and settle peoples from other parts of the empire there: not only do the Assyrian records spell this out, but it was standard practice. Conquered peoples were strategically mixed up and moved around to prevent individual groups from rebelling. It's the *scale* of the repopulation that Kings has exaggerated.

Gary N. Knoppers, author of a 2013 study, *Jews and Samaritans,* adds: "To be sure, tens of thousands of Israelites were deported by the Assyrians to foreign territories and were forced to adjust to living in cultures considerably different from their own. But many others continued to reside in their ancestral homeland, albeit under foreign rule."[77]

Archaeology has found, for example, that the style of pottery—always a defining cultural fingerprint—changed not at all in most of Samaria. As with the Babylonian Exile of the Judahites, the deportations mainly affected the elite. There were plenty of ordinary Samaritans left.

More significantly for us, the Assyrians were not known for imposing their own culture or religion on those they invaded. While they carried off the northern kingdom's "gods"—according to other records standard Assyrian practice to prove who was boss—the idols and cult objects were returned once the conquered people proved they had no intention of trouble-making. And at that point Assyria made no attempt to interfere with local cults.[78]

Undoubtedly, the Samaritans encountered by the returning Judahite exiles, and by Nehemiah and Ezra a few generations later, were Israelite descendants of the northern tribes, primarily Ephraim and Manasseh. Clearly there was a difference between the new monotheistic Yahwism that arose during the Exile and the God of the Samaritans, who presumably retained older aspects of the religion—including honoring the beloved Asherah.

But to confuse matters even further, what *became* the established, official version of the religion in Samaria was basically a copy of the Jerusalem edition—if anything even more uncompromisingly Yahwist. As with most Samaritan history, the exact sequence of events is unclear, but apparently, under the Persians a group of priests from Jerusalem went into exile in Samaria and, with the sanction of the Persian governor, established a rival religious center.

The cult they installed mimicked the Jerusalem setup—becoming even more Yahwist than the original Yahwists. The major difference was that the Samaritans only accepted the Pentateuch—the five "books of Moses"—as scripture. This is hardly surprising, as the other books of the Hebrew Bible are blatantly pro-Jerusalem and anti-Samaritan. Weren't the nasty northerners guilty of corrupting Yahweh's pure religion?

With so many issues about Jerusalem, the Samaritans simply built a rival temple—on Mount Gerizim, traditionally a sacred spot close to Shechem, the very ancient and *original* center of the Yahweh cult.

The Samaritan version posed a real threat to Jerusalem's authority, as the northern sites such as Shechem and Bethel, with their associated legends of the Patriarchs, boasted an older pedigree than Jerusalem. (Jerusalem is mentioned nowhere in the Pentateuch—it only became Israelite territory after its capture by David.) And now the hated Samaritans had a rival temple where sacrifices could be offered to Yahweh. This was totally unacceptable to Jerusalem, which dismissed the despised Samaritan religion as illegitimate.

There was a century or so when the Judahites managed to claw back their independence, after the Maccabean Revolt against Seleucid rule in 167 BCE. The result was the founding of the Hasmonean dynasty by Simon Maccabeus, son of the Temple priest who had instigated the revolt. Although, mindful that the new royal line had no scriptural sanction or ancient lineage, Simon was careful to declare that it would hold the throne only "until a trustworthy prophet should arise."[79]

Under the Hasmoneans, who attempted to create their own empire in the region, the upstart Samaritans were severely dealt with. In 110 BCE, led by their king John Hyrcanus the Judahites invaded and annexed Samaria, destroying the city of Shechem and the precious temple on Mount Gerizim. But despite the traumatic desecration and destruction, the official Samaritan cult found ways of continuing.

Surprisingly, the last Hasmonean ruler—and the last of an independent Judah—was a woman: Salome Alexandra, sometimes Alexandra of Jerusalem, who ruled from 76 to 67 BCE as regent for her two young sons after the death of her husband. When she died, almost as a matter of routine there was a civil war between her sons over who would succeed. Both appealed for support to the Roman general Pompey, who was fighting a campaign in Syria. Drawing attention to their homeland turned out to be a very bad move. Pompey decided it would do rather nicely for Rome, and in 63 BCE he annexed Jerusalem. And what the Romans did for them was not at all amusing.

With the arrival of the Roman Pompey the Jews experienced their third wave of foreign masters in 500 years, while to the Samaritans it was their fourth, after the Assyrians, Persians, and Jews. Judah became the new Roman province of Judea. And that was the end of an independent Jewish state for over 2,000 years . . .

Pompey set up the last Hasmonean king's general, the Idumean Antipater, to administer and control the region for Rome. He was succeeded in 37 BCE by his famous son Herod the Great, to whom the Senate voted the title King of the Jews. Despite claims to the contrary from his own day to the present, Herod was Jewish by religion. His family had been forcibly converted when the Hasmoneans annexed Idumea.

Like every ruler of the time, Herod wanted his kingdom to reflect his personal greatness, overseeing monumental building works in Jerusalem and throughout his lands, including the brand-new seaport of Caesarea Maritima in former Phoenician territory. He had the modest Second Temple completely remodeled and comprehensively burnished and gilded. He also had the old Samaritan sacred city of Shechem—then in ruins—rebuilt and renamed Sebaste, making it the capital of Samaria.

Although under a single ruler, Judea and Samaria were administratively independent. The Samaritans fared pretty well under Rome, with their own council to administer Samaria's internal affairs.

Like the Jews, Samaritans were to be found in many cities outside of Palestine—in Egypt, with a particularly large community in Alexandria, and synagogues in the Syrian towns of Antioch and Damascus, besides many other places throughout the Near East and Asia Minor. The Samaritans—presumably homesick—even named their town in the Faiyum region of Egypt "Samaria."

Undoubtedly—as with the Judahites—the older forms of the religion persisted both in Samaria and their diaspora communities. Although often sidelined, and therefore rarely studied, Samaria holds many secrets—some truly explosive, especially as we turn to the very beginnings of the Christian era.

In their homelands, the Jews and Samaritans shared a major preoccupation. There was a huge expectation that the end of the world as they knew it was imminent, that God was about to intervene to fulfill his covenant with the Israelites, either by enabling their victory over the oppressors and setting them up over other nations, or by remaking the world in an entirely new way—as in Jesus's notion of the "Kingdom of God." The books of the Hebrew Bible were pored over for clues about what would come to pass, and all kinds of prophecies—some crazier than others—were read into their words.

A manifestation of end-times mania was a rash of charismatic cult leaders—often, but not always, connected with fringe sects—who attracted disciples and mass followings, tapping into the popular hysteria. If ever there was a time to get your ideas out there, or even get yourself worshipped, however briefly, this was it.

The end-times fervor often centered on expectations of a magnificent Chosen One sent by God either to lead the people to victory over their oppressors or bring about their salvation in some other way. Today we tend to think that everyone was agog waiting for the same Messiah—in Jewish terms, a divinely backed king and military hero who would lead Israel to victory. But there were many variations on the Last Days theme.

Some thought that God himself would appear, others that he would send a powerful angel, or that one or other of the prophets would return—Elijah being a particular front-runner. The Samaritans were awaiting their own redeemer figure, the Taheb, or "Restorer." A significant legend for what comes next in our story concerns the coming of an individual whom scholars refer to as the "Prophet like Moses," but known at the time simply as "the Prophet" or "the Prophet who is to come." This tradition derives from Deuteronomy, when Moses—the Israelites' ultimate deliverer figure—in his final declaration to the Israelites, says that when the time is right "the LORD will raise up for you a prophet like me from among you."[80]

Given the apocalyptic obsession, many people claimed to be one or other of these figures, or at least to represent them. A particularly maligned and infamous individual, burning with a mission to restore all aspects of the sacred feminine, emerged from Samaria at that time. This time she was no vague metaphor, God's playmate, his cute-but-dependent daughter, or simply another aspect of his greatness. This time she was not even the creatrix nor the Sophia of the Alexandrian Jewish books, her immense potential power hidden between the lines.

This time the sacred feminine was a raunchily sexual *woman,* who celebrated her red-blooded desires in appropriately abandoned rituals.

6

"The Great Revelation"

If the Jewish goddess—as Sophia or otherwise—was to survive into the Christian era and beyond, she needed champions who were not afraid to make a stand in her name. Perhaps many bravely tried to wave her flag, but are now lost to history, whose names we will never know. Fortunately, probably the most high-profile lover of the sacred feminine has not been lost to us, and his words and deeds were recorded and avidly commented upon. Sadly, however, we have no way of knowing just how true many of his reported activities were, as this particular character rapidly became such a byword for evil that today's Harry Potter fans would instantly see him as a sort of Lord Voldemort. He was hated—and indeed feared—as a travesty of Christ himself. Almost everything we know about him was written by his enemies—of which he had a great many.

This extraordinary cult leader of the first century CE became the early Church's greatest bogeyman, but even his reputation as the epitome of demonic degradation does little to detract from the aura of glamor and audacity that still surrounds him. That is, if one has even heard of him. Ironically, this larger-than-life figure, though very familiar to theologians and historians, and who has a memorable cameo in the Acts of the Apostles, often completely escapes the notice of the average twenty-first-century churchgoer. This is extra ironic, as for the best part of the last two millennia, apart from Judas Iscariot, he has been the most hated man in Christendom.

His name is Simon Magus—Simon the magician, or less melodramatically, "Simon the Wise." To put it mildly, he was perceived as disgusting, beyond mere decadence, filth personified. His evil knew no bounds. He was the very embodiment of an anti-Christ.

It's difficult to exaggerate the contempt poured on Simon and his works over the years. And yet, he has a remarkably central part to play in this investigation of the complex and colorful history of the sacred feminine. So just who was this ultrascandalous tour de force? What can we piece together about Christ's evil shadow?

Simon Magus was a Samaritan sect leader, a spiritual teacher with alleged miraculous powers, a contemporary of Jesus, who is mentioned in the New Testament Acts of Apostles and known from the writings of theologians and churchmen of the first three hundred years of the Christian era—the so-called Church Fathers. David R. Cartlidge, professor of religion, Maryville College, Tennessee, writes: "Simon Magus is arguably the worst of the bad guys in the history of the church."[1] To the Church Fathers Simon was "a symbol of everything a Christian should *not* be."[2]

Simon has his uses, however, being "the common enemy who inspires the feuding factions within the earliest church to unite in opposition" because to the churchmen, "Simon Magus is the founder of all Christian heresies, including Gnosticism, and the champion of all wrong thinking and blasphemous worship."[3]

So what was Gnosticism, which caused the early Christians so much trouble—and was such an insult that it was even applied to this Simon? Gnosticism was an umbrella term for a number of related religious philosophies that arose in the Judeo-Christian world of the first and second centuries CE—precisely the time of Simon's rise to fame, or rather infamy. Gnostics believed the ordinary, material world was a delusion created by an imperfect lesser deity, the God of the Old Testament. Human beings, each with their own divine spark, are trapped in physical bodies and can only escape the prison of matter through personal *gnosis*—Greek for personal knowledge, as opposed to intellectual knowing. It's the first-century equivalent of *The Matrix*, with the character of Neo as Everyman slowly experiencing his own gnosis and, though it's often nightmarishly tough, coming to free himself from the restraints of consensus reality. Once gnosis has awakened the divine spark, it can fly free. All of this is found in some form in Simon Magus's belief system.

Already it is clear that believers never held back about Simon. His reputation as an evildoer and corrupter of Christians skyrocketed until he became the medieval Church's go-to archvillain. He wasn't just a heretic, originator of the *heresis simoniaca,* but the "father of all heresy." Commentators really let rip about Simon. One twelfth-century Benedictine cardinal declared, "Simon Magus is not just a great heretic, but the first and worst."[4]

But a closer look at the historical Simon Magus—as far as it's possible to find him among all the paranoid hysteria—reveals him to be a spiritual teacher with a serious message. Indeed, he is still highly relevant today, although his attitude and practices might be rather tough on modern sensibilities.

Basically, Simon was a zealous believer in the Sophia tradition we explored in the last chapter, and a prime mover in an underground Samaritan stream that kept alive the old traditions of the divine feminine—including, indeed emphasizing, her wilder erotic aspects.

If we're looking for the bridge between the Sophia years and the goddess's survival into the early Christian era it is Simon who holds the key. Under the accumulated patina of ancient bias, the story that emerges not only reveals a crucial insight into the continuing goddess tradition but also sheds startling new light on other, much more familiar names of his time. Simon never operated in a hermetically sealed bubble, nor was he inconsequential. Everything he did impacted on early Christianity and its leaders—and to some extent, vice versa.

Simon does not appear fully formed with no religious roots or backstory. His message, while certainly unpalatable to many people over the years, is not random. He is very much a product of the Samaritan belief system, and clearly deeply erudite about the Hebrew Bible. Indeed, several scholars have seen a strange, looking-glass connection between Simon's message and the writing of the pioneer prophet, Hosea. Perhaps it's no coincidence that Hosea's mission, too, took place in the northern kingdom, the future Samaria. Although separated by eight centuries, Simon seems to extol everything that Hosea condemned, including what some term the "whore wisdom."

As we saw earlier that Hosea's message was specifically aimed at a tradition of sacred prostitution involved in the Asherah/Qadesh cult, Simon perpetrating the very thing that Hosea fulminated against indicates it had survived.

To researchers, Simon is something of a gift. Being so controversial and obviously outrageous, his shocked-to-the-core enemies were obsessed with recording his sins and crimes as they saw them. Some of these accounts still exist. However, even better is the fact that Simon himself left writings, although even they come down to us at second hand.

THE GREAT REVELATION

In 1842 there was a momentous discovery in a monastery on the holy Mount Athos in Greece. At first it might not sound particularly sensational, but these copies of long-lost books on heresy by a third-century Christian theologian, Hippolytus of Rome, were to be massively significant—not only to the scholars in their ivory towers but also to the big, bold story of the Hebrew goddess.

Although known to have written ten volumes of his *Refutation of All Heresies,* only the first of Hippolytus's books had survived down the centuries. It was the discovery of seven more at Mount Athos that caused great excitement among historians of the early Church, and we can see why. They are, in their own way, electrifying.

In Book Six he dealt with what was, for him, one of the first and most pernicious of the heresies, which was still causing mayhem and confusion among Christians. And as part of his refutation he included extracts from the book written by its founder—the original having long been consigned to the flames. The irony is huge. In condemning this book and its author Hippolytus is handing future generations the only surviving words of the man whom he calls Simon of Samaria, but is better known as Simon Magus. These rare extracts are from Simon's *Apophasis Megale,* or "Great Revelation," "Great Declaration" or "Great Exposition."

As with all ancient works, no one knows for certain whether the *Great Revelation* was written, or rather dictated, by Simon Magus himself—as Hippolytus believed—or was compiled by his later followers (just like, say, the New Testament Sermon on the Mount). But as we will see, it perfectly matches other information about him, while adding more detail. When put together with other sources, it provides the key to understanding not just what motivated him, but much else about the underground history of the Jewish and Samaritan world of his—and Jesus's—time.

Simon Magus was obviously coming from a very similar place to the Sophia/Chokmah tradition we just explored, adding a vital insight into the perpetuation of ancient ideas about the sacred feminine still current in Samaria. To him, the goddess was an intrinsic part of creation.

The *Great Revelation* outlines Simon's version of the creation of the cosmos, which bears some resemblance to the Gnostic cosmologies of the early Christian centuries, although Simon's is considerably simpler than their characteristically elaborate and often impenetrable systems.

Simon's creation story begins with the universe in a primordial state that he calls the "Unbegotten Fire." Creation of an ordered and structured cosmos begins when two forces, or "roots," appear: The Universal Mind (*Nous*), which is male and corresponds to heaven, and the First Thought (*Epinoia,* or sometimes *Ennoia*), "which is female and brings forth all things," corresponding to the Earth. The two unite, producing a "male-female" power and it is from this that the universe—the "contingent cosmos"—comes into being.[5]

The *Revelation* stresses the yin-yang-like oppositeness but complementarity of this power, which runs through all creation: "that which was revealed from them, though it is one, is however found as two, the male-female in itself."[6]

The union of Mind and Thought produces four more paired powers: voice/name (sun/moon) and reason/reflection (air/water). Simon calls the six pairs together the Boundless Power or Great Power—that is, God—described as "He who has stood, stands, and will stand."[7] This is not only a reflection of God's eternal nature but it's also one of Simon's signature phrases. He elucidates: "a male-female power like the pre-existing Boundless Power, which has neither beginning nor end, existing in oneness."[8]

There's a seventh power that "proceeds from itself, containing all and yet latent in the six powers."[9] It's this that brings into being and orders the material world. The seventh power is in some way identified with the First Thought, although exactly how this works Simon either left as a mystery or Hippolytus thought it wasn't worth quoting.

However, Simon's use of the word *powers* (*dynamis*), particularly when discussing the "angels and lesser powers," is important. "Lord of the Powers" was the translation used in the Greek Pentateuch for "Lord of the Hosts" (*tsava*) in the Hebrew original.[10] The "hosts" in question were originally the lesser gods who assembled around El, but to avoid the polytheistic connotations were later reimagined as angels; in any case, divine entities. Simon's "powers" are therefore gods or angels.

All this is very different from the account of creation in Genesis, but bears some comparison with the Greek and Egyptian cosmologies. Karl Luckert has pointed out the similarity with the creation myth of the Heliopolis religion, which also describes a series of divine male-female pairs being generated from the creator-god Atum.[11]

However, despite other probable influences, Simon's book the *Great Revelation* has a specifically Judaic—or rather Samaritan—setting. He quotes from several books of the Hebrew Bible: Genesis, Numbers, and even (unexpectedly for a Samaritan) the prophetic books of Daniel and Isaiah. He discusses the five books of Moses by name, relating them to the five senses. The Israelite religion is never far from his thought processes and his message.

More significantly for us, Simon conspicuously draws on ideas about Wisdom that had emerged among the Alexandrian Jews—and also presumably Samaritans—as discussed in the last chapter. Hans Jonas, the eminent Jewish-American authority on Gnosticism, writes that Simon's system "depends on the fact that the Greek words *epinoia* and *ennoia,* like the more frequent *sophia* (wisdom) of other systems, are feminine, and the same is true of their Hebrew and Aramaic equivalents."[12]

The identity of the seventh power is revealed when Simon explains it is implied in Wisdom's declaration in the book of Proverbs, "The LORD possessed me at the beginning of his work . . ."[13] Moreover, it is also the "Spirit of God" that hovered over the waters before creation in Genesis, which fits with the seventh power bringing the world of matter into being.[14] Clearly, Simon is drawing on the same concepts that appear in the works of Ben Sira and Philo, linking Sophia with the Holy Spirit.

Simon's cosmology also features a strong sexual element, which is unsurprising as much of his theology depends on the union of the original male-female pair. The cosmos was created, or rather generated, from the "Unbegotten Fire," reflected in the conflagration of physical desire essential for all procreation. "Of all things of which there is generation, the beginning of the desire for their generation is from Fire. For, indeed, the desire of mutable generation is called 'being on fire.'"[15]

Many readers will immediately associate such language with the Eastern idea of the kundalini, the serpentlike coil of potential passion believed to lie invisibly at the base of the spine, waiting to be awakened, when it then rises up through the back—and the awakening psyche—like a flame. While it is impossible to know for certain if Simon ever encountered such a belief on his travels, his words do seem to reflect a similar concept.

In his last passages about "Simon the Samaritan," Hippolytus describes the story that links his cosmic vision to his earthly role. It's unclear whether Hippolytus is still referencing the *Great Revelation* or other early Christian sources. But it does seem that even if not mentioned in the *Great Revelation* this tale is genuinely about Simon and his followers. And it concerns the key to his teachings—and probably his whole life's work.

For Simon, the world was *not* the direct creation of God, or even of the female archetype, First Thought: she first created angels and "lower powers" and it was they who fashioned the world of matter. However, something went badly wrong with the process of creation. The power-seeking angels and other entities turned against Thought, restraining and "defiling" her, and forcing her to use the "fiery power within her" to manifest their own creations. As a result, creation was corrupted, flawed from the beginning.[16]

To keep their power over the material world, the angels imprisoned the First Thought in the material world by trapping her in human form and forcing her to reincarnate from one—always female—body to another. Along her incarnatory journey she became some of the great women of history, including the legendary Helen of Troy.

Eventually, descending further and further into the corruption of matter, she incarnated as a prostitute in the port city of Tyre in Phoenicia. But Mind—the male counterpart of Thought—seeking his "lost sheep" also descended into the world. At this point Mind took on the form of Simon himself, and eventually he found his First Thought in the person of Helen, a sex worker in Tyre. After he purchased her freedom she became his constant companion, thus beginning the process of fixing the flaw in the material world that affects everything in it, including human beings. Surely few human relationships could ever be quite so breathtakingly significant.

This is where the story becomes even more colorful. Hippolytus comments that, because of the relationship between Simon and Helen, his followers claim "that all intercourse should be promiscuous," calling this "perfect love."[17] He quotes from a Simonian text—but, tantalizingly, there's something missing from this page of his manuscript, which reads: "the holy shall be sanctified by the . . . of the holy."[18] Perhaps "sanctified" alludes to the traditional Qadesh aspect of Asherah, though we will never know for certain. But that's all we know about the "perfect love" rationale behind Simon and Helen's protohippie commune. There are no more references to this or even the Simonian text in any other early Christian sources.

To Hippolytus, no doubt pop-eyed with outrage, another proof of the Simonians' immorality concerns their belief about creation. Simon's followers thought the world was created by the lesser powers, not by God. The great divinity of the Old Testament, therefore, isn't the *real* God. The commandments and instructions it insists were laid down by "God" are simply the powers' way of controlling humankind. Similarly, the prophets were not inspired by God but by the bad angels and lesser powers, so their fulminations should be rigorously ignored. Therefore the scriptures had no relevance to the Simonians, who saw them as inauthentic—even ironically, sacrilegious.

Unsurprisingly, there are no references to Jesus in Simon's work, or any references to the books of the New Testament. Except, that is, for one quote that's also found in the Gospels of Luke and Matthew, which makes it more likely that both are quoting from the same source (as is the case with quotes from Isaiah that also appear in the gospels). The line is: "For now the axe is set at the root of the tree. Every tree that fails to bear good fruit is chopped down and flung in the fire."[19] This is identical to Luke and Matthew, where the saying is attributed to John the Baptist, part of his call to the people to mend their ways before God's coming judgment on Israel.[20] However, this seemingly trivial axiom is loaded with importance, as we will see.

Simon is clearly more than a hiss-boo villain, the evil sinner theologians have always loved to hate. With his own understanding of Sophia, and the emphasis on the feminine—and not just in a sanitized form but as a real woman—Simon Magus more than repays further investigation. With Simon nothing is easy, however. There are always going to be many more questions than answers. Where did he get his extraordinary ideas? Although in many ways his thinking parallels his exact contemporary Philo of Alexandria and the earlier Ben Sira. Were they his main inspirations? Or did they all use the same source? And then there's his explosive link between Sophia and a very real fallen woman—the embodiment of the flawed creation, no less. Did he just make it up? Or did that also come from long-hidden Samaritan traditions?

Simon sometimes yields his secrets with great reluctance to the twenty-first-century researcher, especially if there's some doubt about the agendas of those who quote him. As the Theosophist G. R. S. Mead, author of a classic 1892 study, cautions: "We must always remember that every single syllable we possess about Simon comes from the hands of bitter opponents, from men who had no mercy or toleration for the heretic."[21]

But is there anything objective we can wheedle out of the scattered hints and clues? What's the truth about Simon Magus?

"THE POWER OF GOD THAT IS CALLED GREAT"

Famously—or infamously—Simon Magus makes his debut in the Acts of the Apostles, the New Testament book that essentially continues the Gospel of Luke, both being written by the same author. It probably dated from the 80s or 90s of the first century, so about fifty years after the events it describes. (From clues in Luke, we know the two works were composed after 70 CE.)[22]

The first place outside Judea to receive a Christian mission was Samaria, probably within ten years of Jesus's crucifixion—in the 40s CE, perhaps even late 30s. According to Acts, the apostle Philip traveled to the "city of Samaria" where he set about casting out demons, healing people, and winning converts to the new sect (not yet properly a religion).

It was in Samaria that Philip encountered trouble:

But there was a man named Simon who had previously practiced magic in the city and amazed the people of Samaria saying that he himself was somebody great. They all paid attention to him, from the least to the greatest, saying, "This man is the power of God that is called Great." And they paid attention to him because for a long time he had amazed them with his magic. But when they believed Philip as he preached good news about the kingdom of God and the name of Jesus Christ they were baptized, both men and women. Even Simon himself believed, and after being baptized he continued with Philip. And seeing signs and great miracles performed he was amazed.

Now when the apostles at Jerusalem heard that Samaria had received the word of God, they sent to them Peter and John, who came down and prayed for them that they might receive the Holy Spirit, for he had not yet fallen on any of them, but they had only been baptized in the name of the Lord Jesus. Then they laid their hands on them and they received the Holy Spirit. Now when Simon saw that the Spirit was given through the laying on of the apostles' hands, he offered them money, saying, "Give me this power also, so that anyone on whom I lay my hands may receive the Holy Spirit." But Peter said to him "May your silver perish with you, because you thought you could obtain the gift of God with money! You have neither part nor lot in this matter, for your heart is not right before God. Repent, therefore, of this wickedness of yours, and pray to the Lord that, if possible, the intent of your heart may be forgiven you. For I see that you are in the gall of bitterness and in the bond of iniquity." And Simon answered "Pray for me to the Lord, that nothing of what you have said may come upon me."[23]

There are no further mentions of this larger-than-life, but curiously subservient Simon. The next verse just has Peter and John returning to Jerusalem, evangelizing in Samaritan villages on the way. What can we take from this tantalizing passage? Simon had been doing whatever he got up to in Samaria for "a long time," amazing people and building up a large fan base. The apparently throwaway phrase that he was "somebody great" is in fact highly significant: it means he was claiming to be one of the various legendary messianic figures, although we don't know which one.[24]

But when Philip arrives, preaching Jesus's gospel, healing, and casting out demons even Simon is impressed, and like many Samaritans is baptized into the Jesus sect. At this stage, there is no suggestion of a power struggle or animosity, and apparently Simon even accompanied Philip on his mission.

Then the more important apostles Peter and John come down from Jerusalem to bestow the Holy Spirit, which is beyond Philip's remit or ability. According to the story that's when it all unravels for Simon. We are told he commits the huge faux pas of offering them money for this mysterious power. It's not necessarily a bribe: the word is the same as for a sacrificial offering at the Temple. But whatever the nature of his gaffe he is not just harangued, but formally cursed by Peter.[25] Simon, chastened and scared, asks Peter to lift the curse, although Acts stops short of spelling out he did so because he admitted his big mistake.

The story ends there. We are not told how Peter reacted to Simon's request, or what happened next. Had it not been for the later writers, we would assume that this Simon, having repented, carried on as an obscure member of the fledgling Christian community in Samaria. As it is, knowing from later sources that he founded a sect of his own—presumably picking up where he had left off before Philip arrived on the scene—one can assume that Peter's curse had failed to work. And we can take Simon's groveling contrition with a truckload of salt. Besides, we know from other sources that, curse or no, Peter and Simon Magus became great rivals in evangelizing the region.

In fact, the point of the story is *not*—as assumed in later times—about the Church's power over demonic magic. There are many other episodes concerning that. This is really about who within the early Church had the authority to perform "acts of power." One telling inference is that Simon is a Christian insider at this stage. Rick Strelan (associate professor of religious studies, University of Queensland, Australia) emphasizes that the cautionary tale is aimed at those within the community, not outside.[26] And Robert Conner, in *Magic in Christianity* (2014), agrees, saying: "The point of the story is not as much Simon's magic as it is Peter's apostolic authority."[27]

Neither was the fact that Simon offered money for the Holy Spirit so important at the time, although it came to be. In later years he even gave his name to a whole new sin, that of *simony*—a term first used in 1225, so it took a while to catch on. The implication of committing simony, or trying to buy spiritual power, is that you're not only wicked but really rather stupid.

However, we know from other sources that Simon had his own following that was still around centuries later—and therefore must have existed when Acts was written. Presumably, another major point of the New Testament story was to ram home to the Simonians of the 80s or 90s CE that their leader had once acknowledged Christ's superiority.

What is most fascinating is what Simon was doing *before* Jesus's apostles arrived on the scene—and had been for some time, if Acts is to be believed. Apparently, in a similar way to Philip, he had been performing jaw-dropping miracles, together with delivering a spiritual message, seemingly about himself—so the real parallel is with Jesus rather than Philip. To the early Christians, however, Simon's "miracles" were quite different from those of the apostles or Jesus.

The single word translated as "practiced magic" is *mageou,* and for the magic that amazed the folk of Samaria it's *mageia*—the only times either are used in the New Testament. This is the origin of Simon's later name, and the basis for his image of either (depending on your view of magic) a demonic sorcerer or a charlatan who fooled the people with conjuring tricks. However, as Stephen Haar—of the Australian Lutheran College and author of *Simon Magus: The First Gnostic?* (2003)—is careful to point out, at the time Acts was composed the words were not necessarily negative, not even referring to "magic" in today's sense. They literally refer to the practices of the Magi, the Persian Zoroastrian priests (best known from their visit to the baby Jesus), but by extrapolation in the Greek world a wise or learned person. The word used of the "wise men from the east" who attend the Nativity is *magos,* which the Greeks had borrowed from the Persians, at first to describe the Zoroastrian priesthood, and later, since the Magi were renowned for their wisdom, as a general description of a wise or erudite person. In Greece it also took on the contrary meaning of "charlatan"—someone who just pretended to have divinatory or occult powers. But unexpectedly, that is not how it's used in the New Testament, especially *not* in relation to Simon.

Simon is not actually called a *magos,* although the term is applied to another character in Acts—a false prophet named Bar-Jesus whom Paul encounters on Cyprus. But even there, as the text makes clear, it means "wise man," not "magician." Haar's analysis finds the usual translation of "practicing magic," as applied to Simon in Acts, to be "superficial, selective, and responsible for introducing anachronous ideas,"[28] concluding that "the true 'mageia' of the 'magos' was an ancient tradition of wisdom, and a service to the gods, rather than some doubtful dealings of a charlatan."[29] Already the age-old image of Simon is looking rather more intriguing.

On the other hand, the fact that whatever he was doing amazed and impressed the people, and its obvious similarity to Philip's activities, shows he was believed to be a genuine wonder-worker. This is where things get murky, challenging head-on our modern sensibilities about what we would call "the occult." We think of spells and incantations—perhaps lumped together in our imaginations as the sinister "dark arts"—and usually to be avoided at all costs. But as modern research has conclusively proved, even the original Christians were heavily involved in magical practices.

As Haar observes, "a close examination of the original story in light of contemporary Graeco-Roman estimations of magic would reveal Philip, rather than Simon, to be the magician."[30] Conversely, according to David R. Cartlidge, professor of religion at Maryville College, Tennessee, "Simon would have seen in Philip and Peter men akin to himself; they were fellow practitioners of the sacred and magical arts."[31]

In an academic nutshell, that is the point. There was no real distinction in the classical world between using religious rituals and using sorcery for such matters as divination, casting spells, laying curses—or wonder-working and healing.

Several studies—such as Robert Conner's quoted above—have shown that the first Christians not only achieved the same results as pagan sorcerers, such as miraculous healings, but they also employed identical *methods*—as in Peter's curse on Simon. Unpalatable though it might be to modern Christians, the fact remains that "Christian rite and wonder-working shared the presumptions, processes and procedures of Jewish and pagan magic."[32]

But how far up the Christian hierarchy did these practices go? Could the unthinkable be true? Unknown to the average churchgoer, scholars have recognized for some time that *Jesus himself* used specific formulae found in Greek and Egyptian magical texts.[33] Bearing this in mind, clearly whatever really disturbed the early Christians about Simon Magus, almost certainly it was *not* his occult practices and miracle-working.

Quite soon, though—within a generation of Acts—the term *magos* had taken on its modern meaning as a synonym for sorcery, with extra dark and unsavory connotations. That was due to the early Church's desperation to distinguish the apostles' wonder-working from that of the pagans—since to outsiders *they looked identical*.[34] And the tale of Simon Magus conveniently helped underline what was essentially a bogus distinction, while redefining *magos*.

Some have even suggested that the Simon as presented in Acts—where he's an itinerant wonder-worker—and the Simon in the later accounts of the Church Fathers such as Hippolytus in which he is a sophisticated Gnostic teacher, are two completely different people. After all, Simon was a common enough name and Samaria was a big place. It would be easy for later generations to mistakenly conflate the two. But that rather simplistic explanation is easily challenged.

Although at first glance the description in Acts seems to have little in common with the cosmic scheme in Simon's *Great Revelation,* they do share some points of contact, proving they *are* about the same man. Acts has the people hailing Simon (presumably with some encouragement from him) as "the power of God that is called Great"—and in the *Apophasis Megale* he calls the original male principle, with which he identified himself, the "Great Power." Significantly, this was, as the professor of biblical criticism and minister of the Church of Scotland Matthew Black shows, a characteristically northern Palestinian—i.e., Samaritan—term with no Jewish equivalent.[35]

Even more clues lurk in Acts' choice of words. Conspicuously, there's no mention of Simon's companion Helen, the embodiment of the First Thought who is so prominent in other accounts. However, in Peter's condemnation of Simon, where he tells him to pray to the Lord so that "the intent of your heart may be forgiven you," "intent" is *epinoia,* which is more accurately "thought," so the phrase is better rendered as "the thought in your heart." It's the only time in the entire New Testament this word appears. But as the eminent German New Testament scholar Gerd Lüdemann points out, it is the specific term chosen by Simon Magus in the *Great Revelation* to describe the First Thought incarnated as Helen. Lüdemann suggested that Peter's words in Acts are really a veiled reference to her: Simon is being condemned by Peter for his association with his beloved Epinoia.[36]

"FATHER OF ALL HERESIES"

As the man the early Christians loved to loathe, Simon Magus was something of a hot topic. The next work to discuss him is the *First Apology* of Justin Martyr, from as late as the 150s or 160s, so some years after Acts. Clearly Justin used now-lost sources, besides memories about Simon that had been passed down, and presumably he also knew of local tidbits about him, having lived in two places where Simon had operated—and where the Simonian sect still flourished. And Justin's own journey was not irrelevant.

Justin was born around the year 100 in Samaria, where he was raised, though his family came from elsewhere in the Roman Empire. A pagan convert to Christianity—and with all the extra fire in his belly that conversion brings—Justin became a traveling preacher before setting up a school in Rome during the reign of the emperor Antoninus Pius (138–161). His *First Apology*—*apology* then meant "defense"—was aimed at the emperor to explain and defend the new faith. It did Justin little good, as he met his doom—around 165, shortly after the succession of the next emperor, Marcus Aurelius—for refusing to sacrifice to Rome's gods.

In his book, Justin presents a very short, matter-of-fact description of Simon, without any of the hysteria of later Christian writers, or indeed any explicit criticism, although obviously he does not approve. He even fails to mention the episode in Acts, but does add extra biographical information, for example that Simon came from the Samaritan village of Gitton (Gitta, or Gittha). He says that "almost all" of the Samaritans revere him as the "first god," besides some from other nations. Assuming that Justin is not exaggerating the implications are astonishing: Simon Magus was widely believed to *be a living god.*

Justin was the first writer to mention Simon's female companion, Helen. As in the *Great Revelation,* he calls her Simon's First Thought (Ennoia), although omitting the details about her being trapped by the angels. Justin says that Helen "formerly stood on the roof," a slightly bizarre euphemism for an ex-prostitute.[37]

Justin says Simon's mission was not confined to Samaria or even Palestine, but that he went to Rome—he omits to mention whether Helen accompanied him—where he performed acts of magic that built him quite some reputation in the city. To Justin, Simon's wonder-working was naturally aided by demons—although "demons" to Justin usually meant the gods of other nations. He dates Simon's mission to the reign of the emperor Claudius, so between 41 and 54 CE, which fits the timeframe of Acts.

Innocently unaware he was doing so, Justin provides even more juicy information about the Magus for posterity. He claims his followers considered Simon a god, even erecting a statue to him on an island in the river Tiber, inscribed SIMONI SANCTO DEO—"To Simon the Holy God." The statue really existed—discovered in 1574 and now in the Vatican Museum—but as proof of Simon's deification it turned out to be a damp squib. Or so it once seemed . . . the first two words of the inscription were really SEMONI SANCO, referring to the god Semo Sancus, and not Simon Magus at all. Although it is generally assumed that Justin—who would have seen the statue for himself—misread the inscription, possibly it was the current generation of Simonians who associated the statue with their long-dead master. (As it's dated to the second century it could not have been raised in Simon's lifetime.) The matter doesn't quite end there, however.

Justin says Simon founded a sect to continue his work, and that after his death it was led by Menander, another notorious heretic from Samaria, also known only from the condemnations of the Church Fathers. (These early writers would be horrified to their very souls if they knew their writings were the only record of their enemies, keeping their names alive.) According to Justin, Menander also declared himself the Messiah and savior, as well as the Power of God, and taught that the world was created by angels that kept mankind imprisoned. He founded his own sect with baptism as the main ritual—heavily implying that Simon must also have practiced baptism. This, as we will see, is hardly surprising.

About twenty years after Justin's martyrdom—in the late 170s or 180s—Irenaeus, bishop of Lyons wrote about Simon Magus in his *Against Heresies,* dubbing him "father of all heresies."[38] Irenaeus was also the first to describe Simon as the founder of Gnosticism.

But exactly why were the early Christian writers so obsessed with Simon? It transpires he was uniquely important in one particular way, one that today's Christians would find deeply offensive, if not downright unbelievable.

When Irenaeus writes that Simon appeared as a man, although he was not really human, and that he "was thought to have suffered in Judaea, although he did not really suffer"—he is implicitly *equating Simon with Jesus.* Irenaeus goes further, saying that Simon "appeared among the Jews as the Son, while in Samaria he descended as the Father, and in the rest of the nations he came as the Holy Spirit."[39]

Irenaeus does, though, add to our information about the Simonian sect. Because they regard the Jewish scriptures as the work of the power-hungry angels who created the world, not of God, they don't feel bound by them. Simon's followers therefore feel totally free from the usual moral constraints. Liberated, they live immoral lives, being sexually promiscuous, their "mystic priests" in particular being infamous libertines.

To add to the list of their abominations, Irenaeus notes that the Simonians worship Simon and Helen in the form of Zeus and Minerva—which at first seems incongruous but actually makes sense. The Roman equivalent of the Greek Athena, Minerva was the goddess of wisdom and war, said to have sprung fully formed—and armored—from the head of Zeus, the Roman Jupiter. She was therefore a literal expression of the First Thought emerging from Mind. While not linking this directly to Simon, in a separate section of his book Justin Martyr had referred to heretics who "knowing that God conceived and made the world by the Word . . . say that Minerva is the first conception."[40]

If the Simonians worshipped their founder in this guise it might explain the "Semoni" statue, as the god to whom it was dedicated, Semo Sancus, was a form of Zeus/Jupiter. So the confusion—or rather association—of Simon with Semo may have been deliberate on the part of the sect. Which makes Justin right all along.

Another important Church leader and theologian, Clement of Alexandria, added to the swelling chorus of disapproval about Simon. In a book written around 200, he included this brief aside: "Thus Abraham stood in the face of the Lord and when he approached he spoke and to Moses it was said: 'But you, stand here with me.' And those who are around Simon want to adapt their way of living to the Standing One, who they honour."[41] This little reference is clearly to Simon's current followers, who associated him with the title of "Standing One"—here linked with prophets like Moses—which matches clues from other sources.

Next to stand in the Simon-bashing line was our old friend Hippolytus of Rome—a disciple of Irenaeus—who had unknowingly done future researchers a huge favor by leaving us extracts from Simon's *Great Revelation.* Hippolytus's most outspoken ire was aimed at the libertinism of the Simonians—still very much around in his day—denouncing them for indulging in "indiscriminate intercourse."[42] Hippolytus adds a—very much alleged—account of Simon's death, claiming that he got his disciples to bury him alive, announcing that he would rise again on the third day, "yet he remained in the grave because he was not the Christ."[43] Stephen Haar calls this "pure Christian propaganda."[44]

Another major Church Father, Origen of Alexandria in his *Against Celsus,* written around 250 CE, includes some brief mentions of the Simonian sect. Origen's book was written to counter the anti-Christian claims of the pagan philosopher Celsus so his main concern is to disprove everything he said. Origen's main issue is that Celsus classed the Simonians as a Christian heresy, whereas Jesus Christ is conspicuous only by his absence in their doctrines.

Celsus's classification highlights an important issue that obsessed the early Christian writers: Was Simon Magus technically a heretic at all? Strictly speaking, a heretic was somebody whose view of Jesus and/ or his message challenged the Church's official position. Jesus doesn't feature at all, either positively or negatively, in Simon's teachings about what makes the universe tick or how salvation will come about. So technically, as Origen argued, Simon Magus was *not* a heretic. The early Church's antipathy seems to be based more on his claim to possess the same powers and authority as Jesus. None of that would have made much impact on them, but for one gigantic elephant-in-the-room. What really distressed and appalled them so much was that they knew Simon Magus *was uncomfortably like Christ.*

Origen's evidence about Simon continues, although he overdoes his airy downplaying of the Simonian sect. He starts by claiming there probably are no more than thirty Simonians left in the entire world, and even that's probably an overstatement, although he acknowledges that there are a "very few" in Palestine. Later he flatly contradicts this, saying that "nowhere in the world do the Simonians any longer exist."[45] But clearly his bottom line is that the Simonians were of negligible significance and nobody should ever take them seriously.

Origen also reports Celsus's claim that there was a female branch of the sect called the Heleniani, centered around veneration for Simon's constant companion. This is the sole such allegation, but the idea of a line of female initiates descended from Helen is potentially exciting, implying that she belonged to a line of priestesses, whose secret knowledge she handed on to the other Simonian women, initiated into the cult-within-a-cult.

A little over a century after Origen came Epiphanius, bishop of Salamis in Cyprus, in 377 who wrote a mammoth catalog of heresies called the *Panarion* ("medicine chest"—so called because he intended it as "a chest of medicine for the victims of wild beasts' bites").[46] Every mention of Simon Magus is surrounded by a palpable aura of early Christian anxiety. Epiphanius, too, stresses the threat he posed to the nascent religion, writing that his heresy "worked great havoc by the corruption it produced among Christians."[47] Perhaps more provocatively, Simon "said that he was the Father to Samaritans, but Christ to the Jews."[48] *Christ* here presumably means "Messiah" in its original sense, rather than its Christian reimagining. But in any case, Simon is issuing a full-on challenge to his rivals.

Epiphanius describes Simon working "under the cloak of Christ,"[49] implying that in some way he had been intimately associated with the Christian movement, which matches Acts' implication that he had even been a member.

Unsurprisingly, Epiphanius homed in on the Simonians' sexual practices, writing salaciously, perhaps to stir up even more of a scandal: "Simon instituted mysteries consisting of dirt and—to put it more politely—the fluids generated from men's bodies through the seminal emission and women's through the menstrual flux, which are collected for mysteries by a most indecent method."[50]

But we do have Epiphanius to thank for adding to the scant store of information. Apparently Simon "ventured to call his prostitute companion the Holy Spirit," recognizing that when he identifies Helen as the Spirit of God, it is the same as the Christian Holy Spirit.[51]

By this time rumors about Simon's depravities and demon-backed powers were becoming increasingly outrageous, matching the hyperbole surrounding his status as bogeyman and the embodiment of every possible un- and anti-Christian manifestation. Simon might have been bad—but he was also *big*.

In an apocryphal work called the Acts of Peter, Simon—who had been expelled from Judea by Peter—comes to Rome, where people take him to be "the Christ" and he leads astray "all of the great multitude which had been confirmed in the faith."[52] Acting on a message from God, Peter travels to Rome and engages in a series of prayer-against-magic contests. This tale ends in the Magus going for a demon-propelled flight, but Peter's prayer brings about a particularly satisfying ending: Simon crashes down to his death.

The Acts of Peter also includes another strange episode: Marcellus, a senator who was a follower of Simon until Peter won him over, has a dream where he sees dancing before Peter a woman, "according to her appearance an Ethiopian . . . very black" dressed in rags with an iron collar and chains on her hands and feet. Peter tells Marcellus that she is "the whole power of Simon and his God"[53]—and orders Marcellus to behead her. The rather sweet-sounding Marcellus refuses, saying he's never harmed so much as a sparrow, at which point a doppelganger of Peter appears with a sword, beheads her, and dismembers her body. Then Marcellus wakes up.

The dream woman is never actually named as Helen—who never

appears in the Acts of Peter—but as she was known as Simon's "power," she must be associated with the black dancing woman. (And for all we know, Helen was literally a woman of color who danced in chains. Presumably it would have suited her style.)

MANY GODS

The tales about a wonder-working face-off between Simon and the apostle Peter are obvious fantasies, the bastard offspring of their authors' pious imaginations. These sagas are derived from sources such as Justin Martyr that have Simon visiting Rome, and other legends about Peter's adventures in the Imperial capital. But they may be based on a more down-to-earth confrontation between the two men, hinted at in the Acts of the Apostles but elaborated on elsewhere.

All the Church Fathers we have discussed follow in a direct line, taking information about Simon Magus from earlier writers and passing it on, adding their own contribution, and often exaggerating it. They are all leading lights of the Western Church—Rome, Lyon, Cyprus, and Alexandria—all Gentiles, and all part of what became the Roman Catholic Church. What we might call the "Roman Church sources."

But there was another, incredibly important line of traditions about Simon that was transmitted outside the Roman Church world. This came from Syria and was passed down within its own Jewish-Christian communities. Although it was eventually set down in texts that present a radical new picture of early Christianity, they are still woefully little known.

The new faith was greatly divided, both in matters of belief—which is why there were so many heresies—and in matters of authority. One of the major splits was between those who had entered the religion from outside Judaism—pagans or Gentiles—and those from a Jewish background, who saw Christianity as a development of Judaism. As it was the former that eventually won the day, becoming the established religion based in Rome, and Jewish Christianity was to dwindle away, the traditions in the texts we will explore made little impact outside Palestine and Syria until the fourth or fifth centuries.

Handily for future researchers, they also retain information about Simon Magus, and particularly his rivalry with the apostle Peter that doesn't appear in the Roman Church sources, and that fills in the gap between Acts and Simon's appearance in Rome.

These stories reached the West in a series of related tales purportedly written by Clement of Rome, an important figure in the first decades of the Church, telling the story of his conversion to Christianity by Peter and his rise through the ranks.

Clement was either the second or third bishop of Rome, officiating in the last decade of the first century, and is therefore considered one of the first popes, although the title only came later. He certainly existed—he was the author of one of the New Testament epistles. However, the volumes that claim to be his autobiography—although containing genuine information about him and his time—are known to be the work of a later author, or rather authors. For this reason they're known as the "Pseudo-Clementine literature" or the "Pseudo-Clementines."

They're basically novels for the faithful. Stephen Haar even describes them as "an example of early Jewish-Christian religious and philosophical romance."[54] However, they do contain early traditions—and genuine information—from the Syrian branch of Christianity. F. Stanley Jones, professor of the New Testament and ancient Christianity at California State University, writes that they "contain traditions of ancient Syrian Jewish Christianity that have not survived elsewhere."[55] With such rarity value, they are greatly prized by researchers.

There are two main books: the Homilies of Clement, dating from between 300 and 320 CE, and the Recognitions of Clement, from about half a century later. The latter is essentially a rewrite of the former, hastily removing or fudging anything that went against the Church's official version of Christian origins. Even that censorship fell short, so the translation of the Recognitions from Greek into Latin in 410 CE took the much more significant step of actually omitting passages likely to offend Roman Catholic Christians.

Although written nearly three centuries after the events they purportedly describe, the Clementines are clearly based on a lost original—the "basic writing"—thought to date from Syria around 220 or 230. And that, too, was put together from earlier sources that scholars have deduced included an early account of Peter's missionary activity and a work known as the Teaching of Peter.[56] Robert Eisenmann, the American archaeologist best known for exposing the academic conspiracy to restrict access to the Dead Sea Scrolls, argues that the Pseudo-Clementines draw on the same sources as the Acts of the Apostles, but with less editing.[57]

The Homilies begin with Clement, curious about the new faith he has heard about in Rome, traveling to the Palestinian port of Caesarea Maritima on a quest to meet Peter. Handily for our investigation, he arrives at a time when Peter is locked in a battle with Simon Magus for the hearts and minds of the locals.

Eager to know more about this competitor, Clement is briefed by one of Peter's disciples, Aquila, who had previously followed Simon. The account adds information not found elsewhere: Simon's father and mother were called Antonius and Rachel; Simon comes from the village of Gittha, six *schoeni* (approximately 23 miles) from Samaria's capital, Sebaste. He was educated in Alexandria, where he "acquired a large measure of Greek culture and attained to an extensive knowledge of magic and ability in it."[58]

The Homilies of Clement also presents some intriguing insights into Simon's modus operandi. Returning to Samaria, he proclaimed himself as "a mighty power" of God, setting himself up as the Messiah and the "Standing One." He denies that the divine being who created the world is the highest God. He does not believe in the resurrection of the dead, and—unsurprisingly for a Samaritan—considers Mount Gerizim as the true holy place, not Jerusalem.

The Homilies has Simon traveling with Helen whom he claims, "he had brought down to the world from the highest heaven." He lavishes her with titles missing from the "Roman" sources: "Kyria," or

"Queen," but much more significantly the "mistress of all being and Wisdom."[59] Although this is hinted at in the Roman sources—through Simon's association of Ennoia with Wisdom and Helen as Ennoia's incarnation—here he spells it out explicitly. To Simon Magus, Helen *is the final and literal embodiment of Sophia.*

The transgressive twosome travel about inseparably, preaching and wonder-working. Aquila tells Clement that Simon "deceives many in a plausible manner, and at the same time he performs numerous wonderful deeds, by which we would ourselves have been imposed on, had we not known that he works them only by sorcery."[60]

While we can dismiss much of this as pure fantasy, the basic information fits the other sources. Some extra comments not only ring true—it's very hard to imagine a third- or fourth-century writer making them up—but they also shed considerable light on the Magus's own influences.

In the Clementine works Simon's teaching is not dreamed up in isolation, but is very much part of a network of sects known from other, independent sources. They especially associate him with another notorious Samaritan heretic, Dositheus, founder of a sect that survived for at least a thousand years. In fact, the Pseudo-Clementines describe Simon and Dositheus as rivals for leadership of a major, already-existing sect. Their relationship with this, as we will see, is quite sensational in its implications and will amaze and unsettle even those who have never heard of Simon Magus or Dositheus.

The Pseudo-Clementines also has the two great heretics disputing the title of "the Standing One," the Samaritan term mentioned in the Roman Christian sources, but that was also attributed to Dositheus by his followers. So this appears to be based on real information about the two men; if nothing else the novelist had done his homework.

Although we will explore the intriguing Dositheus issue later, for now our focus is on the legendary rivalry between Simon and the leader of another emerging sect, the Christian Apostle Peter. Both men are competing on the same ground for the same audience, trying to win the people over to their respective beliefs. They even use the same methods, preaching a message that promises both individual and universal salvation, while crowd-pleasing by wonder-working—naturally presented as miracles through the Holy Spirit on Peter's side, but as the dark arts on Simon's. However, unlike those tall tales of miracle-against-magic face-offs in Rome, in these texts the main confrontation takes the form of a public debate in Caesarea Maritima, where both leaders present their arguments to an assembled throng.

No one knows whether such an event really took place—although it would make sense in terms of the confrontation between Peter and Simon in Acts (and it would be wonderful if it had). What is important here is that the Homilies include Simon's own explanation of his doctrines—and their contrast with Peter's. This casts further light on what we know from the Roman Church sources, especially the *Great Revelation*. The fact that the Homilies' description of Simon's ideas matches his own description so neatly suggests it comes from real memories of his preaching. And momentously, it also fits our reconstruction of the hidden Samaritan stream.

After an opening statement by Peter, the Magus leaps straight in, accusing Peter of deceiving the assembled audience by claiming there is only one God and that all others are false. His reasoning is very telling. The Jewish scriptures themselves, he says, show Peter to be wrong: "For now in the presence of all I would argue with you from these very books that one must necessarily assume the existence of [other] gods."[61] As we know from our earlier exploration of the meaning of *elohim*, this is perfectly correct.

Simon also says that the scriptures themselves prove that their God—and therefore the God of Christianity—is not only one of many but is not even the supreme deity. Simon reels off a mass of evidence from the Hebrew Bible itself that shows God *not* to be all-knowing, or omniscient. This God is inconsistent and, for that matter, not particularly pleasant or good. Simon concludes that the scriptural God is "imperfect, not without needs, not good, and is subject to innumerable dubious passions."[62] But, Simon goes on, there is another, higher God who *is* all-knowing and free from such passions. It was this God who created the cosmos. Simon says that the God of the scriptures was "chosen by lot" from among the other lesser deities to be the God of the Jews.

Again, it is Simon who is right. As we argued in chapter 1, the evidence is overwhelmingly there in the pages of the Hebrew Bible. The Most High God of Genesis is different from Yahweh, the god of Israel, the lesser deity who takes center stage from Exodus onward, and who is allocated Israel as his special nation out of the seventy countries.

Simon's argument is entirely logical—on the Bible's own terms, at least—and, despite its portrayal in the Homilies, it makes much more sense than Peter's counterargument, which is barely coherent. To Simon's claims of the scriptural God's supposed imperfections and moral dubiousness, Peter responds: "How then can God be bad and wicked if the shameful actions ascribed to him are imputed to him with his consent in all publicity?" and "If of his own will he has incriminated himself, then . . . he cannot be wicked."[63]

In other words, as far as his gabble can be unscrambled, God must be good because he says he is, and we can believe him because he's God, who wouldn't lie because he's good, and we know he's good because he says he is . . . and so it goes on, round and round.

As for the biblical God not being the creator, Peter has a killer argument: "Those statements of the Holy Scriptures which are in keeping with the creation wrought by God must be counted as genuine and those which contradict them as false."[64] Put mercifully briefly, Peter is saying anything that doesn't agree with him must be wrong.

But should we take these particular passages in the Homilies seriously, when obviously so much of the story is obvious fiction? We probably should. It's simply not credible that a fourth-century Christian would have been *capable* of making up the arguments put into Simon's mouth. And they dovetail in ways that are not immediately obvious with what we know of Simon's teaching from the other sources. So they *must* be based on genuine memories of what he taught in that region.

THE GNOSTIC IMPERATIVE

Simon is often linked to the then-blossoming Gnostic movement, even being seen as—or accused of being, depending on one's viewpoint—the inspiration for the entire philosophy. If true, it would be yet another nail in the coffin of his reputation to the early Church, for Gnosticism had caused them no end of problems. While the debate has kept generations of academics very busy, can we shed any light on the subject? Was Simon, as his Christian opponents claim, a Gnostic—even the founder of Gnosticism?

Simon's cosmology is obviously similar to Gnostic systems, although mercifully his is much simpler, given their usual convolutions. His cosmos still consists of several different levels, though, with our world of matter as the lowest. Each level is inhabited by various supernatural beings including angels. Another obvious link with Gnosticism was Simon's belief that the material world was inherently flawed, and this defect ran through everything in it, including humankind.

This ties in with another concept Simon shared with later Gnostics: Every human being houses a "divine spark," a "blessed and incorruptible" aspect that can be activated. He claimed his system enables the believer to do this, reintegrating with the divine source. In Haar's words, there is a "divinely created potentiality in all humankind that perishes at death unless it is actualised."[65] Being a follower of Simon, naturally, helped actualize it. (So, in a way he promised eternal life.)

It is too complex to explore in depth here, but put briefly, the most likely conclusion is outlined by Jarl Fossum (his emphases): "although there definitely *is* a relationship between the teaching of Simon and the Gnostic systems of the 2nd century, Simonianism contains some remarkably *un*-Gnostic elements. I would therefore suggest to call Simon a *proto*-Gnostic. In Simonianism we can discern the transition from Jewish-Samaritan heresy to Gnosticism."[66]

Clearly, Simon was key in the evolution of Gnosticism—so in that at least the Church Fathers were correct. And his teaching extended well beyond his own time and place. The French scholar J. M. A. Salles-Dabadie has even detected Simon's influence on the Hermetic texts that had such an influence on the Western mystery tradition.[67]

However, not even Simon Magus exists in a vacuum. Even he must have learned from someone else, so what—or who—made him such a force to be reckoned with?

While always centered on the Hebrew scriptures, Simon never adhered to the established Samaritan religion. But what about the wider world? Just how much did Simon depend on sources such as the Greek and Egyptian mysteries? Perhaps in his fervent devotion to the sacred feminine he owed a debt to the cult of Isis—which he would have known well, having lived in Egypt. And although—as the likes of Fossum and Stephen Haar have shown—Simon certainly drew upon Hellenistic ideas (as did others such as Philo), his teachings are firmly rooted in Hebrew thought. But being him, often its most controversial and unconventional byways.

THE LESSER GOD

A fundamental difference between Simon's cosmology and "official" Yahwism is his belief in the imperfection of the material world. The Judaism and Samaritanism of Simon's day wanted their worshippers to believe that the God of Israel—the creator and only God—is good and perfect, and yet a glance around the world he allegedly created, and especially the species he made in his own image, tells a different story. (The Yahwists traditionally wriggled out of that by blaming the bad things on Israel's lack of faith.)

Simon could have taken that basic concept from Greek philosophies, such as Platonism, or from Zoroastrian dualism, but—we would expect nothing less—molded it his own way, trying to explain the paradoxes and inconsistencies in the Hebrew version of God's history.

But was Simon, as has been suggested, literally a Magus in the Persian sense? His ancestors could have been among Magi who were settled in Samaria during the Assyrian period, or he could simply have been their pupil.[68] Remember that the words Acts use to describe him derive from the Magi, so logistically either is possible.

Romantic though it would be to think of Simon as one of the Magi, unless he had rejected most of their ideas utterly, he wasn't. Their basic cosmologies are too different. The Zoroastrian system is based on the preexistence of two opposing principles, with the conflict between light and dark present from the beginning and affecting every level of the cosmos. In Simon's system, it all begins with a divine unity: the negative forces appear because of an error in the process of creation, and only apply to the lower regions. And, again, the core of Simon's thinking—which everything always returns to—is firmly Hebraic, proving it was still his spiritual bedrock.

Nevertheless, Simon undoubtedly trawled other cultures around the Samaritan/Jewish world for concepts and insights that would help shed light on his own religion—particularly its problems as he saw them—in the same way that Ben Sira and the writer of the Wisdom of Solomon drew on beliefs about Isis to amplify and expand on the Jewish Chokmah/Sophia.

Karl Luckert—the professor of religious history who argued for the influence of Egyptian religion on the Israelites—discerns a strong influence of Egyptian spirituality on Simon: His teaching had "its ideological roots deep in the theology of ancient Egypt."[69] As our own research has revealed the Heliopolitan religion as the ultimate origin of Hermeticism, which fits with Salles-Dabadie's theory of a Simonian influence on the Hermetic texts, Luckert is probably not far wrong.[70]

Karl Luckert sees signs of the Heliopolitan cosmology specifically in Simon's concept of the feminine entity in the divine pairing of Mind and Thought, "the self-willed feminine hypostasis of the godhead."[71] The Heliopolitan system also begins with the generation of a male and female pair, Shu and Tefnut, from the original creator deity Atum, who contains both male and female within himself or herself. From the union of Shu and Tefnut further god/goddess pairs emerge.

In the end there is a series of goddesses at each level of the cosmos—all expressions of the same divine feminine power—from the origin of all to the material world: Maat (Mahet in Luckert's spelling), Neith (Nut), and Isis.

But as proved by Simon and Peter's public spats, the Magus found the solution to the imperfect world right there in the Hebrews' own sacred books. He seized on their explicit mention of other gods. Even El and Yahweh are different deities, El being higher, to whom Yahweh is subordinate. In Simon's *Revelation,* Yahweh—although Simon never uses the name—is a second-rank deity who deludedly *thinks* he is the God of all. He's even unaware there is a First God.

The idea of the world being created by a lesser deity was not new. Four centuries before, Plato had introduced the *demiurge*—originally meaning "craftsman"—responsible for creating the world but, not being the supreme god, inevitably he gets it slightly wrong, which explains its imperfections. Simon adapted the concept to the Israelite myth of creation—perhaps inspired by the term *craftsman* in relation to Wisdom in Proverbs.

The Magus takes this to its logical conclusion: if the sacred texts of the Israelites mistake the lesser god for the real/only one then they are untrustworthy about what they claim is the word of God, whether via Moses or the prophets. Having turned their backs on the cornerstone of Judaism, Simon and his followers felt completely free of the Law.

To the Christians who stood by the Old Testament, seeing anyone who rejected its ethical code as morally lost, this meant that the Simonians considered themselves free to commit any crime. Indeed, their enemies had to present them as beyond the pale to their flock, as otherwise it undermined the very foundation of their religion. If you could be good without the Bible what was the point of believing?

There was another problem that drove a wedge between the Simonians and an increasingly uneasy Church. Feeling free of the Law meant thinking and choosing for oneself—and the Church, and for that matter, the Temple *really* couldn't allow that.

THE SUFFERING OF HELEN

Other Gnostic systems that emerged over the next 200 years also blamed the existence of evil, and bad things happening in a supposedly divinely created world, on a lesser god or demiurge. But Simon's demiurge figure, Ennoia/Wisdom, does not fall through her own actions or error, but is *forced* down into the world of matter. Fossum explains: "The angels not only detained Wisdom, but also brought her down into the material world. That Wisdom had descended from heaven is told in Jewish tradition, where according to the Book of Sirach ch. 24, for instance, she is said to have come down from heaven, traversed the lower regions and, finally, taken up her abode in Israel. Here Wisdom is interpreted as the Law, but this is obviously a secondary conception meant to call a halt to the tendency to view her as a hypostasis or a goddess."[72]

Simon had no such qualms about a goddess in a Samaritan/Jewish setting, seeing it as only right. His Ennoia is, like Sophia/Chokmah, the being through whom God creates—who brings into material form what God conceives. Simon is swimming in the same stream as Ben Sira and Philo.

Simon's complex, female-based theology has been meticulously picked over by researchers for many years. Focusing on Ennoia's human incarnation, G. R. S. Mead described Simon's Helen story as "an adaption of the Sophia-mythos."[73] Haar agrees (his emphasis): "It is a *Sophia* myth which is the basis of the Simonian myth of Ennoia-Helen."[74]

And it's not just Helen Simon is honoring. Referring to the work of other scholars, Haar writes, "The conclusion is that Helen—as the *ennoia* of Simon—should be considered as part of widespread early traditions that emphasise woman as principle of knowledge."[75]

As Jarl Fossum shows in his 1987 study, "The Simonian Sophia Myth," although Simon's cult relates him to Zeus and Helen to Athena, the primary source is Jewish/Samaritan: "The identification of Simon and Helen with Zeus and Athena apparently is secondary and may be connected with the fact that Hadrian in the beginning of the 2nd century C.E. erected a temple to Zeus on Mt. Gerizim. Syncretistic

Samaritans apparently were attracted to this cult and identified Zeus and YHWH, and later Simonians could assert that their cult hero was Zeus as well as 'the Great Power,' a genuinely Samaritan divine name."[76]

Haar argues that Sophia/Wisdom is a sort of demiurge "that is analogous to the allegory of Athena/Helen as 'creative thought.'" While this is often thought of as a purely Gnostic principle "it should not be overlooked that there are similar conceptual connections already to be found in Jewish literature."[77] However, unlike in Ben Sira or Philo—and certainly Proverbs—Simon's Ennoia is a more explicitly goddesslike figure. After all, he had constant access to his own *very* explicit goddess.

What Simon's version had—writ large—which the Sophia writers lacked was the sexual, erotic Qadesh element formerly demonized in Proverbs' Strange Woman. Simon Magus's Helen was the Strange Woman in the flesh but reintegrated with Chokmah. She was the lost goddess herself, walking among them, her every gesture, word, and deed a living rebuke for their neglect and demonization.

There are still some big questions. Fossum asks: "But why was Wisdom incarnated as a *prostitute?* It would seem that the female deity in Simonianism has roots in the figure of the Near Eastern mother— and lovegoddess, for Tyre—the city where Simon ransomed Helen— was an important centre for the cult of the goddess, who had temple prostitutes in her service and was even herself said to be a prostitute."[78]

Fossum sees the metaphorical Wisdom as a Hebrew substitute for the Great Goddess, adding: "In *Proverbs* the libidinous traits of the latter are delegated to the 'adulteress' or the 'strange woman,' apparently a harlot in the service of the goddess, . . . but it is not so difficult to see that the picture of Wisdom has been painted with the same colours as those used to portray these figures. . . . It would seem that already Simon comprehended the deeper nature of Wisdom."[79]

Helen's role also relates to another vilified woman: Gomer, the wanton wife of the prophet Hosea. Helen has the same function, except that her sexuality, and even her wantonness, is depicted in a positive light.[80] Hosea's fulminations were not just the usual mix of sexual frustration and religious mania. He was describing something real and highly significant: a tradition of sacred prostitution—in which his own wife was involved—and which he blamed for the situation in his land, by diverting people from Yahweh. It was probably no coincidence that the prophet Hosea was from the land that became Samaria. Both he and Simon rose to prominence there and both linked whoredom with divinity. Simon, however, turned Hosea's condemnation on its head, claiming that the bad things were not due to the sacred whore tradition, but to rejecting it.

Judging by the "libertinism" and "promiscuity" condemned by the Church Fathers (even if we make allowances for some of their more overheated claims), Simon's sect probably did practice sacred sex. As we—and others—believe Hosea described the sexual rites of the Asherah/Qadesh priesthood of his day, probably Simon's sect was his own version of it. To the Simonians, the "whore wisdom" was all-important, and demanded their complete attention. It was nothing less than a matter of personal salvation.

In Simon's *Revelation,* the fall of Ennoia/Wisdom—God's Holy Spirit—is the reason for the imperfection in the world, a metaphor for the consequences of the elimination of the divine feminine from Judaism. And through Helen, the Magus symbolically links the flaw in creation to the mistreatment and devaluation of womankind in general. Through his image of Ennoia's violation and control by the lesser powers, Simon makes *the material world the product of rape.*

The Magus's message is surprisingly modern, and not just because of its powerful "think for yourself" subtext: The world is flawed because of the way the feminine is treated, both cosmically and individually. The female creative force, Thought or Sophia, was used, abused, and denigrated. Likewise, her incarnation Helen, symbol for women in general, has been violated and degraded.

In Simon's system the establishment cults of Judaism and Samaritanism are imperfect because they eliminated the sacred feminine—which as we now know is historically accurate, through the suppression of the Asherah cult and its priesthood. In Simon's theology the salvation of everything and everyone depends on recognizing the horrors visited on the sacred feminine—and by implication the secular feminine. This is not just about the rightful place of women in society: their sexual power must also be understood and respected. This is symbolized by the Magus's act of freeing Helen from prostitution.

There is no suggestion that the newly freed Helen embraced a life of chastity. Sex plays a big part, symbolically and physically, in Simonianism. But now Helen has *control* of her sexuality. She may choose to dispense her favors freely, which she never could as a sex worker—especially in a sailor's town. In a very real way, this neatly encapsulates the difference between sacred prostitution and the profane kind. Even as an allegory, it's potent—and still highly relevant in the #MeToo world.

Karl Luckert suggests that through his familiarity with Heliopolitan theology, Simon not only saw parallels with the original Israelite religion—in the scriptures he read for himself, not as peddled by priests—but also found an answer to the problems of creation: "It became Simon's mission to fix that which had at first possibly, and then definitely, must have gone wrong; namely, the estrangement of the entire female Tefnut-Mahet-Nut-Isis dimension from the masculine godhead."[81]

This makes sense and has huge implications. With increased contact with other Hellenistic cultures—especially the intellectual and spiritual melting pot of Alexandria—it would have been natural for Jews and Samaritans to explore the roots of their religion. The Samaritans would have been especially interested that according to their sacred texts, the progenitors of the tribes Ephraim and Manasseh from whom they were descended were the children of Joseph and also his Egyptian wife Asenath, daughter of the priest of Heliopolis. So, while the tribes proudly traced their ancestry back to an Israelite icon, they were also descended from an Egyptian with a strong connection to her ancient religion.

This was a powerful reason to explore their maternal ancestry, and we know from the writings of Greek travelers in Egypt the Heliopolitan priesthood still existed in their day. Luckert seems to have assumed that Simon learned the Heliopolitan concepts simply through study, but if we are right, and Moses's religion had Egyptian roots, perhaps the memory was still alive in Samaria. Maybe it was passed down, at first within the priesthood itself, but later, after the Asherah cult had been driven underground, in secret. It is not a huge leap to speculate that *Simon Magus and Helen were, essentially, the first-century face of the ancient Asherah priesthood.*

SIMON'S NETWORK

The Magus as poster boy for Asherah's underground cult makes sense, but was he alone, a voice crying in the wilderness? Or could he have been at the center of a well-established network, even its prophet? As we have seen, he fits snugly into the traditions incorporated into the Pseudo-Clementine literature, in the context of other sects and charismatic leaders. But, at least in the beginning, he was clearly a leading light of an already-existing movement.

First, the Clementines link him with another sectarian leader—or another blaspheming heretic—known from other sources. This is Dositheus, the first-century Samaritan schismatic and another "miracle worker" with messianic pretensions. In *Against Celsus,* Origen wrote that Dositheus "wanted to persuade the Samaritans that he was the Christ prophesied by Moses."[82] In another work Origen said: "there are Dositheans to this day who originate from him; they read books by Dositheus and interpret myths about him to the effect that he did not taste death, but is still alive somewhere."[83]

Although Dositheus is discussed by other Church Fathers, none of them connect him directly with Simon. Only one other source besides the Pseudo-Clementines, the fourth-century *Apostolic Constitutions,* has Simon and another heretic named Cleobius starting out as pupils of Dositheus but ousting him from leadership of his sect.

Origen, though, does hint at a connection between the two cult leaders, saying: "the one [Simon] said that he was the so-called Great Power of God, while the other [Dositheus] said that he himself was son of God."[84] Tellingly, at least subconsciously he is associating the two men.

Another of Origen's subliminal links comes in the passage about Dositheus's sect where he repeats exactly what he claimed about Simon's cult: there were no more than thirty members left. This is manifestly untrue—Dositheans outlived Origen by at least a thousand years, and author of *The Theology of the Samaritans* John MacDonald calls the Dositheans a "powerful and influential sect."[85] But linking the number thirty to both men's followings shows Origen was aware of some kind of relationship.

As we have examined Dositheus elsewhere,[86] suffice it to say here that the schismatic Dositheans posed a real threat to the mainstream Samaritan religion. Far from being an inconsequential little bunch that soon fizzled out, they were mentioned in Samaritan, Muslim, and Persian sources as late as the twelfth century.

There are few hard facts about Dositheus and his cult, and the little we have is garbled. The main source are the writings of the fourteenth-century Samaritan historian Abu'l-Fath, but as he uses the past tense it had obviously disappeared by his day. Still, he does explain that in the Dositheans' version of the scriptures they replaced "Yahweh" with "Elohim," and that they adopted a thirty-day calendar of their own.[87] That number again . . .

Simon and Dositheus being part of the same group of decadent occultists, or even being lightbearers for an ancient truth—depending on one's viewpoint—might be interesting but not earth-shattering. But then Dositheus was not the only name associated with the Magus. According to the Pseudo-Clementine books, incongruously, both Dositheus and Simon Magus began their careers as disciples of none other than John the Baptist.

In the Homilies of Clement, where Peter's disciple Aquila explains Simon Magus to Clement, it is stated matter-of-factly that he and Dositheus were members of the Baptist's inner circle of disciples. It was even, apparently, Simon's entry into the "doctrines of religion" after his studies in Alexandria.[88]

In fact, according to the Homilies, the wild Simon Magus *was John the Baptist's favorite disciple*. Even more jaw-droppingly, he was also John's appointed successor. Yet more improbably the Homilies also names *Helen* as one of his disciples . . . What on earth is going on?

The Homilies tell how, just as Jesus had twelve disciples representing the twelve months of the year, John's inner circle was made up of thirty disciples to represent the lunar month. However, one of them was a woman—Helen—although the implication is that she was included just to make the numbers come out right. As a woman is only equal to half a man, and the lunar month is actually 29½ days, she was needed to make the figures work.

Other clues suggest that some association with the moon was behind this, even if the Homilies has invented that bizarre—not to say offensive—explanation. A strong streak of misogyny runs through the Pseudo-Clementine works, which matches its depiction of Peter perfectly. Even for the time, Peter's own woman-hatred was so fanatical it is also highlighted in other early writings. Part of the reason the Homilies opposed both Simon Magus and John the Baptist is that they dared give a pivotal role to a woman.

The writer of the Homilies clearly dreamed up the silly, insulting "half-person" explanation to explain Helen's presence in the inner circle of disciples, not vice versa (i.e., he didn't start with his stupid line and then exploit Helen's role to make it work). This implies that in the Homilies' early Syrian Jewish-Christian sources, Helen really was one of the Baptist's leading disciples.

Perhaps it's all connected with Origen's odd but conspicuous mention of the number thirty when discussing the discipleships of both Simon Magus and Dositheus. The extremely eminent—and Very Reverend—theologian and Anglican priest, Henry Chadwick, in a note to his translation of Origen's *Against Celsus*, picks up on the statement that both Simon Magus and Dositheus had no more than thirty disciples. Chadwick relates this to the thirty disciples of John the Baptist in the Homilies, which he takes as a clue that Origen, writing around

250, "seems to have known the second-century document laying behind the Clementine writings."[89]

What do we really have here? If nothing else, the mysterious thirty disciples link the Baptist, Simon Magus, and Dositheus—and show how all three cults were held in great disfavor by the early Christian writers. Yet John is a Christian saint, not to mention being honored as the forerunner of Christ. Obviously, if the Clementines are correct, there was much more to him than the brief passages in the New Testament would suggest.

According to the Clementines, although Simon was John's designated successor at the time John was beheaded in Herod's dungeon, he was away in Alexandria, so Dositheus took over. When Simon returned, he pretended to accept his authority, feigning allegiance while secretly circulating slanders about him among the others. Eventually, Dositheus confronted Simon and attempted to strike him with his staff, which passed through him like smoke. Simon declared to a stunned Dositheus that he, Simon, was the "Standing One." This seemed to be enough to persuade him, though the staff-and-smoke trick was probably also a factor. Dositheus conceded the leadership and bowed to Simon. It seemed all too much for Dositheus, as he died just a few days later.

The term "Standing One," which features in the Roman Church sources on Simon Magus, is Samaritan, describing God and the angels. Fossum argues that it was a messianic title among the Samaritans, while Haar relates it to the "prophet like Moses," who is to stand before God and receive his revelation.[90] "Standing One" also appears in Philo of Alexandria's writings, both about God and the "true philosopher." As God is "immutable and unchangeable," so "the true philosopher who approaches him also must be a 'Standing One,'" that is, be mentally disciplined and remain unaffected by the changes in the material world.[91] Philo refers to Abraham and Moses as perfect examples of "standing ones" in this context.

The Homilies of Clement says it was after Dositheus's ousting that Simon started pursuing his mission together with Helen, with whom he was besotted. If that chronology is correct, then Helen and Simon must have been working together in Samaria between John's and Jesus's death and the advent of Philip. Remember Gerd Lüdemann's suggestion that there is a coded reference to Helen's presence during the Acts episode, through Peter's covert use of the word *epinoia*.

As the Christian religion picked up speed, and the Baptist's alleged role in the ministry of Jesus was becoming an iconic part of the story, the early spin doctors went into overdrive. One thing they just couldn't have in their shiny new epic was Christ's subservient herald being the mentor of Simon Magus. That would be bad news indeed. So they reworded the relevant part in the later Recognitions of Clement to downplay any connection between Simon and the Baptist. As Fossum observes dryly: "the author of the *Recognitions* has preserved the orthodox reputation of John by certain alterations of the original."[92] The Recognitions of Clement skips the discipleship of Simon in John's group, going straight to Simon's confrontation with Dositheus (making the thirty disciples his), creating a conspicuous non sequitur. Suddenly it is very obvious something has gone: "For after that John the Baptist was killed, as you yourself [i.e., Clement] also know, when Dositheus had broached his heresy, with thirty other chief disciples, and one woman, who was called Luna."[93]

Helen is named "Luna"—Latin for "moon"—throughout the Recognitions, which some explain as a reference to her involvement in moon goddess rituals. Hans Jonas sees an interesting connection: "In the gnostic spiritualization, 'Moon' is merely the exoteric name of the figure: her true name is Epinoia, Ennoia, Sophia, and Holy Spirit. Her representation as a harlot is intended to show the depth to which the divine principle has sunk by becoming involved in creation."[94]

Although the Recognitions downplays any suggestion of heterodoxy about John the Baptist, it does include something that the Homilies lacks and that points in the same direction. In an earlier section (where Peter explains to Clement the background to the appearance of Christ) Simon, Dositheus, and John are set within a network of related, heretical sects that had erupted in schisms.

The Recognitions says the first schism, a century or two before

Simon and Dositheus, was that of the "Sadducees." For years historians cited this as a reason to dismiss the Pseudo-Clementine works as pure fantasy: the Sadducees, as known from the New Testament and elsewhere, were the Jerusalem Temple establishment—certainly not Samaritan heretics. However, discoveries in the nineteenth and twentieth centuries—including some Dead Sea Scrolls—show there was an entirely separate group that called itself the Sons of Zadok, or Zadokites, which in Greek would be Sadducees. Like the Temple Sadducees, they claimed descent from the ancient high priest, but denounced the Jerusalem versions as imposters. These unorthodox Sadducees were founded by a figure known only as the "Teacher of Righteousness" at around the time of Maccabean revolt, matching the timescale of the Recognitions.[95] So the Recognitions' sources were not so ridiculous, after all.

According to the Recognitions, within this Zadokite movement emerged first Dositheus and then Simon. All these schisms were deliberate ploys by the "enemy"—presumably Satan—to prevent the masses from accepting Christ.

And although the Recognitions itself never describes Simon and Dositheus as disciples of John the Baptist, it still includes *John's own sect* among the heretics that seek to lure people from Christianity. To soften any suggestion of a rift between John and Jesus themselves, the Recognitions blames the heresy on John's disciples after his death: it is they who claim *he* is the true Christ. The Recognitions also has them alleging the Baptist is not really dead but "concealed," presumably about to return one day.

But Simon Magus and Dositheus as followers of John the Baptist, the apparently puritanical holy man who played such an important role in Jesus's ministry? Where did the writers of the Homilies get such a crazy, even blasphemous idea? After all, the Baptist's usual image is of an uncompromising puritan, striding forth with blazing eyes, dressed in animal skins, often being alone in the wilderness to fast and pray. He is the ultimate ascetic, calling the people to repent and baptizing them in the river Jordan. This seems a world away from the likes of Simon

Magus, Helen, and Dositheus, unless these three had turned rogue after they left his side. However, as we will see, the New Testament simply cannot be trusted when it comes to John the Baptist. And there are similar parallels with John's most famous disciple.

THE JOHANNITES

As we discovered for ourselves over the course of thirty years' research, the truth about John the Baptist—or "the Baptizer"—is breathtakingly at odds with the Christian story. In fact, the Pseudo-Clementines scenario is an accurate reflection of the time they were written. Although unimaginable to modern believers, early Christianity in Palestine and Syria—where these books originated—was really locked in deadly competition with a movement that upheld John the Baptist. John posed a very real threat to the spread of the Jesus gospel, because to his followers *he was the true Christ.*[96]

The New Testament implies that after John had pointed out Jesus as the "one who is to come"—whom he had prophesied—his following switched to Jesus down to the last man or woman. The reality is that the Baptist's following continued, not just after Jesus's appearance but even after John's execution by Herod Antipas. This unpalatable truth is found not just in early Christian sources but even in the New Testament itself.

The gospels have Jesus's disciples engaging in disputes with John's, and the Acts of the Apostles tells us that during Paul's journeys around the Roman Empire, in both Ephesus and Corinth he encountered groups who followed "the baptism of John" (and, tellingly, they knew nothing about him predicting the coming of "he who is mightier than I").[97]

Because his sect represented such a threat, when the gospels were written John the Baptist had to be marginalized as much as possible. He was reduced merely to Christ's forerunner, even though the gospels reveal that his influence on Jesus as teacher and mentor was considerably more important. Because of this comprehensive rewriting—almost rebranding—it is difficult to know the real Baptist, where he came from or what he was trying to achieve. The gospels simply have him divinely inspired to proclaim Jesus's imminent coming, and then disappearing into the shadows before being executed.

Yet that was by no means the end of the John the Baptist story. We know from other sources his sect survived for many centuries in the Middle East. It even exists today in the form of the Mandaeans, the Gnostic sect whose homeland is in today's southern Iraq and Iran.[98]

Nothing in all our thirty years of co-authorship has intrigued us more than the conspiracy to cover up the Baptist's true status and purpose. In our 1997 book *The Templar Revelation* we presented evidence that this "Johannite heresy" was brought to Europe at the time of the Crusades, lying like a timebomb at the heart of groups such as the Knights Templar, flowing through the underground stream of the Western mystery tradition.

So the Pseudo-Clementines' claims are correct: there really was a rival sect to early Christianity based on John as the true Christ. But what about the alleged link between John the Baptist and Simon Magus? Is there any other evidence? Given the threat that Simon and the Simonians posed through the "confusion" they caused, besides the necessity of promoting a Jesus-friendly image of Baptist, if there was a connection between the two the Church would have worked tirelessly to suppress it. However, there are some hints.

We recall that line in Simon's *Great Revelation,* which also appears in the Gospels of Luke and Matthew as part of John the Baptist's call to the crowds who come to him for baptism to repent: "Even now the axe is laid to the root of the trees. Every tree therefore that does not bear good fruit is cut down and thrown into the fire." The "trees that don't bear good fruit" are those people who fail to live as God commands (or more accurately by God's commands as interpreted by John).

It seems something of a coincidence that the only lines shared by Simon and the gospels happen to be a teaching of John the Baptist. It suggests that either Simon was quoting John—though he never quotes Jesus—or that both John and Simon took the imagery from the same source. Which would make most sense if they were members of the same movement.

Also, according to Justin Martyr, Simon's successor Menander set up a sect in Antioch that used baptism as a ritual, which implies that Simon had also baptized. Then again, earlier we referred to the intriguing episodes where Paul and his companions encountered followers of the "baptism of John." At Ephesus they met the Jew Apollos who had come from Alexandria to the city, preaching John's baptism—and the Homilies of Clement suggests a connection between John's movement and Alexandria, through Simon Magus. The web is undeniable, linking baptism, Alexandria, John—and Simon Magus.

Morton Smith observed a telling parallel between Acts' other account of the John sect and that of Simon Magus. In Corinth, Paul encounters the "John" group—about twelve men (no women are mentioned)—and not only rebaptizes them into the Jesus movement, but also bestows the Holy Spirit by the laying on of hands. In the conversions in Samaria of those who had been "amazed" by Simon Magus, baptism is also followed by the laying on of hands to bestow the Holy Spirit. Smith points out that "the other instance in Acts where a baptism is followed by a separate gift of the spirit is the case where the first baptism was Johannite,"[99] suggesting an association of ideas by the writer of Acts between what happened on the one hand with John's followers in Corinth and on the other with Simon in Samaria.

It's also suggestive that John, although customarily associated with the river Jordan in Judea, also preached and baptized in Samaria, at Aenon ("Springs"), just a few miles from the capital Sebaste.[100] According to an early tradition, John's headless body was buried at Sebaste, where his tomb was venerated until destroyed in the fourth century. Even if not a Samaritan himself, John obviously had no problem with Simon's country. The Samaritan link is just something else few people knew about John the Baptist. But how could we all have got him so wrong?

We can hardly blame ourselves. For two millennia Christians' only source of information about the Baptist was the New Testament. For someone with an apparently key role in Jesus's ministry, the gospel accounts tell us the bare minimum about the Baptist. In fact, it's clear they would have left him out of the story entirely had his influence on Jesus not been too well known. The only thing we can be sure of is that the gospels tell us as little as possible about John the Baptist.

A strong point in favor of the Homilies' scenario is that it is difficult (to say the least) to imagine Christian authors inventing a connection between John the Baptist and Simon Magus. After all, wasn't Simon the polar opposite of another protégé of John—Jesus Christ? At least that's how the early Church would have it. As Stephen Haar says of the Church Father's portrayal: "the image of Simon is painted with the shades of villainy and ignominy, and by some he is framed even as an anti-apostle if not an anti-Christ."[101]

However . . .

A DANGEROUS LIKENESS

Hans Jonas sums up the description of the Magus in the early sources: "Simon traveled around as a prophet, miracle-worker, and magician, apparently with a great deal of showmanship."[102] We can add to this profile. Simon claimed a special insight into the mind of God, offering the masses salvation and the transformation of the world for the better. He presented himself either as God incarnate or was believed to have been God incarnate by his later followers. As well as being surrounded by acolytes in his lifetime, Simon attracted disciples who evolved into a sect that survived him and continued to spread his message. Does that remind us of anyone?

Morton Smith, in his analysis of Simon Magus in the Acts of the Apostles, pithily adds to the story of his baptism into Christianity (our emphasis): "We have another example of a first-century Palestinian figure who was baptized into one Jewish sect and then proceeded to set up his own in competition. *This was Jesus.*"[103]

Although the similarities between Simon and Christ are often noted in passing by scholars—Haar, for example, sees the parallel between Simon the *magos* being transformed into the "first god" and Jesus's deification—surprisingly few seem to truly realize just how startlingly alike they were.

Early Christianity was certainly startled by the similarity. As we have suggested elsewhere, this is the real reason it devoted so much time and energy to—literally—demonizing Simon Magus, and why they were so terrified of him: Precisely because he was so like Jesus. He did the same things Christ was said to have done and appealed to the people's same needs and expectations.

The academic world, while being familiar with many of the facts, seems reluctant to push them to their logical conclusion. Although Haar notes that some scholars do acknowledge the real threat Simonianism posed to Christianity in the second century, to us the extent of the threat is surprisingly underappreciated.[104]

As usual, however, one particular scholar *gets it*. Karl Luckert writes that Simon Magus "must be restudied not merely as an opponent, but also as a conspicuous competitor of Christ in the early Christian church"[105] and that "the danger [to the Church] amounted to the possibility that he could be confused with the Christ figure himself. The teachings of Simon therefore had to be differentiated unequivocally from the Christian gospel."[106]

And now, in the teacher/master they shared, John the Baptist, we have yet another—previously rarely acknowledged—point of contact.

But for most of Christian history commentators believed there was one glaring difference between the Simon Magus and Jesus Christ. Infamously, Simon not only traveled and worked in partnership with, but also extolled the "virtues" of a woman of dubious reputation. Indeed, he based his whole message around her. On the other hand, of course, Jesus was famously an unmarried celibate who, while he might forgive *repentant* prostitutes, could never possibly have had personal dealings with such women. That's what Christians have fervently believed for two millennia.

However . . .

7

Jesus and His Goddess

By now, few readers will not be wondering where Mary Magdalene fits into this story. Ever since the publication of *Holy Blood, Holy Grail* by Michael Baigent, Richard Leigh, and Henry Lincoln in 1982 and then *The Da Vinci Code* by Dan Brown in 2003—not to mention our own *Templar Revelation* and *Mary Magdalene: Christianity's Hidden Goddess* in 1997 and 2002 respectively—seekers of the truth have been buzzing with theories about this long-maligned companion of Christ. Suddenly this long-dead woman is a hot topic, a tsunami of long-repressed questions tumbling out. Was she Jesus's wife, lover, mother of his children, or partner in the sacred mysteries? Exactly why was she marginalized by the Bible writers, and her reputation smeared for centuries as a prostitute? What was her true role in Jesus's mission? Whatever the details of her life and work, among the most open-minded of today's seekers Mary Magdalene is by now almost automatically seen as an embodiment of sacred sexuality. In that respect, they believe, the Magdalene stands alone.

However, the fact is, she does *not* stand alone—as we have just seen. As the British Egyptologist John Romer observed in *Testament* (1988): "Helen the Harlot, as the Christians called her, was Simon Magus' Mary Magdalene."[1] Or put it another way: Mary Magdalene was Jesus's Helen the Harlot, perhaps in her sacred role if not in profession.

Once we allow Simon Magus and his Helen to assume their rightful places in this story, our usual view not only of the Magdalene but also—momentously—Jesus Christ himself, is turned on its head. Suddenly we can put them in *context*. And once we see them as part of something bigger, something much more ancient, their joint mission leaps into focus. And it's very different than Christians usually believe.

First, we must revisit Jesus himself.

THE MAN BELIEVED TO BE GOD

There are many mysteries, contradictions, and unsolved questions about Christ. To name just a few: his origins; his objectives; the relationship of Jewish and pagan elements in his teaching; his relationship to John the Baptist; whether he claimed to be the Messiah; what happened at the crucifixion; and his alleged resurrection. Not to mention his relationship with the mysterious "Mary called Magdalene."

Jesus isn't just an enigma to us today because much potentially enlightening information has been lost over time, or because of the vast and vexed theological baggage that has accumulated around him. He was an enigma in his own time, too. According to the gospels even his closest disciples often failed to understand what he was about.

Almost immediately after his death, disappearance from the scene for whatever reason, or Ascension into heaven (depending on one's beliefs), differences arose among his followers about precisely who he was and what he had stood for. These only multiplied in succeeding generations, erupting into new rifts and schisms, which is why so many heresies blossomed in the early Christian centuries.

Our own research—first, for *The Templar Revelation* ("*Templar*") and even more so for its 2008 sequel *Masks of Christ* ("*Masks*")—made us realize just how the real Jesus differed from the Christ of traditional faith, where he is worshipped as God incarnate, unique in every way. As we doggedly delved, it soon became obvious that one reason Jesus was such an enigma was that he was not operating alone. He was part of something—a movement or sect—that lay behind him, shaping and at times facilitating his actions, but about which even his closest disciples were not always aware. Shadowy figures lurked behind the man believed to be God—who could even have been puppet masters who pulled his strings.

A major clue is the gospels' curiously abrupt mention of certain individuals, often without any introduction or explanation, who are more in tune with his agenda than his famous twelve disciples. The classic example is the family of Bethany of Lazarus, Martha, and Mary—particularly the last, as we'll see.

Although we tried to answer all the puzzles in *Masks,* right now we are focusing on aspects we have clarified by our ongoing research. In some cases this has meant modifying our conclusions in *Masks* and *Templar,* especially about Jesus and the sacred feminine. Our newest insights concern his place in the timeline of the sacred feminine in the Israelite religion.

In *Templar,* in a chapter entitled "Son of the Goddess," we argued that Jesus and Mary Magdalene were attempting to reintroduce the divine feminine to the Jews, in the same way that Karl Luckert suggests Simon Magus and Helen in Samaria were trying to fix the problems in the Israelite religion. We assumed that this great forgetting and the elimination of the divine feminine—at least from the established cult—had happened way back in the mists of time. We thought these memories were only just being recovered during the Hellenistic period, when Jews and Samaritans were thrown together with other theologies and philosophies.

Our ongoing research made us realize that the goddess had been part of the religion until much later in Israel's history than we once believed. She had only been eliminated from the official cult after the return of the exiles from Babylon in the late 500s BCE—probably not until after the reforms of Nehemiah and Ezra in the mid-400s. Even then it probably took some time to eradicate the worship of a goddess alongside Yahweh among the ordinary folk of Judea. Although, given the Temple's tighter central control via the network of synagogues, and the fact that Judea was a fairly small nation, they probably managed to do so eventually.

In Samaria the original form of the Israelite religion continued for much longer. As in Judea, an official movement had been established—apparently a copy of the Jerusalem Temple cult—in the 300s BCE. But even though it too set up synagogues, it had nowhere near the same control of religious practices throughout the whole land, which was in any case far larger than Judea.

Then there were the Jewish and Samaritan communities outside the Israelite nations, particularly in Egypt. When we wrote *Templar* we had assumed, like most people, that the Hebrews of Elephantine had adopted the worship of the goddess Anat alongside Yahweh because of their isolation from Israel and living so closely with the polytheistic Egyptians. In other words, they had introduced Anat into their worship after settling in Elephantine. However, now we see that the Elephantine Hebrews represented a continuation of the *original* religion and that it was the now-mainstream form, as practiced at the Jerusalem Temple, that had changed by eliminating the goddess. If anything, the official cult was the heresy. The same applied to the Jews encountered by Jeremiah in southern Egypt, who worshipped the Queen of Heaven.

By Jesus's day the memory of a goddess in the religion was not so very distant. She had only been removed from the official faith at most four centuries before in Judea and three centuries previously in Samaria. Because people tend to cling to their cherished beliefs for generations, that's hardly any time at all. More importantly, she was almost certainly still around in the non-mainstream cults and the expatriate communities of Egypt.

It also makes sense that the impetus to restore the goddess would come from the communities in Egypt. It was in Alexandria, after all, that the Sophia tradition emerged in Jewish thought. This was not the result of importing Egyptian and Greek ideas about the sacred feminine, particularly from the Isis cult, as used to be assumed. It represented the resurfacing of the Hebrew goddess into open discussion and thought—even if they had to be discreet about her Qadesh aspect.

And this aspect was, it seems, inextricably linked with Simon Magus. The Pseudo-Clementine literature links Simon, who attempted to reintroduce the goddess to his fellow Samaritans, with the great Egyptian melting pot of Alexandria. Indeed, early Jewish traditions about Jesus, found in the Talmud, claimed he was a magician who learned his techniques in Egypt.[2] Which is exactly how the Christians described Simon.

We have also modified our conclusions about Jesus since *Templar*—not because we have changed our mind about him, but because we have discovered more about Judaism.

JESUS SOPHIA

Something that became increasingly obvious as we researched this subject is that the Wisdom tradition—where Sophia/Chokmah was regarded as a female deity, taking Asherah's place—played an important part in Jesus's mission. Indeed, as several scholars have also concluded, Jesus presented himself as the messenger of Sophia.

Two specialists in this aspect of Jesus's ministry, Elizabeth Schüssler Fiorenza and Martin Scott, both use the term "Jesus Sophia" to describe him in this mode. Fiorenza summarizes her conclusions about Christ and the Wisdom tradition: "The earliest Palestinian theological remembrances and interpretations of Jesus' life and death understand him as Sophia's messenger and later as Sophia herself. The earliest Christian theology is sophialogy. It was possible to understand Jesus' ministry and death in terms of God-Sophia, because Jesus probably understood himself as the prophet and child of Sophia."[3] Similarly, Scott observes that Jesus "thought of himself as a messenger of Wisdom."[4]

The source for the teachings of Jesus in the Gospels of Matthew and Luke was a now-lost book designated Q (from the German *Quelle* for "source"). Both Matthew and Luke incorporated Q into an account of

Jesus's career drawn from Mark's gospel and other sources. In Matthew it became the passage known as the Sermon on the Mount. These texts saw Jesus "as the messenger and teacher of Wisdom."[5]

John Dominic Crossan, the New Testament scholar and ex-Catholic priest notes: "In the Q Gospel's vision, divine Wisdom came down to earth and spoke through the prophets of old, spoke through John the Baptist and Jesus recently, and continues to do so today through the Q community."[6]

However, through most of the two millennia since the New Testament took shape, the relationship between Jesus and Sophia has been fudged to disguise the fact that Jesus himself claimed to be conveying the wisdom not of himself, nor even of God, but of a divine female figure. Early on, Christians made Jesus himself the source of the wisdom he taught, rather than being merely a vehicle for Sophia. Paul, in his First Letter to the Corinthians in the mid-50s called Jesus "the power of God and the wisdom of God." (Titles Jesus shares with Simon Magus and Helen.)

This process started very early. In Q, Jesus attributes his teachings to Wisdom/Sophia and while Luke did too, Matthew changed it. So, in Luke Jesus says, "Therefore also the Wisdom of God said, 'I will send them prophets and apostles some of whom they will kill and persecute,'"[7] while Matthew has it as "Therefore I send you . . ."[8]

Earlier English translations, such as in the King James Bible, rendered "Wisdom of God" (*sophia tou theou*) as "God in his wisdom," disguising the fact that it is not God himself who carries out the action, but a separate—*female*—entity who executes or manifests God's wishes (assuming they are not her own initiative in the first place).

This obfuscation may even have helped with the identification of Jesus with God. Sophia's wisdom was attributed to Jesus himself, and because, to conventional Jews, Sophia was an aspect of God, so Jesus became part of God. Christ came to be thought of as preexistent with God just like Wisdom—which found its ultimate expression in the "Logos" prologue to the Gospel of John.

More importantly for us, the fudging of early texts such as Q and—as we're about to see—the original version of the Gospel of John, suggests that Jesus's presentation of himself as the messenger of Sophia is authentic. *That is how he described himself.*

Clearly, Jesus was as much a Sophia sympathizer as others such as (in their own way) Philo of Alexandria, Ben Sira, and the author of the Wisdom of Solomon—although they were not entirely free from the mainstream religion. The best parallel is with Simon Magus, to whom his Helen/First Thought *was* Sophia.

In our ongoing research, Jesus's relationship with the sacred feminine is becoming clearer, as is his mission. And the same applies to Mary Magdalene—which is only to be expected, as she was the other half of the team.

THE WOMAN WHOM JESUS LOVED

In the Victorian era gentlemen seeking amusement would visit brothels to watch tableaux or plays about the penitence of Mary Magdalene. Played by a prostitute, robes hanging off her shoulders and bosom on show, she would sob uncontrollably and even invite the all-male audience to whip and otherwise abuse her. After all, the logic was, she was a penitent sinner, and sinners deserve anything you care to do to them—especially if they're women.

Abuse has become almost synonymous with Mary Magdalene over the years. Even up until the 1990s, in Catholic institutions in Ireland and elsewhere unmarried mothers were imprisoned in laundries where they were tortured and enslaved as "Magdalenes," for whom any punishment was justified.[9] All over Christendom "fallen women" were known as "Magdalenes" and expected to live oppressed, cringing lives at the mercy of the more righteous members of society. The Magdalene had become the brand name for female shame, when the facts that can be teased out of certain ancient documents suggest she was, in fact, one of the least ashamed women of history.

Then, in the late twentieth century, something astounding happened. Mary Magdalene suddenly *trended,* not as a pathologically blubbering wreck, but as a proud role model for girls and women. With one of religion's more jaw-dropping ironies, her rehabilitation to the wider world has come about not through theological studies, but—ironically—from "fringe" books, including our own. While routinely dismissed and vilified by traditionalists, such works have helped present the Magdalene in an entirely different light. Now, looking back, we realize just how Mary's "brand" was deliberately exploited over the millennia, becoming the symbol for the marginalization of all women. But the pendulum is swinging, and her day has finally arrived. And if she is rehabilitated, so are we.

Mary Magdalene was marginalized—intensely and persistently—in two main ways. Back at the very beginning of her story, the biblical gospel writers devoted almost no column inches to her, despite her obvious importance. And the later Church explained the scant New Testament references simply because she was only an example of Jesus's forgiveness and the virtues of repentance. From the start, these men found the Magdalene very, very useful, but only if they completely misrepresented her.

Ask most people in the West today about Mary Magdalene and they will probably reply she was a prostitute who followed Christ. In fact, she was declared a sex worker by Pope Gregory I in 591 CE, simply because as both a sinner and a woman she *must* have been a streetwalker. Few people, even among Catholics, know that this belief was officially retracted in 1969. Presumably there was so little fanfare at the time because her myth was still useful in keeping uppity women down.

It was very convenient to have a sort of negative role model like this crazy caricature of a penitent whore, usually presented as so hysterical with grief that she never had a moment's peace for the rest of her life. That just shows you what happens to bad women who come to their senses! That shows you where female vanity and weakness lands you!

No one seems to notice the flaws in this fantasy version of the

Magdalene. We are not specifically told Mary-the-prostitute repented of her wicked ways once she met Christ and became reformed. We are expected to take that for granted. But even supposing this former harlot *had* been forgiven and absolved, what on earth was she doing still maintaining this over-the-top penitence act? Why all the sobbing and rending of garments? Why didn't the new, clean-living Magdalene leap out of bed every morning with a song in her heart and the urge to rush out and do good works, radiating a gloriously happy energy? None of this makes any sense, except that this sordid, mentally sick, everlasting penitent with robes that strangely tended to fall off at any given moment, was incredibly appealing to the men who ran the world. And she offered them *such* an excuse to oppress and violate the women around them, "fallen" or not.

Yet the Magdalene was much more than the was-she-or-wasn't-she-a-whore controversy, though that is important, as we will see. In recent years many commentators have admitted that she was a much more significant figure than has been believed, and for considerably more positive reasons. In some circles she's now spoken of as the "First Apostle," with the suggestion that she, not Peter, was the real continuator of Jesus's movement. (Though hardcore traditionalists will only unbend so far as to admit that she might have been leader of Christ's female followers. It's a start.)

But what exactly was her significance? And how do new discoveries change her traditional depiction?

Even a brief glance at what little there is in the New Testament about the Magdalene shows she's important in the Jesus story. She is that strange and rare creature, a biblical alpha woman, the only one mentioned by name in all four gospels, always first in the list of Christ's female devotees. And of course she plays the pivotal role in the events of the resurrection.

Most momentously, she is also the first person to encounter and talk to the risen Jesus—which alone should have marked her out as special. But shamefully it very much did *not*, until recently. It was a blind spot that developed quickly: in fact, the Magdalene features not at all in Paul's list of people who saw the risen Jesus.[10] (Although perhaps that shouldn't surprise us. Infamously, Paul was not exactly a feminist sympathizer. Apart from his fulsome thanks to the rich women who funded his mission, his writings are almost completely devoid of women.)

Yet the gospel writers include little specific information about Mary, while being manifestly evasive. *Why?*

In Mark, the earliest gospel, she's first mentioned as one of the women present at the crucifixion, with the brief explanation: "When he [Jesus] was in Galilee, they followed him and ministered to him."[11] Then she is present at the discovery of the empty tomb, apparently the leader of the women who go to prepare his body for burial.

Once again, the language is telling. "Follow" is *akaloutheo,* which while it does mean literally to follow (i.e., behind someone) or accompany them, it is also used figuratively, as in "to follow or be a disciple of a leader's teaching." The same word describes the male disciples who leave their fishing nets to "follow" Jesus. Although it is also used about the crowds who follow after Jesus to hear him speak, in the context of Mary Magdalene and the women, "disciple" makes more sense. Indeed, the only sense, despite the fact that over the years the churches have presented the women as mere followers, while the men have always been the more important disciples.

"Minister to," *diakonio,* means to serve or attend, and is the origin of *deacon.* Although used when Martha complains that her sister has left her to "serve alone," again in context it means more than just helping serve the boys refreshments. As American professor of religion and philosophy William E. Phipps observes: "The position of the women who followed him was no more demeaning than that of their leader, for Luke uses the same verb *daikonein* ('to wait on') to refer to the ministry of both Jesus and the women with him."[12]

The treatment of Mary in Matthew is much the same as in Mark. But Luke introduces her and the other women earlier in the story, accompanying Jesus and his twelve male disciples in their wanderings around Galilee. She's "Mary, called Magdalene, from who seven demons had gone out," although this tantalizing vignette is never elaborated on. It expands the women's role slightly by adding they "provided for them [Jesus and the twelve] out of their means."[13] The word translated as "means" elsewhere becomes "possessions" or "property," as when Jesus tells his followers to "sell your possessions and give them to the needy."[14]

So, the women, including the Magdalene, basically funded Christ's mission. This is potentially explosive stuff, since *if* she had been a prostitute, then Jesus and the twelve would have been living off immoral earnings—as we always enjoy pointing out in our talks.

It's clear that Mary and the other women belonged to Jesus's following in Galilee and were as much disciples as the men. Given the flat denial over the centuries that women *could* be disciples, even this single revelation is remarkable.

In the culture of that time and place, for women to travel with a religious teacher was not just unheard of but actually scandalous.[15] That's one reason their presence was downplayed in the gospels, to avoid upsetting their Jewish readers' sense of propriety—and also to prevent them wondering too much about Jesus's own behavior. Presumably it is only the women's presence at the empty tomb that made mentioning them unavoidable.

It's also apparent that the Magdalene was the leader of the female disciples, as Peter was of the men. Several things mark her out as special among the women. For a start, the way she is named is unusual. Unlike every other woman in the gospels, she is not defined by her relationship with a man. Whereas all the others are labelled "wife of" or "daughter of," she just remains, enigmatically, "Mary called Magdalene."

Even her name is mysterious. Traditionally it's explained as referring to the town of Magdala on Lake Galilee, but that is by no means certain. It is probably related to the Hebrew *migdal,* meaning "tower." There are several place names with Migdal as a prefix because there was a tower there, such as Migdal-el, "Tower of God," in Naphtali and Migdal-eder, "Tower of the Flock," near Bethlehem, so called because

there was a shepherd's watchtower. Besides, there was an Egyptian for-
tified town on the border called Migdol. It's also used of the Tower
of Babel. Perhaps significantly, the city of Samaria, which by the first
century had given its name to the whole country, also originally derived
from *shomron,* "watchtower." By extension, *migdal* is also used figuratively, relating to words meaning "great," "greatness," "powerful," and
"magnify."

As the latest translation is "Mary *called* Magdalene," this suggests
some kind of title—or maybe even a nickname. Jesus had a fondness
for handing them out, after all—calling Simon "Peter," which means
"rock," and naming two other disciples "sons of thunder." Maybe he
called Mary "Magdalene" to honor her "greatness," either metaphorically or literally, because she was unusually tall!

Tall or not, she was certainly great in Jesus's mission. At the very
least she was his top female disciple—and there is no doubt that he *had*
female disciples. Even to acknowledge that marks a seismic shift in our
understanding of Christian origins, though we need to look outside the
New Testament to discover more about her heart and soul.

BLOODLINES

The great upsurge of modern interest in Mary Magdalene really began
with *Holy Blood, Holy Grail* by Baigent, Leigh, and Lincoln, which
famously theorized that Jesus and Mary were married and had children,
giving rise to a bloodline that continues to this day. The idea reached an
even bigger global audience thanks to *The Da Vinci Code* in 2003 (and
the movie in 2005, in which we have cameo roles). These days in certain circles the idea that Christ and the Magdalene were man and wife
is little less than the new orthodoxy. For Baigent, Leigh, and Lincoln,
Mary's significance was simply that she was Jesus's wife and the mother
of his children: she had no relevance to his teaching or mission.

Despite the many problems with the theory—indeed with any theory based on reverence for a line of "special" genetic inheritance—*Holy*

Blood created a veritable bloodline-mania in alternative and esoteric circles.[16] By now it's something of a cliché for people to claim to be of "The Bloodline" (or, for that matter, the reincarnation of Mary Magdalene).

Despite that, *Holy Blood* did its huge readership a major service in alerting them to the existence of alternative sources about the origins of Christianity outside of the New Testament—the "gnostic gospels"— and what they said about Mary Magdalene. For the next generation of readers it was Dan Brown's airport thriller that poleaxed them with new, exciting ideas about her status, and the explosive potential of the once-forbidden gnostic gospels. For at least a decade, you could even feel this excitement in the air.

Suddenly there was a near-global debate about Mary Magdalene, and the way she is portrayed in the gnostic gospels besides the New Testament. This led a new wave of researchers and writers to explore her significance in her own right, not simply as Jesus's wife or girlfriend, as in books such as Margaret Starbird's *The Woman with the Alabaster Jar* and Susan Haskins's *Mary Magdalen* (both 1993), besides Lynn's *Mary Magdalene: Christianity's Hidden Goddess*.

Lynn had been inspired to trace not only the Magdalene's own importance, but also the terrible atrocities visited upon women throughout the ages in her name, as touched upon above. The more she delved into her legacy—made toxic by those who hated her and all she stood for—the more furious she became. Mary's restoration to a position of female power and simple human dignity was long overdue.

However, Lynn has to take issue with those who see her as some kind of untouchable living goddess whom one must only ever discuss in reverential whispers. If, as we firmly believed, she was a flesh-and-blood woman, then she was not perfect. She might have *represented* a goddess, as we will see, but she was *not* herself divine. One can, therefore, feel free to criticize her, though of course only if the facts permit. She emerges from such data as we have as feisty, extrovert, articulate, wealthy, and perhaps slightly controlling and manipulative. But as Princess Diana showed, when all around the male establishment is determined to suppress you, it's only by using cunning that you can ever hope to win through. Sometimes manipulation is the only tool you possess. It is the Magdalene's *humanity* that calls to us across the millennia, and her desperate need to be heard above the catcalls and jeers of the male-dominated religion that, with a unique irony, she helped to found.

But the Magdalene is important not just as a much-maligned individual whose rehabilitation is long, long overdue. All the above-mentioned books widened the picture to throw light on the sacred feminine in general—and on its suppression.

To us, any putative bloodline was not significant because it might still be around, but that it had started in the first place, given the conventional conception of Jesus as unmarried and celibate, a view reinforced by Pope Paul VI's declaration in 1967: "Christ remained his whole life in a state of celibacy."[17] It was what the *idea* of the bloodline might tell us about Jesus that was important.

Although in our view the evidence in *Holy Blood* for the continuation of the bloodline down the ages is seriously flawed, the authors did base their argument about the marriage of Jesus and Mary on the work of scholars previously restricted to a specialized audience. In particular, William E. Phipps, whose 1970 *Was Jesus Married?* argued first that, contrary to Church teaching, Jesus was not celibate and had taken a wife and, secondly, that his spouse was most likely Mary Magdalene.

When we began our own in-depth research, we soon realized that Mary had *not* (as *Holy Blood* argued) been written out of the gospels because the existence of Jesus's—putative—descendants threatened the Church's traditional teaching of his celibacy, which led to the concept of chastity becoming the model for priests, monks, and nuns, and underpinned the Church's denigration of sex and women in general. Nor was the Magdalene almost written out of the Bible just because she was a woman; the Church could have coped with a married Jesus, probably by treating his wife as irrelevant (just as the spouses of the prophets and Jewish holy men—and even Peter—were not considered important). As we argued in *Templar,* the Church's institutional misogyny and the trashing of women and sex were a consequence, not a cause, of airbrushing Mary Magdalene out of Jesus's story, and leaving us with a celibate Savior.

No, it was clearly something about Mary herself, and what her true role might reveal about the *religion* of Jesus, that was behind her millennia-long marginalization.

As far as Jesus and Mary's personal relationship was concerned, we concluded—for reasons detailed in *Masks*—they were indeed in a sexual relationship, but they were *not* legally married. But Jesus must have been, and maybe still was, married to somebody else. As it was the inflexible custom that all men married by age twenty at the latest, Jesus *must* have been married, though of course he could have been separated from his wife or have become a widower by the time he took the Magdalene on his mission.

But we also agreed with others that because of the emphasis on that sexual relationship in the gnostic texts, which gave it a religious connotation, there must have been a ritualistic element involved. Margaret Starbird was the first author to link the Magdalene, and therefore Jesus, with the practice of sacred sexuality and the *hieros gamos* ritual, viewing Mary not just as one of Jesus's disciples, or even his wife or lover, but as a priestess.[18] (Baigent, Leigh, and Lincoln had speculated that Mary may have once belonged to a pagan cult—which is what the "casting out of seven devils" referred to—but to them it had no particular significance.)[19]

Other writers, researchers, and historians, mostly from the alternative community, also explored this aspect of the Magdalene, and our own research was to take us in the same direction. As described in the Gnostic sources—and even reading between the lines of the biblical gospels—she amply fits the profile of a priestess and sexual initiatrix.

THE WOMAN WHO CREATED CHRIST

A key part of Mary's initiatrix role is her identification with another woman in the gospels, one who carried out a vital ritual—with sexual overtones—for, or rather on, Jesus. This was Mary, the sister of

Martha and Lazarus with whom he stayed at Bethany, on the outskirts of Jerusalem, in the days leading up to his Passion. Today few doubt that Mary, Martha, and Lazarus were disciples of Jesus, rather than just friends.[20]

Of the three, Mary is the most obviously a disciple: she "sat at the Lord's feet" as he was teaching.[21] She may well have been among the women who traveled with Jesus, as nowhere does it say she lived in Bethany with her siblings. (In fact, we are told the house belonged to Martha.) It makes sense that one of the women who traveled with Jesus and provided for him should offer to put him and the men up at her family home.

In turn, this Mary is identified with another woman, unnamed in three of the gospels, who anoints Jesus. In Luke she is a "sinner" although we're not told the exact nature of her sin.[22] The word is *hamartolos*—an archery term meaning "to miss the target"—which applied to Jews who failed to keep the Law and also those who needn't observe it simply because they were not Jewish. The translation as "sinner" in a Christian sense is seriously misleading.

The evidence is that the Mary who anoints Jesus is one and the same as Mary Magdalene. For one thing, it seems to be stretching things a little too far that Jesus would have two *specially* devoted female disciples named Mary. And that the Mary who showed such an understanding of his purpose, and was so close to him, a few days before should vanish when a woman is needed to prepare his body for burial. And then another Mary who we have never heard of until the crucifixion should abruptly appear to undertake the task. Because of this, Phipps concludes: "Magdalene and the sister of Martha are probably not two different characters. . . . Except for the conflicting towns of Magdala and Bethany with which the various stories are associated, there is considerable reason for coalescing them into an account referring to one person."[23]

As the Bible never calls Mary, the sister of Lazarus and Martha, "Mary of Bethany"—she's simply "Mary"—this could easily be the

Magdalene. After all, the gospel writers don't refer to Jesus as "Jesus the Nazarene" every single time.

The "sinner" label, and the identification of this anointing Mary with the Magdalene, was why the Church traditionally represented her as a prostitute, although the pope changed his mind about that in 1969, as mentioned above. But whatever her profession, clearly there was something a little dubious about the anointing woman.

John's gospel explicitly identifies the woman with Mary, the sister of Lazarus and Martha, and locates the event at Bethany. (So do Mark and Matthew, but don't name her.)

Famously, this Mary anoints Jesus with *nard,* a very expensive oil extracted from the spikenard plant, imported from India, from her alabaster flask. While this is certainly ritualistic, it has no echoes in any known Jewish rite.

On the other hand, the episode is very unlikely to have been invented—simply because it is so baffling and falls well short of the image of Jesus the gospels wanted to promote. They seem to have no clues about its meaning, just like the male disciples who were there at the time.

It's ironic, to say the least, that Jesus announces the anointing woman will always be remembered for what she has done—when the Bible doesn't even mention her name. As the Roman Catholic feminist theologian, and professor at Harvard Divinity School, Elizabeth Schüssler Fiorenza, says in her book *In Memory of Her* (1983), "The name of the betrayer is remembered, but the name of the faithful disciple is forgotten because she was a woman."[24] Yet in context it's very clear that the anointing woman is Mary called Magdalene.

In the earliest gospel, Mark, and also in Matthew, Mary anoints Jesus's head, while in Luke and John it is his feet. Luke and John also have her wiping his feet with her hair. Either way it has some kind of ritualistic meaning. If she anointed his head then there is a stupendous implication: as "Christ" means "anointed one," this is the only anointing ritual in the entire New Testament. Therefore *Jesus's "Christ-ening" was performed by a woman.*

In order to wipe Jesus's feet with her hair presumably Mary would have had to loosen it first. A woman unbinding her hair in the presence of men was disgraceful to the point of actual scandal. It's certainly not what one would expect from a woman who is supposed to have been a devoted, and doting, disciple. As Martin Scott puts it, "The picture of Mary as a virtuous, believing member of the household in which Lazarus had been raised from the dead, not to mention the devoted Mary of Luke's account, may be tainted by the impropriety of such an action."[25] The other possibility is that she had no need of loosening her hair as it wasn't tied up in the first place—though for an adult woman to wander around with unbound hair was off the scale of outrage.

The anointing of a man's feet (and a woman wiping it off with her hair) was so unusual as to be downright weird—and very distasteful. There is something sensual, not to say erotic, in the image of a woman wiping her hair on a man's feet. This was not just a matter of the eye of the beholder, or personal interpretation. The sexual subtext of "feet" already had a long tradition. After all, as we have seen, in the story of Jael and Sheba feet was a euphemism for genitals. Likewise, in the story of Ruth when, after washing and anointing herself, she goes to Boaz, "uncovers his feet," and gets into bed with him.[26] Even for a woman to "lay at a man's feet" was a euphemism. (And we are told Mary, let us not forget, also sat at Jesus's feet at Bethany.)

Whatever really lay behind the anointing, one thing is clear: As Jesus points out to his male disciples, through her deed the woman shows she has a far deeper understanding of what he is about than they had. She's therefore a better disciple, to say the least.

But how did she know his greater purpose if it was a closed book even to Peter? Had Jesus given her special teaching? Or—more likely—did she belong to the same mysterious movement as he did, but the other disciples did not? They seem to have no clue about such a thing. Was she a member of an inner circle of initiates kept secret even from Peter and the other men?

With her ritual use of expensive oils, her scandalously unbound hair, and erotic foot rubbing—if it *was* his feet—Mary Magdalene emphatically fits the profile of the sacred prostitute. Almost certainly she was a priestess who played sexual initiatrix in some kind of *hieros gamos* ritual with Jesus. If it had been in any other Near Eastern culture, that would be the logical—perhaps the only—conclusion. It is only centuries of conditioning about Judaism, and indeed Christianity, that make such an act seem unlikely, even blasphemous. But the obvious question is: What was she a priestess of?

Over three decades ago, when we first explored the subject of this highly charged erotic ritual, it was obviously very un-Jewish. That, and other indications of pagan elements in Jesus's behavior—most conspicuously the rite of the Eucharist, which smacks of Greek or Egyptian mystery cults—sent us searching for clues outside Judaism. Because of the many similarities, we concluded that Jesus and Mary Magdalene were initiates of the Isis and Osiris cult, suggesting that Western culture was really "Egypto-Christian" rather than Judeo-Christian.

The twenty-first century sees us with a different perspective. We know now there *was* a tradition of sacred sexuality and assertive priestesses within the Israelite religion, associated with the Asherah cult, or rather Asherah in her Qadesh aspect. But we were only partly wrong previously, as this Jewish cult was not mutually exclusive with the Isis cult. The relationship between the Hebrew divine feminine—as Chokmah/Sophia—and the Egyptian goddess Isis was being explored within Judaism a century or two before Jesus's day. And if we are right, the memory of the Yahweh cult's Egyptian origins still echoed down to the first century. So today we are more inclined to label it "Egypto-Judeo-Christian."

But was the Magdalene's role similar in any other ways to the ancient Hebrew goddess?

GNOSTIC MAGDALENE

The New Testament gospels are not exactly generous with their information about Mary called Magdalene, and the early Church was keen to airbrush her out of the picture as much as possible. There was a determined Church conspiracy to prevent the masses from knowing the truth about her importance in Jesus's mission—not to mention his private, emotional, and even sexual life. But now, largely thanks to a certain airport thriller and alternative nonfiction, most people are aware that the books of Matthew, Mark, Luke, and John—the backbone of the New Testament—are not the only gospels ever written. There are other important texts, long-hidden but recently recovered and translated. These are the "gnostic gospels," such as the Gospel of Thomas, the Gospel of Philip—and the Gospel of Mary (Magdalene). Above all, what most of them have in common is that, unlike the biblical books, in these books Mary is *the star*. (Nominally, of course, Jesus is the main character, but somehow even his depiction lacks her immediacy and vitality.)

Written on papyrus in Coptic (the Egyptian language using Greek characters), these gospels date from the third to the fifth centuries but are obviously translations of older Greek originals. The most famous were found among the codices discovered at Nag Hammadi in Egypt in 1945, though some had been known since the eighteenth century.

Those "alternative" gospels that feature Mary share certain themes: they portray her as a leading and favorite disciple of Jesus, who understands his teaching better than the male disciples—as with the New Testament's Mary of Bethany. Some of these books suggest, or even explicitly state, that they were in an intimate physical and romantic relationship. And they portray Peter as being deeply hostile to her. In fact, Peter hated—not too strong a word—all women, as the gnostic gospels repeatedly stress. But he reserved his most extreme venom for the Magdalene, presumably because he was dangerously jealous of her bond with his teacher. Why would Jesus want to spend so much time with a mere woman, when he could have enjoyed the company of himself, Peter?

For a start, there is the Gospel of Mary, a fifth-century Coptic codex, which was discovered in Cairo in 1896. A couple of other fragments have been found since. Unlike the New Testament gospels this one is about a disciple who, although just called "Mary," can only be the Magdalene—though the book never purports she wrote it. This describes her rallying the despairing disciples after Jesus's crucifixion and, while not suggesting an intimate physical relationship, she is the one who truly understands him, and there's a clear emotional attachment. It also has one of the other common themes, Peter's intense hatred of her, although it does have him admit—presumably through gritted teeth—"the Savior loved you more than the rest of women."[27] This isn't much of an admission as elsewhere Jesus is said to love her more than all the other disciples, female *and* male.

Like all these Coptic texts, the Gospel of Mary is a translation of a Greek original, which was dated on linguistic grounds to between 150 and the early 200s, although Karen L. King of Harvard Divinity School argued in *The Gospel of Mary of Magdala* (2003) that it was actually written during Jesus's lifetime.

Clues from its structure suggests the gospel was put together from at least two sources.[28] One of those was a lost work called the Questions of Mary, which we know existed because our old friend Epiphanius of Salamis wrote about it, therefore before 150—close to the canonical gospels.[29]

From Epiphanius, we know the Questions of Mary *did* describe the Magdalene in a physical relationship with Jesus. It transpires that the Gospel of Mary was an edited version of the Questions, specifically downplaying that controversial angle.

Another example of Peter's blatant antiwoman bigotry—jaw-dropping even for its time and place—is in another book based on the Questions of Mary, the Pistis Sophia (Faith-Wisdom), which was discovered in the eighteenth century and is now in the British Library. Although this particular manuscript is dated to the third or possibly fourth century, it has a much older pedigree, being a translation of a Greek work compiled from several sources. In other words, its depiction of the dynamic among Jesus's disciples is likely to be based on real memories.

Pistis Sophia tells of the fall in matter and the redemption of Sophia, in typical Gnostic fashion—as in Simon Magus's system. It takes the form of a lengthy question-and-answer session between Jesus and his disciples, which sounds innocent enough, except that it becomes the cause of immense friction between the Magdalene and the men, especially Peter. Of the forty-two questions in the session, she manages to ask or answer thirty-nine and is clearly indulged by Jesus, who heaps praise on her.

Taking center stage in this way was astounding for first-century Judea, where women were expected to shut up and put up, hair decently tied away out of sight and opinions kept to themselves. None of that was for the Magdalene. In this text, Jesus obviously has no problem with this at all, also allowing other female disciples such as Salome and Martha to chip in with their own contributions to the discussion. Obviously this relaxed and egalitarian attitude matches that of Simon Magus, and almost certainly of their shared teacher, John the Baptist. After all, John bestowed the sacrament of baptism on women as well as men—which in itself has enormously radical implications, rarely even noticed by churchgoers. But while John, Simon, and Jesus might think nothing of letting their sisters-in-God find their authentic voices, equal to the menfolk, it clearly outraged Peter. Perhaps he and the other Galileans had never had the benefit of Egypto-Judean understanding and he had never had the opportunity to forge a relationship with the goddess.

Peter was not afraid to speak his mind, and the *Pistis Sophia* recorded Mary confiding in Jesus: "I am afraid of Peter, because he threatened me and hateth our sex."[30]

A similar sentiment is also found in another gnostic text, the Gospel of Thomas—from the Nag Hammadi trove—a collection of Jesus's sayings purportedly compiled by the disciple Thomas. (Some date it as early as the canonical gospels, others say it was written a couple of centuries later but used some very early sources. Some of its sayings are also found in the New Testament, though a few of them appear to be earlier versions.) In the Gospel of Thomas, Peter utters this astonishing line: "Lord, let Mary leave us, for women are not worthy of life."[31] Not only is this beyond offensive to women, but the man is being very ill advised to insult Jesus's beloved Magdalene to his face, especially as Jesus quite clearly was a sort of protofeminist. Elsewhere in the gnostic gospels Christ loses his temper with Peter, saying, basically, that he's too dim to understand the gospel even though it is explained to him repeatedly. So much for the Catholic—and traditional Christian—view that Peter was Jesus's second-in-command and therefore his chosen successor! In fact, there is a much better case for Christ's successor being Mary Magdalene.

The usual explanation for Peter being the original pope is that he was the first person to witness the resurrected Christ. A quick glance at the New Testament will instantly blow that apart. It was clearly Mary Magdalene, though the Catholic Church has over the years tried to wriggle out of it by saying that as she was a woman she didn't count. When in a hole, stop digging . . . Which one would Jesus prefer to carry his message into the future? His beloved goddess-on-earth, quick-thinking, feisty, and clued-up Mary from Jesus's *very* inner circle? Or dim, ignorant, hot-tempered, and women-hating Peter? But look who won, and what happened to the lives of women as a result.

PETER, WOMEN, AND JOHN

There is another element of the Pseudo-Clementine literature that chimes with the gnostic gospels in which Mary Magdalene stars, and their consistency suggests they are all based on genuine memories of real events and of the personalities involved. It also gels with our conclusions about the relationship between early Christianity and the rival sect that upheld John the Baptist as the true Christ (besides our conclusions about the real relationship between Jesus and John).

When we discussed the Homilies of Clement in the last chapter we saw that scholars have deduced from its language that it incorporates a much earlier document that was used as source. This was a text setting out Peter's beliefs and teaching compiled by his early followers. Experts have managed to reconstruct what they call the "Teachings of Peter" (*Kerygmata Petrou*). It is the oldest element of the Homilies that, in the words of Lutheran theologian Oscar Cullmann, "preserved very early material from primitive Jewish Christianity."[32]

The Teachings of Peter, if only by what it opposes, makes sense of a great deal about Jesus, John, Mary Magdalene, and Simon Magus. It also confirms the rift between what became mainstream Christianity represented by Peter on the one hand, and the version represented by Mary Magdalene, John the Baptist, Simon Magus—and even Jesus Christ—on the other.

The author of the Homilies used the Teachings in the episode when Peter clarifies his mission to Clement of Rome. To explain his conflict with Simon, Peter says that prophecy is governed by the law of *syzygies*—pairs of opposites, every prophet having an "anti-prophet," a kind of evil twin. The bad prophet comes first so that the good one's mission is to correct the errors into which they're leading people—and so ultimately God's work is advanced. God's true prophets are defined by those they come to oppose. That's why, Peter explains, he has been preceded by Simon Magus, and why they must have their momentous showdown. It is also, he says, why the anti-Christ will have to appear before Christ's second coming, in order to make it happen.

Peter explains that there are two kinds of prophecy, one male and one female. And—no surprises here—the bad prophets are inspired by the female kind: only the male kind is *real* prophecy; the female version is just a bad imitation.

He traces the law of syzygies all the way back to Adam and Eve, who were the first prophets. As a result of the Fall from Eden, precipitated by Eve, this world is the province of woman, but its salvation lies in becoming more male. (This is a blatant, and exact, reversal of Simon's philosophy, which is built around male-female pairs of powers, and where the salvation of the world is found in a woman.)

This is Peter's theological justification for such misogyny, apparently in his own words:

Along with the true prophet [Adam] there has been created as a companion a female being [Eve] who is as far inferior to him . . . as the moon is to the sun, as fire is to light. As a female she rules over the present world, which is like to her, and counts as the first prophetess; she proclaims her prophecy with all *amongst those born of woman.* . . .

There are two kinds of prophecy, the one is male . . . the other is found *amongst those who are born of woman.* Proclaiming what pertains to the present world, female prophecy desires to be considered male. On this account she steals the seed of the male, envelops them with her own seed of the flesh and lets them—that is, her words—come forth as her own creations. . . . She not only ventures to speak and hear of many gods, but also believes that she herself will be deified; and because she hopes to become something that contradicts her nature, she destroys what she has. Pretending to make sacrifice, she stains herself with blood at the time of her menses and thus pollutes those who touch her. . . . Those who desire to get to know the truth from her, are led by many opposing and varied statements and hints to seek it perpetually without finding it, even unto death.[33]

We have to remind ourselves that Peter is supposed to be the hero of the Homilies, and Simon the villain . . .

In the context of the Homilies this is obviously a not-too-subtle dig at Simon and Helen—the Magus being under her power. This is why, according to Peter, he spouts all his pro-woman garbage. But remember this is from the *Kerygma Petrou,* the older, separate text that the author of the Homilies has incorporated into his story; he hasn't made it up as part of his plot, rather the other way around.

Something else is hinted at through the repetition of the words "born of woman"—the phrase famously used by Jesus of John the

Baptist: "Truly, I say to you, among those born of women there has arisen no one greater than John the Baptist."[34] Recall the Homilies describes Simon Magus as a disciple of John, and the Recognitions of Clement, while clumsily fudging that part, also has Peter's group locked in rivalry with the Baptist's followers, who cite Jesus's praise for John to support their claim that he is the Christ:

> And, behold, one of the disciples of John asserted that John was the Christ, and not Jesus, inasmuch as Jesus Himself declared that John was greater than all men and all prophets. "If, then," said he, "he be greater than all, he must be held to be greater than Moses, and than Jesus himself. But if he be the greatest of all, then must he be the Christ."[35]

By using the phrase "born of woman" Peter is obviously trying to link John with the false, deceptive type of prophecy—the female kind. And from the law of syzygies, it follows that in his thinking John the Baptist was the anti-prophet who came ahead of Jesus and who Jesus came to correct: John was not, in Peter's thinking, Jesus's forerunner in the normally understood way, sent by God to pave the way for Christ. John was the forerunner of Jesus in the same way that the anti-Christ will foreshadow the return of Christ. As F. Stanley Jones puts it in his study of the Recognitions of Clement, in the Homilies "John is considered the evil forerunner of Jesus."[36] (Also note Peter's sly reference to the moon, presumably a sideswipe at Helen/Luna and the lunar symbolism of John's discipleship.)

We see that the Teachings of Peter is consistent with his bigotry in the gnostic texts against Mary Magdalene. And here he's using that prejudice to trash John, which in itself is remarkable—given the Christian belief that the Baptist was the subservient herald of Christ—but also proves that in Peter's mind, John's movement was inseparable from a profound reverence for the sacred feminine, and women in general. To Peter, John the Baptist was a filthy heretic.

Peter's entrenched hatred of the Magdalene and the other women Jesus encouraged to voice their opinions equally with the men is presumably also due to his bafflement as to why his beloved Savior would even think them worth noticing. Much, much worse to Peter was the fact that—as in the gnostic gospels—the Magdalene was clearly a figure of *authority*. And one doesn't have to think too hard about just what she might have represented. Robert M. Price, the American theologian and self-styled "Christian atheist," explains boldly: "Mary is a symbolic figurehead for Gnostic and other sects who claimed her as their authorization. She clearly takes the place of the divine consort who resurrects the dying god in various salvation myths, the Christian version of Cybele, Isis, Ishtar and Anath."[37]

However, there is one obvious difference: Mary is *not* claimed by the Gnostics as a goddess or a divine figure, but a human follower of, and in some texts virtually a prophet of Jesus. The parallel is more properly with the *priestesses* of the goddesses Price mentions—although they did enact the goddesses' roles ritually. But did the Gnostics invent this version of the Magdalene specifically to link her with the dying-and-rising-god cults—or were they simply describing what had really happened? Was she a priestess? And just how close was Jesus and Mary's relationship?

With tedious inevitability, the conventional Christian line on the gnostic gospels' claims of a physical relationship—their only way out of it really—is that it was an invention of the Gnostics as a consequence of their theology: they needed a female figure to fill that role, and the Magdalene was the obvious, indeed only, choice. But it makes more sense the other way around: the theology evolved because people knew Jesus had a consort. And they knew about their physical relationship from very early on.

The main gnostic text to portray Jesus and Mary as lovers is the Gospel of Philip, one of the Nag Hamadi collection. This purports to be the work of the apostle Philip (the evangelizer of Samaria who had the mixed blessing of converting Simon Magus—albeit briefly), although it was almost certainly written at least a century after he lived.

The Gospel of Philip was really from the Valentinian school of Gnosticism—which is important as its founder, Valentinus (ca. 100–160 CE) was a prominent member of the early Christian Church in Rome—so therefore basically mainstream. When he was passed over for the position of bishop of Rome (i.e., pope) he flounced off to form a breakaway movement. According to the likes of Epiphanius, Valentinus was born in Egypt and educated in Alexandria, which puts him in exactly the same place as certain heretical movements, formerly including Simon Magus and John the Baptist. Valentinus's group was very successful and widespread, but it was eradicated when the Roman Church became the official religion of the Roman Empire in the fourth century.

As Valentinus was originally close to the heart of mainstream Christianity the texts attributed to him and his sect are not so different from the canonical gospels. He fell out with the Roman Church over an issue of authority and organization, not doctrine. The original Gospel of Philip is dated to at least 150 CE—though some think a century or two later—but its ideas about Mary would have been older, and were presumably current in Rome in Valentinus's day. In any case, we know they were around from the Questions of Mary.

The Gospel of Philip has two now-famous verses—or "sayings"—relating to Mary Magdalene, who is the only disciple apart from Philip himself mentioned by name: "There were three who walked with the Lord at all times, Mary his mother and his sister and Magdalene, whom they called his consort. For Mary was his sister and his mother and his consort."[38]

"Consort" is very telling. The word is *koinonos*—an Egyptian borrowing from the Greek, which explains the apparently male ending, as they never followed the same grammatical rules as the Greeks. The word has several meanings but in this context the only one that works is "sexual partner."

Later a verb based on the same word, *koinonein,* is used to describe the "union" of "unclean spirits" with the souls of people who have not undergone the required rites.[39] Since male spirits try to "unite" with the souls of women, and female spirits with men, it clearly refers to a sexual union.

The other relevant saying in the Gospel of Philip—with assumed words in brackets to fill the gaps caused by damage to the manuscript—is as follows: "The Sophia whom they call barren is the mother of the angels. And the consort of [Christ is] Mary Magdalene. [The Lord loved Mary] more than [all] the disciples, and kissed her on her [mouth] often. The others too [. . .] they said to him 'Why do you love her more than all of us?' The Saviour answered and said to them 'Why do I not love you like her?'"[40]

(The reference to Sophia being barren while also the mother of angels is, frankly, obscure. It refers to an earlier saying that discusses, and presumably explains, Sophia's barrenness but annoyingly this part of the text is too badly damaged to read. It does contain the words "Holy Spirit" and "many are her children," so perhaps it makes some gnomic and paradoxical statement about Sophia having many children even though she's barren, and likening her to the Holy Spirit.)

The first thing to strike modern readers is the blatantly sexual image it conjures of Mary and Christ's relationship. Not only is she described as his *koinonos,* or consort, but he is often kissing her. Note that the fragment of manuscript that would tell us *where* he kissed her is missing, though of course it's assumed it was her mouth. But what if it wasn't? Supposing Jesus often kissed her, say, on the hand? In the twenty-first century that would be quaintly gallant in an old-fashioned sort of way, but in Jesus's time and place for a man to do that to a woman—and in public—would seem almost subservient. If hand kissing today would imply "my lady," then in first-century Judea it might well imply "my goddess."

We simply don't know where Christ kissed Mary Magdalene. But we do know that he did it often and in front of the male disciples, upsetting them, especially Peter. (Traditional Christians often claim he just pecked her on the cheek, but then why would that distress the men so much? And as for the question about why Jesus loves her more than them, you can hear the incredulity in his voice as he repeats their question. It really is a case of, why do you *think,* boys?) The picture that builds up from the gnostic gospels is—and it is hard to avoid—that Jesus was *besotted* with Mary Magdalene. Another parallel with Simon and Helen.

In this extract from the Gospel of Philip we quoted above there is something else of great importance. Although other researchers rarely notice it, clearly it equates Sophia with Mary Magdalene, in the same way that Simon Magus's Helen was the earthly incarnation of the First Thought.

GNOSTIC SOPHIA

Other gnostic texts, although not featuring the Magdalene, clearly owe much to the Sophia tradition of Simon Magus, Helen, Jesus, and Mary herself. They often underline Sophia's dual nature, as in Simon's system but also hinted at in earlier Jewish texts, where her wildly erotic side is honored alongside her aspect as goddess of wisdom. For example, Sophia is frequently called *prounikos,* "lewd" or "lustful."[41]

Epiphanius writes about a sect called the Nicolaitans, whose sacred texts were the Gospel of Eve and the Gospel of Perfection. He gives few details, but the Gospel of Eve suggests it concerned the tradition of female wisdom—condemned by Peter in the *Kerygma Petrou.* And it wasn't just wisdom that attracted the condemnation of mainstream Christians.

The Nicolaitans were believed to indulge in sexual rites and to have shared their wives in common—or put another way, the women shared their husbands. Unexpectedly, originally this sect seems to exist *within* the early Christian community—Revelation condemns the Pergamum faithful for harboring Nicolaitans.[42] Revelation also has the sect being active in Ephesus, although it commends the Ephesian Christians for rejecting its teaching.[43] As Revelation was written as early as 70–100 CE, the Nicolaitans must have been one of the first or second generation of Christian sects.

Later writers say its founder was Nicolas, who was converted by

Peter in Jerusalem. Some think he's the Nicolaus who appears in Acts as one of the very first converts, shortly after the crucifixion.[44] Nicolaus is described as a "proselyte from Antioch"—a convert to Judaism, which means he was a Gentile.

According to Epiphanius, Nicolas had tried to abstain from sex with his wife, but when that was impossible he rocketed to the other extreme, declaring "unless one copulates every day, he cannot have eternal life."[45] It's interesting that an early Christian convert—initiated by Peter, no less—should think exactly like Simon Magus. Although inevitably the Church Fathers would have dismissed this as wicked libertinism—no doubt with much salivation and fantasizing—possibly Nicolas was simply continuing the ritual sex tradition of the old Qadesh rites.

Epiphanius says of the Nicolaitans' Gospel of Perfection that it was a revelation given to its author by a voice like thunder. It is thought it became the Nag Hammadi text called Thunder: Perfect Mind, which contained revelations from an anonymous female figure.[46]

The Coptic manuscript of Thunder: Perfect Mind dates from around 350 CE, but it is a translation of an earlier Greek original— possibly from even 200 years before. It's thought to have been composed in Alexandria, although that is hardly surprising. The great Egyptian seaport was the hub of heresy, a breeding ground for audacious challenges to the religious status quo.

The leading Yale University scholar of Gnosticism Bentley Layton points out the similarities between Thunder: Perfect Mind and the Nicolaitans' other sacred book, the Gospel of Eve.[47] Robert M. Price explains that both books seem to be announcements from Eve herself, who "reflects on the paradoxes of her twin existence as the heavenly power who animated the inert Adam and the earthly substitute she created to throw the lustful archons off her trail when they wanted to rape her."[48] In fact, they did rape her counterpart. The "double Eve" was a version of the divine Wisdom or Sophia, "her fallen counterpart Achamoth." Significantly, Thunder: Perfect Mind explicitly refers to Egyptian stelae dedicated to Isis, underlying her significance here.

Some Gnostic systems—as here—saw Sophia divided into two, the heavenly and the fallen, called Achamoth, a word that may come from *chokmah*. The scenario in Thunder: Perfect Mind—the fall of Sophia/ Achamoth into matter and her rape by the lower powers—is obviously similar to Simon Magus's teaching. However, there seems an attempt to soften his version by having a substitute Sophia suffering the fate of Simon's First Thought, though it does use the same word, *epinoia,* for her. And as the text probably originated from a sect founded by early Christians that practiced sexual rites, it is hard to ignore a connection with Simon Magus. The sentiments expressed in Thunder: Perfect Mind are unashamedly centered on the feminine:

> *For it is I, who am the first: I am the first and the last.*
> *It is I who am the revered: and the despised.*
> *It is I who am the harlot: and the holy.*
> *It is I who am the wife: and the virgin.*[49]

Probably not coincidentally, Thunder: Perfect Mind is also very similar to one of the Mandaeans' sacred texts, providing a link to John the Baptist.[50] Once again, we find Sophia, sex rites, heretical sects, Simon, and John linked across the years.

A similar "fall" to Simon's First Thought, as incarnated in Helen the prostitute, is reflected in another Nag Hammadi tractate, Exegesis of the Soul. This traces the soul's descent—originally an androgynous form who lives with their father, God, but who then enters a female body. She falls prey to "wanton men" who through rape or seduction reduce her to prostitution. Eventually, as a destitute widow, she calls upon God for help, repenting of her sordid profession. He has mercy, restoring her to her "house" in heaven.

The text blames the Soul for desiring to incarnate, although it also condemns the men who abuse, trick, or abandon her. Again, it could be about Simon and Helen—but it has much older roots in Jewish writings.[51] Stephen Haar likens the soul's journey in the Exegesis of the

Soul to the "stories of various Jewish women; namely, Rahab, Tamar, Ruth, and Gomer."[52] Gomer was the prophet Hosea's wife, while— interestingly—the other three women are named in Jesus's genealogy. While it is tempting to infer that this is a coded reference to Jesus's family connection to the underground line of priestesses, sadly, as Jane Schaberg argues in her 1995 *The Illegitimacy of Jesus,* this could simply allude to the rumors of his uncertain parentage.

THE BRIDEGROOM

Although as already discussed we believe they were not legally married, Christ and the Magdalene were almost certainly sexual partners in both their private lives and in highly charged sacred rituals. There are further clues, hidden in the New Testament.

Tellingly, in the canonical gospels Jesus speaks of himself as a bridegroom—what Karl Luckert calls "divine marriage" imagery.[53] In Mark and Luke, he says in answer to a question from John's disciples about why they have to fast and his never do: "Can the wedding guests fast as long as the bridegroom is with them?" (Matthew changes "fast" to "mourn.")[54]

But who was the bride? Traditionally it is identified as the Church, but we can dismiss that as wishful thinking on their part. Given Jesus's self-identification as Sophia's messenger, we can make a shrewd guess she was "the Bride." Which is exactly what the Valentinian Gnostics— those behind the Gospel of Philip—said. And they equated Sophia with Mary Magdalene.

The Valentinian system, as described in the Gospel of Philip, had five sacraments. The first was baptism—obviously marking entry into the religion—followed by chrism, eucharist, redemption, and the last and highest, the mysterious "bridal chamber," which is rather tantalizing.

In this, the Savior—the divine being of whom Jesus was the earthly manifestation—was the bridegroom and Sophia the bride.[55] But presumably the roles were acted out by the supplicant, the would-be initiate, in dramas that conveyed the higher mysteries. To an outsider, however, there would be only one interpretation of all this colorful drama.

Irenaeus, in his condemnation of the Valentinians, hinted that the bridal chamber rite was simply an excuse by Valentinian priests to have sex with female members but—although he would say that, wouldn't he?—it does seem it really included a sexual element.

In the bridal chamber ritual, Sophia is the bride. The equation of Mary Magdalene with Sophia in the Gospel of Philip *could* therefore be taken as support for her being Jesus's wife. However, the bridal chamber is clearly a religious ritual or initiation, not a literal wedding, so the participants would only *assume* the roles of bride and bridegroom—though of course they could still have enjoyed the benefits. Even though she was acting the part of Sophia, Mary was still a flesh-and-blood woman, and Jesus as the Logos still a flesh-and-blood man.

THE SEX SECRETS OF JOHN'S GOSPEL

Another great surprise is that the Sophia tradition also underpins John's gospel, although again all sorts of hasty amendments have obscured its original message.

Martin Scott observed in his study *Sophia and the Johannine Jesus* (1992) that, unlike in the other gospels, women play key roles at crucial points in the story, particularly in relation to the unfolding of Jesus's nature as Christ. For example, Jesus chooses to make his first declaration of being the Christ to a woman—a Samaritan woman at that; John's gospel has Jesus's mother with the women at the cross (unlike the other three biblical gospels in which she is absent) and Mary Magdalene's role is expanded at the resurrection and in recognizing the risen Christ.

This led Scott to "the recognition of the crucial influence of Wisdom speculation on the Johannine picture of Jesus"—which has been noted by other specialists in John's gospel.[56] It made Scott realize there was a link between Wisdom's gender and the presence of the important women in John.

The influence of the Sophia tradition on John's gospel is more indirect, or perhaps hidden, than it is on Q. As Scott points out, although it has been known for years that Sophia was a big influence on the gospel, it never spells out the connection between her and Jesus. He is not overtly her messenger as he is in Q. The word *wisdom* is even conspicuous by its absence in the entire gospel, and yet, according to Scott this is the book that sits most easily with the Sophia tradition.

It's an extraordinary scenario. On the one hand, the writer of John was very careful to avoid any direct reference to the sacred feminine, but on the other he studs the gospel with references to the Sophia tradition—for example, there's evidence that he used the book of Ben Sira,[57] as well as the prominent roles given to women throughout the gospel—resulting in a palpable tension.

From the very beginning in the famous prologue, the gospel writer often heavy-handedly refashions Sophia's role. This is a deliberate parallel with the book of Proverbs where Wisdom declares she was present at the dawn of creation, but here her role is given to the Word/Logos, which is identified with Jesus. Scott argues that the writer used the Logos because Sophia, being feminine, was simply inappropriate for a man.[58] The prologue reads in full:

In the beginning was the Word, and the Word was with God, and the Word was God. He was in the beginning with God. All things were made through him, and without him was not any thing made that was made.[59]

There's no doubt about it: here it is not Sophia that was with God at the beginning but the Word—and the Word is male. Yet throughout John there is a peculiar tussle between aligning the gospel to the Sophia tradition and deliberately obscuring it. This odd tension might be explained by the fact that the gospel was written in two stages—the prologue and the final chapter, including the testimony of the "beloved disciple" being added later.[60]

Some experts have also argued for years that the original gospel was intended for an early Christian community in Samaria.[61] If so, they were rivals to Simon Magus's movement, and needed to address the burning issues, such as Simon equating Helen with the Sophia theology, and the participation of women in religious rites. It makes sense that a more mainstream Christian community, horrified by the vaguest link with Simon Magus, would have done everything to tone down and subvert the female-elevating elements. Hence the necessity for a substantial, if sometimes awkward, rewrite.

This would explain a curiosity about the Word, which we have discussed elsewhere but were never able to resolve. Although "Word" is male, the phrase "was with" in "the Word was with God" more literally means "was attracted to"—in the sense that a man is attracted to a woman, or vice versa, which could even be described as "erotic."[62] It makes sense—in a strictly heterosexual sense, at least—if it was originally about Sophia, but was changed to the Logos. (The Logos is not feminine as we argued in *Masks,* but was substituted for Sophia, who most definitely is.)

One really telling difference from the other three New Testament gospels is that in John Jesus gives the first revelation of his Messiahship to a Samaritan—and a woman at that. Jesus is passing through Samaria on his way to Galilee.[63] By Jacob's Well, close to the town of Sychar (perhaps Shechem, the ancient holy city), he waits while the disciples go into the city to buy food. He starts chatting to a Samaritan woman, whom he asks to get him a drink from the well. But he turns the conversation to himself.

Jesus says if she had the "gift of God" she would recognize him. (Elsewhere this phrase refers to the Holy Spirit, as in the episode when Simon Magus tries to buy it.) After Jesus reveals his psychic powers by telling her that she's had five husbands and is not married to the man she is now living with, the conversation turns to the difference between Samaritans and Jews over the proper place to worship—Mount Gerizim or Jerusalem. (Their encounter takes place near the former.) Jesus tells the woman that the time is approaching when such differences will no longer matter. She refers to the coming of the Messiah, and Jesus reveals to her that is precisely who he is.

After the woman tells them about this somewhat bizarre encounter, "many Samaritans" believe in Christ, so he stays there for two days preaching—obviously with some success, because they then declare him the "Savior of the world."

This story is unlikely to be the literal truth, as the Samaritans didn't believe in the Messiah (as he was of the line of David, which they rejected). They had their own redeemer figure in the form of the Taheb, but they saw him more as a teacher and giver of the law. They also had the "prophet like Moses" and the "Standing One," so—if the encounter happened at all—the woman and her compatriots would have recognized Jesus as one of those legendary figures.

The important point about this curious incident is what the gospel writer wanted his intended readership to take away from it: "The Samaritan woman is therefore the recipient of a direct revelation of who Jesus is."[64] And the first people to recognize him as Messiah and Savior in this version are Samaritans—a good reason to believe they were the original target audience for the Gospel of John.

Martin Scott sees a parallel to the Wisdom literature in the conversation's central theme of living waters. He also deduces the influence of the Sophia tradition in the Samaritans' recognition of Jesus as "Savior of the world," pointing out he was only called "savior" by the first generation of Christians, struggling to make sense of his death.[65]

Brief as it is, the Samaritan well scene seethes with significance. When the disciples return from their shopping, Jesus tells them that this land is ripe for harvesting: "For here the saying holds true 'One sows and another reaps.' I sent you to reap that for which you did not labor. Others have labored and you have entered into their labor."[66] In other words, the ground has been prepared for their missionary work—but by whom? John the Baptist would seem to be the obvious answer—as we saw in the last chapter, he preached in Samaria. But could Jesus be referring to Simon Magus? Simon clearly recognized the first Jesus-evangelist in Samaria, Philip, as part of the same move-ment as himself. It is only later, when Peter and the apostle John muscle in, that the toxic friction develops.

There's something else in this weird encounter with the woman of Samaria, something totally unexpected—and even shocking. That little scene contains clear sexual undertones. This was picked up by Andrew T. Lincoln, the leading British New Testament scholar and a specialist in John's gospel, and also noted by Martin Scott.[67]

The story has clear parallels, which would have been very obvious to a Jewish/Samaritan reader, with two Old Testament episodes where couples who meet at wells become betrothed—Jacob and Rachel, and Isaac and Rebekah. The first even happens at the very same well. And Jesus and the woman use what were common sexual innuen-does and euphemisms.[68]

It is not the only example of such an undercurrent in John's gos-pel. We have already noted the erotic subtext when Mary of Bethany anointed Jesus's feet. Although to modern Christians this will be off the scale of blasphemy, a sexual subtext has even been suggested in Jesus and the Magdalene's encounter after his resurrection, when an overcome Mary clings to him and he tells her to stop.[69] (The ESV has "Do not cling to me," rather than the more traditional "Do not touch me.")

The word translated as "cling" in the ESV is *hapto,* literally "to kindle a fire," often used figuratively to mean "to touch" sexually.[70] In Paul's First Letter to the Corinthians, for example, it is "have sex-ual relations with." ("It is good for a man not to have sexual relations [*hapto*] with a woman.")[71]

What's going on? How can the story of Christ be either so embroidered or so disgustingly degraded—depending on one's point of view—with erotic undertones? Martin Scott thinks the sexual undercurrent in both the episodes of the Samaritan woman and the Anointing was only subconscious on the part of the writer. He con-cludes (his emphasis):

It is difficult to assess the extent to which sexual attraction plays a role in the formation of the stories about women disciples in the Fourth Gospel. It is clear that much of the appeal of Sophia tradition rests on her overt sexuality, which is meant to attract *men* over-against the wiles of the sluttish Dame Folly. It may be dangerous simply to suggest that the Fourth Evangelist reverses this role by having the women attracted to Jesus Sophia incarnate as a *man*. That is certainly not the focus which the Fourth Evangelist wants to bring, but it may be something of a sub-plot which results from the technique used.[72]

Scott goes on:

There are undoubtedly sexual overtones in the meeting of a man and a woman at a well, especially when the discussion gets round to her previous sex life! We might also find hints of sexual innuendo in the scene where Mary anoints Jesus' feet.[73]

Today, all we can do is speculate about the reasons for John's erotic subtext. But to the first readers in Judea and Samaria, it would have been both obvious and reasonable. Jesus in an erotic context was neither blasphemous nor ludicrous. And presumably to his *very* first followers, his well-known personal links with the living Sophia helped explain everything.

FATHER, SON—AND (FEMALE) HOLY SPIRIT

The Holy Spirit plays a central part in the gospels and therefore Christianity. As we noted earlier, although the concept of God's Spirit (Hebrew *ruach*, Greek *pneuma*) is found in the Hebrew Bible, it has more of a pivotal role in Christianity. We have also seen that in Alexandria the Holy Spirit evolved in parallel with Sophia, and as the two were equated the Spirit was also thought of as female.

Today even among some believers, the Holy Spirit is a source of some bafflement. (As is the concept of the Trinity as a whole.) But its function was clear to the first Christians. It was the force or power through which at first Jesus, and then the apostles, performed their healing and miracles. And, of course, it ended up as part of the mysterious Trinity, along with the Father and Son.

Although the Holy Spirit became synonymous with the presence of the resurrected Jesus, like Sophia it was originally quite separate. For example, he declares "everyone who speaks a word against the Son of Man [i.e., 'me'] will be forgiven, but the one who blasphemes against the Holy Spirit will not be forgiven."[74] (This is Luke—but it appears in all three synoptics, with slightly different wording.)

Clearly, to the very early Christians the Holy Spirit was female, but she soon suffered a forcible sex change, becoming part of the all-male Trinity. However, her role was remembered, retained, and honored—but only by the heretics.

The lost Gospel of the Hebrews—known from Church Fathers like Origen—emphasizes that the Holy Spirit is the mother of God, God presumably meaning Jesus.[75] It is generally dated to the early 100s and thought to have been written in Alexandria, hothouse of most exciting—and authentic—ideas that surround Christianity. The gnostic Gospel of Philip has no doubt about the issue, saying unequivocally, "Some said: Mary [the Mother] conceived of the Holy Spirit. They are in error. What they are saying they do not know. When did a woman ever conceive of a woman?"[76]

Indeed.

ASHERAH'S LEGACY

Traditionalists have always objected that the texts in which Mary Magdalene stars are later elaborations by the Gnostics: the "heretics" created a fantasy woman to fit their crazy system, picking the biblical Magdalene because of her importance in the resurrection narratives. In other words, to the critics the Gnostics wrote their gospels to fit their theologies, rather than basing their theology on the gospels—as they claim their own Church had done. The Gnostics' enemies claimed that, for example, the Gospel of Philip equating Mary Magdalene with Sophia is all part of the fantasizing. Sophia might have been important to the Gnostics but was not nearly so central to Jesus. That, as we now know, is simply untrue.

Sophia was so central to Jesus that he even presented himself as her messenger or prophet. Although the early Church determinedly played this down—or tried to totally obscure it—it is now being recovered by the likes of Elizabeth Schüssler Fiorenza and Martin Scott. Sophia was important in Jesus's teaching; Mary Magdalene was important in Jesus's mission. The New Testament gospels—unsurprisingly—do not specifically equate her with Sophia, but then mentions of both female figures were kept to a minimum.

There are also the similarities between Jesus and Simon Magus, who infamously equated his Helen with Sophia. Jesus's Helen was obviously Mary Magdalene, who also fitted the role of Sophia to perfection—or at least she did before the early Church began its long game of airbrushing her out.

Presumably one reason Mary was edited out as far as possible was because of her similarity to Helen, which would also reinforce the striking likeness between Christ and Simon Magus. And no doubt the traditionalists shuddered to think what would happen if their flocks knew that Jesus was only too like a goddess-worshipping sex magician! Not to mention one who was so besotted with his female partner that he was almost in thrall to her.

Was that why almost all hints of the divine feminine were erased from the Jesus story? It wouldn't be merely ironic if the Church reinvented Jesus to make him less like Simon. It would be an insult to both Jesus himself and his beloved Sophia, his *koinonos,* his Magdalene. But the Church was only too willing to implicitly insult their alleged Lord—by ignoring, demeaning, and degrading his Great Lady—if they would be safe from generations of women demanding to be empowered in their all-male Church. Insulting Jesus was worth it to them. Without strong and sacred women in the picture these churchmen could breathe a sigh of relief. Their Church could feel safe from Magdalene-inspired harridans.

The gnostic texts in which the Magdalene starred were forbidden and brutally suppressed and have only come down to our time through sheer serendipity. But how many other documents failed to survive the millennia, being forever lost to us?

It's hard to exaggerate the disdain felt by the Church over the millennia for the Gnostics and their texts, which is why of course the gnostic gospels recovered in the nineteenth and twentieth centuries had to be hidden in the first place. If you valued your life, and did not greatly relish the idea of an agonizing death, once Pauline Christianity became the established religion of the Roman Empire it was not very wise to possess the likes of the Gospel of Philip or the Gospel of Thomas. The very early Roman Church was on a mission to stamp out every last vestige of Gnosticism. We have to be very grateful that they failed—at least in the long term.

The Church Fathers didn't just loathe the gnostic books, they also clearly feared them. If people were allowed free access to such texts their own carefully constructed version of Christianity would soon be questioned, perhaps even challenged head-on. In that sense little has changed in over 2,000 years. When Dan Brown's *Da Vinci Code* took the world—not much of an overstatement—by storm, suddenly his millions upon millions of readers across the globe discovered that the biblical books of Matthew, Mark, Luke, and John were not the only gospels ever written. Amazon was flooded with orders for translations of the likes of the Gospel of Thomas—not a development relished by the established churches. We experienced this at first hand, as we found ourselves in the eye of the storm, being invited on platforms and radio and television debates to discuss the gnostic books with priests, professors, and the media.

The traditionalists took two lines. First, they denied such books existed. Then, when pressed, they admitted they knew of them but they were such rubbish that no decent Christian would soil their eyes by reading them. Others said they were written too long after Christ's life to be taken seriously—even though their dating in many cases is very similar to the canonical gospels. Even theologians shied away from discussing these gospels with what was obviously suspicious vehemence. *What were they frightened of?*

Undoubtedly, the gnostic gospels contain a potential tsunami of antiestablishment revelations. Clearly, there is the consistent presentation of Jesus and Mary in a close, even intimate relationship. There's also her obviously starring role in his mission, while Peter is shown up as an oafish, misogynist dimwit, who threatens Mary and who is *not* Christ's chosen successor. But beyond that, there is the implication that the gnostic gospels, as we have just seen, are more faithful to Jesus's own beliefs.

As we have shown, even the biblical gospels hide what believers today would consider to be startling, even heretical beliefs: the "Christen-ing" of Jesus by the Magdalene in an ancient, sacred ritual and the sexual innuendoes of John's gospel; Jesus's association with Sophia—to name but a few secrets one can uncover using clues from the academic world and careful, painstaking analysis. Put Matthew, Mark, Luke, and John together with the gnostic gospels plus what we know about other major players, such as Simon Magus and John the Baptist—and an almost entirely different picture emerges. Much of the new revelations depend, not only on close analysis and deduction, but also on context, on how Jesus's mission fits with the history of Judaism—and, of course, specifically with the remarkable story of the Jewish goddess, be she Asherah, Anat, the Queen of Heaven, Chokmah, or Sophia. She is never far away and still very much present even in the Christian story, demanding our attention. And our love.

Equal Rites

The great calamity of the last two thousand years is that the goddess's fate in Judaism was repeated in Christianity. The religious movement in which the divine feminine was supposed to be a cornerstone hastily airbrushed her out, leaving the spiritually incomplete faith we see today.

The main reason was that the new movement operated within a male-dominated environment—in both Judea and the Roman world—meaning Jesus was unable to make his bring-back-the-goddess agenda too obvious. Especially given the emphatically male, monotheistic Yahweh cult of his day, he had to drip-feed his discreet Sophia message very slowly, which is probably why he remained such an enigma even to most around him.

The early Church's attitude to women was hardly helped by Christ keeping something back from even his close disciples. If we are right, that "something" was related to a bigger movement behind him—together with the Baptist and Simon Magus—working to bring the goddess back into the religion of Israel.

Key to early Christians' attitudes was Mary Magdalene. While they obviously knew Jesus wanted women to be prominent, most failed to understand her role both in Jesus's mission and his personal life—and that, we argue, is because it was kept semisecret, even from his closest disciples. Restoring the divine feminine to Judaism was a covert part of Jesus's agenda—which he undertook together with the Magdalene. The gnostic texts consistently portray Mary as his closest confidante who understood his teachings way more profoundly than the male disciples.

In our reconstruction both Mary and Helen were priestesses of Sophia—who was a repackaged Asherah, whose cult had survived underground since its removal from the established religion some four centuries before Jesus's day (removed in Judea, that is, but more recently in Samaria and probably not at all in the expatriate communities in Egypt). Asherah's place alongside Yahweh was remembered, and her rites still practiced, but necessarily in secret. Asherah's worship was no longer perpetuated openly through folk practices, but as a covert survival of the priesthood that had once served her in the Temple but had been suppressed. It may have been secret, but it was organized.

Although she could no longer be called Asherah, she had been given a new lease on life as Wisdom/Sophia. While Sophia might have originated from an attempt to sanitize Asherah and bring her under the control of the Temple, she began to repossess more and more of Asherah's attributes and functions. The similarities with Isis were also recognized and imported into Sophia's cult.

It is unclear if worship of the Hebrew goddess survived in Judea, the heartland of the new Yahwism. The persistent Samaritan connection suggests that's where the restoration movement emerged. The development of the Sophia tradition in Alexandria also suggests that the Hebrew communities in Egypt—the worshippers of Anat-Yahu and the Queen of Heaven—played their own part.

It wasn't just the cozy cake-baking rites that continued. As is shown by the emphasis on female sexuality in Helen's relationship with Simon and—less overtly but still discernibly—Mary's with Jesus, clearly the erotic Qadesh aspect was still practiced, with the priestess as sexual initiatrix.

However, the restoration of the goddess in Jesus's mission was a major embarrassment to the sect that survived him. It was totally unacceptable, especially to those who saw him in more traditional Jewish terms—and who much preferred to emphasize his role as Messiah, the deliverer and restorer of Israel.

That tension seethes through the confrontations between Peter and Mary in the gnostic works, although Peter's unreconstructed misogyny presumably evolved from his traditional view of a woman's place in Jewish society. His bigotry hammers throughout the Teachings of Peter, the early text that inspired the Homilies of Clement. Of course it was the women who would have the greatest interest in restoring Asherah to her rightful place in their religion—and Peter would do anything in his power to stop them.

There was also the uncomfortable parallel between the Magdalene and Helen, which threatened to expose awkward aspects of Christ's mission. As the similarities with Simon Magus challenged the early Christians' claims concerning Jesus's uniqueness, anything that made the two men *too* alike had to be explained away—Simon using demonic magic rather than the Holy Spirit—minimized, or edited out completely. The danger posed by Simon to the Jesus movement was present right from the beginning, which is why Peter had to oppose the Magus so stridently. But because the Simonians continued, it remained a challenge to the Church for at least two centuries, leading to further editing. Ironically, the traditional image of Jesus may owe a great deal to the rewriting campaign to make him less like Simon Magus.

As a result—either because her role was never properly understood or maybe because it *was*—Mary Magdalene's place in Jesus's story had to be minimized. We see the result in the gospels: a woman who was central to Jesus's discipleship and also had a ritual function, yet who is never satisfactorily explained. The gospels' references to her, in the double guise of Magdalene and Mary of Bethany, are evasive, vague, and confusing. Precisely, one suspects, as the authors intended.

Both her ritual role as Asherah/Sophia and her personal relationship with Jesus were reasons for her marginalization. There was no way they would allow Christ to be known as her lover, either ritually or personally, especially if she was *not* his legal wife.

As mentioned earlier, had Jesus been conventionally married, the early Church could have handled it. The wives—and children—of prophets and holy men were never accorded any particular significance in Hebrew tradition (or for that matter Greek and Roman); they had no concept of sacred bloodlines—as opposed to royal or priestly dynastic lineages. Peter was married, and presumably had children, but the only reason we know is because of a single mention of his mother-in-law being healed by Jesus. (His poor wife . . .) Perhaps some of the women who "ministered" to Jesus were the wives of his disciples.

A major consequence of minimizing Magdalene's role and the other female disciples was a shiny new image of Jesus. Despite his teachings about Sophia and the importance of the Holy Spirit, suddenly he was transmuted into an unmarried celibate. This had a knock-on effect down the generations, causing untold psychological damage, and arguably underpinning much of the pernicious child abuse that infects churches today.

Christianity soon came to extol virginity and life-long celibacy—using Jesus and Mary the Mother as role models. As the British historian Robin Lane Fox points out, this was something entirely new in both the pagan and Jewish worlds.[1] He explains: "From its very beginnings, Christianity has considered an orderly sex life to be a clear second best to no sex life at all."[2]

This was advantageous to Christian communities in one major respect: it brought in more revenue. There were a great many widows in the Roman world, as young women tended to marry older men, inheriting from their husbands. Christianity had a particular attraction to well-off women—they vastly outnumbered men—and the celibacy ideal discouraged them from remarrying. Similarly, unmarried women inherited from their parents. To be fair, the money was often used for charity, so it benefited the poorer members of the community.[3]

THE RISE OF PAUL'S CHURCH

Ironically, today's Christian Church did not properly begin with Jesus. For one of the most famous and beloved men of all time, he was so enigmatic that the movement he founded quickly splintered into many rival groups, each convinced their interpretation of his role and message was right—and all the others wrong.

Within at most a decade of his crucifixion his discipleship split between what the Acts of the Apostles calls the Hebrews (*hebraios*) and Hellenists (*hellenistes*—those who lived "according to the Greek manner").[4] It was one of the Hellenists, Philip, who undertook the first Christian mission outside of Judea, to Samaria (where he met a certain larger-than-life wonder-worker), while the Hebrew faction remained based in Jerusalem.

Then came Paul with his own, very different take on Christianity. This was entirely based on his vision on the road to Damascus of the resurrected Jesus and his claim to be guided by Christ's voice. Paul's interpretation of Jesus's mission, which transformed the Messiah of Judaism into the Christ of Christianity, was seriously at odds with Peter's. And for once, we might sympathize with Peter.

It's hard to exaggerate just how bizarre Paul's story is. He had never even met his Lord, but his version of a transcendent Jesus, who came to save humankind through his sacrifice and was still accessible to those who believed in him, won out over Peter's. For all his manifest faults, at least Peter had traveled with Jesus on his Judean mission, and knew him well. Jesus possibly even appointed him chief disciple. Yet as the years passed believers lapped up Paul's version, and "Pauline" Christianity is still triumphant today.

Within a couple of generations there was a multitude of different "Christian" sects, with varied views about Jesus's aims, message, and true nature. They all addressed some very big questions, but in markedly different ways. Was he the human agent of God, a divine figure sent by God, or God himself? Had he come to save just the Jews or all humankind? They all thought he was special, but few could agree exactly why. And that's without even considering all the sects derived from the likes of Simon Magus, Dositheus, and of course, John the Baptist.

Eventually one interpretation of Jesus triumphed: largely, Paul's.

But this new dogmatic certainty had some terrible consequences, creating centuries of suppression of all the other sects, declaring them not only mistaken but actively anti-Christian, agents of the Devil. The concept of heresy was born.

"Heresy" is derived from the Greek *haireseis,* simply meaning "school of thought," which was often used to describe a sect within a wider religion or philosophy. This rather vague definition rapidly hardened, as Matthew Black explains: "The pejorative use of the term is a later Christian development, as Catholic orthodoxy began to define itself over against opposing forms of belief."[5]

Robin Lane Fox in his *Pagans and Christians* (1986) notes: "schism, like heresy, was entirely alien to the pagan religiousness."[6] In the pagan world, the whole concept of the "witch hunt"—either metaphorical or literal—was unknown. Fox adds: "Pagan society knew no 'Devil' with whom individuals could make a pact, and thus no torture and persecutions of 'false' prophets and prophetesses. These features were a consequence of Christianity."[7]

Of course, eventually Christianity became the official religion of the Roman Empire. Although this is popularly believed to have started with the emperor Constantine's vision in 312 CE, in fact that only led to him recognizing Christianity as a legitimate religion, equal to the many pagan ones. Much more significant was the edict of the later emperor Theodosius I who called a council together in Constantinople in 381 CE to resolve the major Christian split over the nature of Christ and his relationship to God.

The row was between those who accepted the Nicene Creed, formulated at the Council of Nicaea in 325 CE, which held that Jesus Christ is essentially one and the same as God—"consubstantial" in the Creed—and the followers of Arianism. The latter believed that Jesus, though a divine being, was distinct from God, who created him at a definite point in time, rather than being co-eternal with him as in the Nicene version.

As the Greek and Roman specialist Charles Freeman shows in his

AD 381: Heretics, Pagans and the Christian State (2008), Theodosius's edict and the Constantinople Council marked the true turning point in Christianity's rise, and the emergence of the Roman Church as an authoritarian institution. Although, as he points out, these have been "airbrushed from the narrative" of the emerging Church.[8]

Theodosius's edict declared that Christianity was the only religion permitted in the empire, and also recognized only those who accepted the Nicene Creed as true Christians. All other gatherings for worship or ordination of priests were forbidden under pain of grim punishment. (Death—usually a particularly agonizing variety—soon became the standard penalty.)

So, the citizens of the Roman Empire had to be not only Christians but the right *sort* of Christians. Theodosius's decree marked the end of religious tolerance—indeed of any free discussion within Christianity or about religion—and the beginning of the persecution of heretics and pagans.

Theodosius backed the Nicene Creed not out of religion conviction, but for reasons of political expediency. As he had begun his reign as a co-emperor with an Arian Christian, he adopted the Nicene version to mark himself out as different. Another reason was to prevent civil unrest, as the Nicene and Arian Christians frequently clashed violently.

But where was the goddess in all this male posturing? Very largely, she simply wasn't. But even before the Council of Nicaea, the new Church authorities had rejected the gnostic gospels—and Gnosticism in general. It's not an exaggeration to say that with them went much of the sacred feminine, and the truth about Mary Magdalene. And very soon the people began to miss their goddess.

THE BLESSED VIRGIN AND JESUS-ISIS

The previously female Holy Spirit, now absorbed into the Trinity, officially became one of the three "natures" of God—all resolutely male. The process was completed at Theodosius's Council of

Constantinople, which equated the Holy Spirit with the Father and the Son.

Even so, there remained that age-old spiritual and psychological need for the feminine, which the Church eventually tried to satisfy, but clumsily and halfheartedly, with little awareness of the damage they were doing to future generations. To placate the masses desperate for a goddess, they invented the Virgin Mary.

Obviously Jesus had a mother—that much they needn't invent. We know she was called Mary (Miriam, or Mariam), a common enough name. But surprising as it seems today, the early Church paid her little attention. After all, she scarcely appears in the gospels; she was obviously unimportant to Jesus's religious agenda. Early Christians respected her as his mother, for being chosen by God and because of the miracle of the virgin birth—important, that is, for the implications of her role about Jesus and God's plan in Christian theology—but not in her own right.

Official recognition of the cult of the Blessed Virgin Mary happened almost by accident at the end of the fifth century, as a by-product of yet another split over the nature of Jesus. One school, championed by Nestorius, Patriarch of Constantinople, believed that Jesus was part human and part divine, whereas the other, championed by Cyril, Patriarch of Alexandria, argued that he was wholly divine. The row centered on how he had come into the world, which obviously concerned Mary.

The debate reached a climax over whether Mary should be given the title *Theotokos,* "God-bearer": Nestorius said no, Cyril yes. In 481 a Church council was held in Ephesus—once the cult center of the goddess Diana—to rule on the issue. It was decided that Jesus was wholly divine, and so Mary should be called *Theotokos.* (At which point the Nestorians broke away from the Catholic Church.)

Tellingly, while the council was locked away in debate, crowds of Ephesians gathered outside. When the decision was announced on June 22, 481, they went wild with joy—not because Jesus had been declared divine but because they were now allowed to worship Mary as *Theotokos*. After the announcement Cyril gave a sermon, setting out what became the traditional concepts of Marianism: because she was chosen to bear Jesus, and Jesus saved the world, Mary the Mother had a significant role in salvation. Cyril's sermon was calculated to appeal to the Ephesians, playing on their need for a goddess.

Although this demonstrates the spiritual and psychological desire for a female archetype, what the Church gave them was a pale imitation. In one way the *Virgin* Mary was a clever choice. The fact that she was a sexless and improbably virgin mother, rather than the earthier Magdalene, reveals the Church's distaste for some of the most vital characteristics of the feminine—and perhaps simply their fear of it. But this compromise goddess was calculated to keep women down, to prevent them from achieving independence and load them with guilt. After all, what flesh-and-blood woman could possibly live up to the standards set by a *virgin mother?* The new image of the sacred feminine was of a woman who wept—not for her sin, like the Church's insanely guilt-ridden Magdalene, but for *your* sin. Every day just by living a normal life you were hurting God's Mother. And if you had problems in your love or sex life, if you suffered from postnatal depression, if you had negative feelings about your children or the man you had promised to obey, you would think twice about confiding them to this new "goddess," who would uncomprehendingly blame you for your weakness. Whether or not that was a conscious factor in the men's decision to invent the Virgin Mary, it rapidly became a fact of life for her worshippers. The terrible effects are suffered to this day.

Jane Schaberg, professor of religious studies at the Roman Catholic University of Detroit Mercy—a member of the Society of the Sacred Heart of Jesus who renounced her vows but remained a Catholic—calls her "a tool of the institutional sexism" of Roman Catholicism, having never been used to promote women's liberation.[9]

Ironically, the Church also tried to satisfy the need for a goddess by giving Jesus himself some of Sophia's and other goddesses' qualities.

Even the goddess's titles and attributes were applied to Jesus—for example *kyria* (queen or lady) became *kyrios*.[10]

The denigration and near-elimination of female power was to continue, gathering speed. In medieval times churchmen seriously debated whether women had souls, relegating them to the same level as animals. And as chastity became the go-to state for all those who sought salvation, monasteries and nunneries heaved with sexual frustration, with sadomasochism often the only permissible outlets—flagellating or otherwise "mortifying" the flesh.

Out of this sick miasma grew such a prevalent woman-hatred that it was just a small step to the historical witch-persecution hysteria—even up to the eighteenth century. Fueled in part by personal spite—that row with your neighbor conveniently becomes an accusation of witchcraft—mostly by institutional misogyny, innocent women were condemned as witches and suffered the most excruciating tortures and death by burning.

Although the numbers involved have been greatly inflated, surely even if just one innocent woman died, that was one too many. And it is true that, as the witch hysteria continued, men also fell victim to the madness. So did tiny children. So did animals—a cockerel was burned because it was thought to be a witch's "familiar," or unholy pet. A horse was also similarly killed. On and on it went . . . in parts of Germany virtually whole villages were wiped out by the witchfinders in their insane zeal. Grotesquely, the walls of houses nearest to the human pyres were inches thick in human fat.

In England and the new country of America, witches were hanged, not burnt, which is perhaps a small mercy, although sometimes they were pressed to death under increasingly huge weights. None of this was humane, none of it was justified, none of it was *right*. And none of it was remotely necessary.

Perhaps some small similar outbreak might have happened even if Christians had been allowed to keep a reverence for a more robust sacred feminine, and not just encouraged to feel inferior and guilty in front the Virgin Mary—though one doubts it. The witch hysteria was largely born out of men's hatred and fear of women, fueled in the first place by the Church, right down to the local parish priests. Things were not much better among the later Protestants, especially the hardcore Puritans. Look what happened in Salem.

And the one name that should have put all that right was being smeared with accusations of prostitution. In convents and monasteries, in churches and in God-fearing homes, Mary Magdalene was presented as a pathetic sinner who should provoke pity, not admiration or reverence. She had nothing to teach us except that being a sinner condemned you to a dreadful life of shame and guilt. In the lofty world of the spirit, she was simply irrelevant.

But there were still those who knew the truth.

THE CHURCH OF MARY MAGDALENE

While Mary Magdalene's true place in the Jesus sect was all but erased by the emerging Church, her memory was perpetuated through the gnostic texts they suppressed. Their existence was scarcely even suspected until the eighteenth century, and not widely known until the twentieth. That is, not known among mainstream Christians.

As we discussed in *Templar Revelation* and *Mary Magdalene: Christianity's Hidden Goddess,* Mary's secrets did not die out altogether, even during the Roman Church's apparently unstoppable rise to power. Even in the very Catholic Middle Ages, a heretical cult of the Magdalene flourished in southern France, which plays a major part in *Holy Blood, Holy Grail*'s historical reconstruction, besides Margaret Starbird's research. Dubbed by some the "Underground Church of Mary Magdalene," it has been linked with the famous heretical Gnostic group of southern France, the Cathars—at least some of whom believed her to be Jesus's partner—and the mysterious cult of the Black Madonnas.[11]

There are ancient legends, which we believe are probably basically true, that the Magdalene traveled to Gaul—today's France—after the crucifixion to escape the Jews, but to us, it's more likely she was fleeing from Peter. (Without Jesus to protect her, he might have acted on his former threats.) Once there we're told she preached and even baptized, like the male apostles on their far-flung missions.

Not only was Mary personally active in France, but there is strong evidence that some gnostic gospels, in which she features so heavily, were also known in Europe in the Middle Ages.[12] One way or another, freethinkers in southern Europe had access to her secrets.

SHE SURVIVES

While the sacred feminine desperately tried to maintain a presence in Christianity, it did manage to cling on in Judaism, taking more mystical and underground forms.

The Jewish religion suffered major changes after the destruction wrought on Judea by the Roman suppression of the two great revolts. The first, 66–70 AD, ended in the utter ruin of the Second Temple. A second uprising in 132–136 AD resulted in the decimation of Jews in Judea through mass executions and enslavement, while the religion was banned in Syria and Palestine. Of the lands once inhabited by the twelve tribes, only Galilee was still home to Jewish communities, although there were also diaspora settlements scattered around the Roman world and in Mesopotamia.

The loss of the Temple was traumatic. Judaism struggled to adjust, as it was still the only place where Yahweh could be directly worshipped by the masses—and where he could be offered sacrifices. With the Temple also went the faith's central authority: it was as if the Catholic Church were to lose the Vatican and the pope at the hands of a sworn enemy. As a result, the Pharisees, who lived and worked among the ordinary people, emerged as the custodians and teachers of the religion.

The Jewish faith necessarily changed, becoming centered less on the Hebrew Bible than on the Talmud ("Instruction"), the core text by a succession of Jewish scholars that began as an exposition of the Hebrew Bible—applying it to religious practice and daily life—but which took on a life of its own. From this emerged Rabbinic Judaism, still prominent today.

Within mainstream Judaism, aspects of the sacred feminine that had resurfaced in forms such as Wisdom were transferred to Yahweh, being absorbed into his godhood, just as Sophia had been assimilated to Jesus. So Yahweh could be said to have his feminine side—or even to be both male and female—although this was never exactly emphasized down the centuries. However, it did inspire a feminist movement within Judaism in the late twentieth century.

In Rabbinic Judaism, women were largely forbidden from studying the Torah and Talmud, and excluded from participation in much Jewish worship. One of the "three blessings" of God that the Talmud requires men to say daily includes blessing God "who has not made me a woman" (the others are not being a Gentile or a slave).

Although moves to make women worshippers equal began in the mid-nineteenth century they only had a real impact a hundred or so years later. Reconstructionist Judaism, established in the United States in the 1930s, upheld gender equality in worship—although its first female rabbi was appointed as late as 1974. She, however, was not the first woman to be ordained.

This was the amazing Regina Jonas, in Germany in 1935, who became a rabbi after writing a thesis arguing that there was no biblical or talmudic objection to females in the role. She was to die in Auschwitz in 1944, scandalously forgotten until a historian discovered her rabbinical diploma and thesis in an East Berlin archive in 1991, the archive being newly open to Western researchers because of the end of the Cold War.

On the mystical and esoteric level, meditation on the feminine aspect of divinity continued alongside the mainstream. Perhaps this movement even echoed the old cults of Asherah, Anat, and the Queen of Heaven.

The undercurrent of the goddess manifested most obviously in the mystical system known as the Kabbalah. The earliest known kabbalistic treatises are from medieval Europe, emerging in twelfth-century Jewish communities in Spain and southern France, although certainly compiled from much more ancient texts. Kabbalist tradition traces its mythical origins back to Eden, claiming its doctrines were transmitted down the ages by a select line of initiates. (The existence of a secret, esoteric line of Judaism, whose teachings are not for public consumption, is acknowledged in the Mishnah, the collection of oral traditions compiled in the third century CE that forms part of the Talmud. One of this line was said to be Rabbi Akiva, who declared the Song of Songs the "Holy of Holies" of Hebrew scripture.)

The Shekinah—the presence of God, closely associated with the Holy Spirit—plays an important role in the Kabbalah's cosmology, and is explicitly female. One of the aims of the medieval Kabbalah was to reintegrate her with God: by interrupting the flow of the divine light or creative energy to the material world, their separation had brought sin into the world. This acknowledges the loss of the divine feminine from Judaism—but it also echoes Simon Magus's teaching.

The feminine aspect of God/creation plays an important part in the Kabbalah's Tree of Life. The lowest of the ten sephiroth, where the system reaches completion by manifesting the divine light into the material plane, is *Malkuth*. Although conventionally translated as "Kingship" or "Kingdom," Malkuth is female, and is explicitly identified with the Shekinah.

Making the connections crystal clear, the sixteenth-century Moses of Cordoba, founder of an important kabbalistic school in Galilee, stated that "Kingdom is called Asherah."[13] She is also present in another female deity, the Shekinah. As Patai explains, she is "a distinct female deity, possessing a will and desire of her own, acting independently of the traditional but somewhat shrunken masculine God." She confronts and sometimes even challenges him head-on, even "occasionally . . . playing a greater role than He in the affairs of Her children, the people of Israel."[14] Her dealings with God recall Asherah's way of handling El in the Canaanite mythology.

Rabbi Léah Novick of the Jewish Renewal Movement, which was started in the United States in the 1970s, adds her voice: "The idea of Shekhinah as mother, sister, daughter, and bride emerged with the arrival of the mystical *Sefir Bahir* (Book of Illumination) in medieval Europe, bringing the Divine Feminine into the thinking of the great scholars of that age." It was the goddess's resurgence, no less, though not described as such. Rabbi Novick adds, "Like a shadow figure from behind the curtain, Shekhinah as the Great Lady began to come onto scholarly Judaism's center stage." Rabbi Novick also points out that the late thirteenth-century *Zohar* (Book of Brilliance) audaciously described the Godhead's sexual dynamics, emphasizing the female role in the Tree of Life.[15]

The kabbalistic literature describes a divine tetrad of Father, Mother, Son, and Daughter (associated with the four letters of the Tetragrammaton), emphasizing that the last two were the product of the Father and Mother's sexual union. Raphael Patai sees echoes of the ancient Egyptian Heliopolitan tetrad of Shu and Tefnut and their offspring Geb and Nut.[16] (Remember Karl Luckert drew parallels between the Heliopolitan cosmology and Simon Magus's.)

The kabbalistic texts also have the divine Son and Daughter marrying each other; apparently the divine realm does not recognize the sin of incest. Their marriage is described, very explicitly, in terms reminiscent of the *hieros gamos*—with their sexual positions seen as highly significant on a mystical level.

Among the many names of the divine Daughter were, unsurprisingly, Shekinah and Malkuth. She was also known as Matronit ("Matron" or "Lady"), who Patai describes as the "goddess of the Kabbalah." Matronit has remarkable similarities to the warrior goddess Anat—she has "the same four traits of chastity and promiscuity, motherliness and bloodthirstiness."[17] Her tempestuous relationship—fierce arguments followed by passionate reconciliations—with her brother-husband also resembles Anat and Baal's.

In his *Man and Temple* (1947), Patai relates a kabbalist legend from the *Zohar Chadash* ("New Zohar" or "New Light"), published in the

1580s but based on earlier writings. After the destruction of the Jerusalem Temple, Matronit descends nightly into the ruins of the Holy of Holies in search of her husband. Rather weirdly she addresses her couch:

> in thee came unto me the Lord of the World, my husband, and he would lie in my arms and all that I wished for he would give me. At this hour he used to come unto me, he left his dwelling-place and played betwixt my breasts. My couch, my couch, dost thou not remember how I came to thee rejoicing and happy, and those youths (the Cherubs) came forth to meet me, beating their wings in welcome . . . how came to be forgotten the Ark of the Covenant which stood here.[18]

Matronit is conceived as the wife of the God of the Temple, or Yahweh. And as she is the Daughter of the divine tetrad, and her husband is her brother, he must be God's son. Although this legend is very late it chimes perfectly with ideas that were supposedly suppressed over a millennium and a half previously.

Against all the odds, the Jewish goddess survived.

THE PROBLEM WITH MONOTHEISM

For centuries the worship of just one God has been seen as the ultimate in religious sophistication, exemplifying the progress of civilization. But the most cursory glance at monotheism's track record tells a very different story.

Throughout history humans have almost always worshipped something, or someone. From the earliest cave dwellers to modern sophisticates, priests, shamans, and cults have found rapt believers. During World War Two even the arch-atheist Josef Stalin, despotic opponent of religion in Communist USSR, reopened the churches when the Nazis invaded, to give the people hope and the impetus to fight on. When Hitler's troops were defeated, he closed the churches and forbade the practice of Christianity once again. But he knew there comes a time when the people need God.

However, history shows that it's not so much God people have needed, as *gods*. Polytheism seems to come much more naturally. That's why even in monotheism worshippers include angels and patron saints, each acting like a minor god. Our polytheistic instinct might well have sound psychological and social implications. And we deny it at our peril.

The elevation of one God—and the rejection of all others—creates an "us and them" attitude. It goes hand in hand with intolerance of outsiders or those with a different perspective—though which is the cause and which the effect is quite another question. (And that's not to say that the old pagan cultures were never intolerant and prejudiced; it just seems not to be linked to their religion.)

This is reflected in how, for example, Ezra condemned "foreign" wives after the reformulation of Yahwism into a one-God religion. Then there was the intolerance that followed Theodosius's edict and that characterized Christianity for most of its history—and still does in some places.

Of all types of religion, it is usually monotheism that results in rigid authoritarianism. Very soon the faithful are ruled with a rod of iron and any deviations are punished severely. If on the other hand, the religion is already polytheistic, there is scope within the pantheon of deities for people to pick and choose their own path. Polytheism implies a certain religious freedom that monotheism can never possess.

And as the sad, mad, bad story of the last two millennia makes only too clear, monotheism also encourages a sense of superiority and moral smugness. This is never good, as it can be used to justify all kinds of abuses, especially if some of the deities who are missing from people's lives and hearts are female.

THE COMEBACK: #SHETOO

In the past century or so Westerners have begun to emerge—often hesitantly and shakily—from the shadow of totalitarian belief systems. Certainly in our own country, the distinctly secular United Kingdom, freethinking is taken for granted as a way of life. It has been very hard-earned—it was the trauma of two World Wars that caused many to question religious certainties for the first time—but spiritual freedom here is now largely a given.

Today we can practice any faith, from Islam and Judaism through the various Christian denominations such as Catholicism and Mormonism to "fringe" religions including Theosophy, Wicca, and even Thelema. All without living in fear of the Inquisitor coming to call. That's not to say that religious practices never cause raised eyebrows, while the media still enjoys holding some beliefs, such as reincarnation, up to ridicule.

Few would deny, though, that one sector of society that has benefited most from the new freedom is women. Running parallel with other sorts of equality—education and employment, for example—women are increasingly demanding a voice in synagogues, churches, temples, and covens.

In Judaism there has been an upsurge in women rabbis and in many forms of Christianity a new wave of female ministers, even bishops. (Though of course, Peter's Catholic Church is still absolutely male-dominated. He would be so proud.)

Away from the mainstream religions—and even aside from female-friendly faiths such as Wicca—ordinary women have been quietly discovering the goddess for themselves. As we have pointed out, much of the change in popular perception of the role of women in Christianity—particularly Mary Magdalene—began with critically derided "alternative" books such as *Holy Blood, Holy Grail* and *The Templar Revelation*. Almost a generation later, it was *The Da Vinci Code* that seized the imagination and made women reconsider not only Mary's real status but also their own. Individual readers can have their own relationship with the goddess, knowing this is not new, but hallowed by the ages.

She was here. She was abandoned and defiled. But now she is back . . .

However, her return was not random or unexpected. As we have shown, even the most spiritual beliefs need a political and historical framework. It's rarely appreciated that even the return of the goddess has been driven by academic and archaeological research—even if most people only know about it through alternative books and even fiction. Her historical roots give her substance.

Think of the archaeological discoveries about Asherah that seriously changed our view of the Israelite religion. As William G. Dever observes (his italics): "in time orthodoxy drove the Great Mother underground, where she was almost forgotten for centuries, until popular piety *and* archaeology rediscovered and revived her. Asherah, in whatever guise, appears to be alive and well."[19]

She does indeed have many guises. But call her Asherah. Call her Isis. See her priestesses clamor for recognition across the millennia— Mary, called Magdalene; Helen the prostitute; and many more whose names we will never know, besides their devoted priests. We honor them by trying to get their stories right. And by welcoming them into the twenty-first century, we implicitly salute all those women who suffered neglect, humiliation, abuse, and hideous death over the years. For how we treat women is how we treat the goddess—but not just women . . .

There is something else to bear in mind, which many goddess-worshipping modern feminists often choose to ignore. If by ignoring Mary Magdalene people were insulting Jesus Christ, who clearly longed for her to be admired and loved by the whole world, then this also works the other way. He was her Lord, her other half, the essential male balance to her female power, as she was to his. Asherah had her Yahweh. Isis had her Osiris. Helen had her Simon. Whatever they were about, it centered on *balance* between the opposite and equal powers of the two. After Helen was saved, she partnered the Magus. Magdalene anointed Jesus and the couple then shared a mission, as the gnostic gospels make clear. Even Asherah and El were once a team, as were Yahweh and the Shekinah. The story we have traced shows a perpetual yin-yang-like balance to be cosmically important.

And what the world needs now more than anything is balance. But as ever, hidden in the story of the goddess is the secret of how to make it happen.

Notes

CHAPTER ONE. OUT OF EGYPT

1. Dever, *Early Israelites,* 8.
2. Dever, *Early Israelites,* 150.
3. Dever, *Did God Have a Wife?,* 70.
4. Brenner, *The Israelite Woman,* 17.
5. Exodus 15:20–21. All Bible references are to the English Standard Version (ESV).
6. McCarter, "Exodus," 146.
7. Numbers 12.
8. Brenner, *The Israelite Woman,* 55.
9. Exum, "Judges," 250.
10. Judges 5.
11. Exum, "Judges," 250.
12. Brenner, *The Israelite Woman,* 55.
13. Exodus 38:8.
14. 1 Samuel 2:22.
15. Numbers 25.
16. Exodus 12:37.
17. McCarter, "Exodus," 132.
18. Dever, *Early Israelites,* 19.
19. Dever, *Early Israelites,* 45–46; Stager, "Forging an Identity," 129.
20. Stager, "Forging an Identity," 129.
21. Stager, "Forging an Identity," 129–31.
22. Stager, "Forging an Identity," 130–34.

23. Stager, "Forging an Identity," 134.

24. Dever, *Early Israelites,* 98.

25. Kitchen, review of *Egypt, Canaan, and Israel in Ancient Times,* 124.

26. Dever, *Biblical Writers,* 266.

27. Feather, *Where Moses Stood,* 10.

28. Numbers 25:13.

29. 1 Samuel 4:1–10.

30. Mark S. Smith, *Origins of Biblical Monotheism,* 147.

31. Genesis 46:11.

32. Albright, *Stone Age to Christianity,* 282.

33. Genesis 48.

34. Hooke, "Genesis," 198.

35. Dever, *Early Israelites,* 230.

36. Dever, *Early Israelites,* 231.

37. Joshua 24:25–27.

38. Hooke, "Genesis," 199.

39. Rast, "Joshua," 243.

40. Judges 9:46.

41. Dever, *Did God Have a Wife?,* 167–70.

42. Schama, *The Story of the Jews,* 16.

43. Albright, *Stone Age to Christianity,* 266.

44. Kitchen, review of *Egypt, Canaan, and Israel in Ancient Times,* 124.

45. Hancock, *The Sign and the Seal,* 288.

46. Niehr, "In Search of YHWH's Cult Statue in the First Temple," 82.

47. Exodus 25:17–22.

48. Botterweck, Ringgren, and Fabry, *Theological Dictionary of the Old Testament,* 315.

49. Dever, *Biblical Writers,* 150.

50. Hancock, *The Sign and the Seal,* 288.

51. Patai, *Hebrew Goddess,* 68, plate 26.

52. Redford, *Egypt, Canaan, and Israel in Ancient Times,* 378.

53. Exodus 15:11.

54. Exodus 20:3.

55. Dever, *Did God Have a Wife?,* 263.

56. Dever, *Did God Have a Wife?,* 263.

57. Schama, *The Story of the Jews,* 47.

58. Isaiah 44:6.

59. Sanders, *The Provenance of Deuteronomy 32*, 426.

60. Sanders, *The Provenance of Deuteronomy 32*, 371.

61. John Day, *Yahweh and the Gods and Goddesses of Canaan*, 22.

62. Genesis 6:1–4.

63. Psalms 82:6–7.

64. 1 Kings 22; Isaiah 6.

65. Dijkstra, "El, the God of Israel," 100.

66. Mark S. Smith, *Origins of Biblical Monotheism*, 145.

67. E.g., Peggy L. Day, *Gender Difference in Ancient Israel*, chapter 1.

68. McLaughlin, *What Are They Saying about Ancient Israelite Religion?*, 6–7.

69. Dever, *Did God Have a Wife?*, 259.

70. Sanders, *The Provenance of Deuteronomy 32*, 371.

71. Deuteronomy 32:8–9.

72. Exodus 33:20.

73. Lang, *Hebrew God*, 207.

74. See Cornelius, "The Many Images of God"; Niehr, "In Search of YHWH's Cult Statue in the First Temple."

75. Quoted in Luckert, *Egyptian Light and Hebrew Fire*, 112.

76. Pritchard, *Ancient Near Eastern Texts Relating to the Old Testament*, 12–18.

77. Quoted in Luckert, *Egyptian Light and Hebrew Fire*, 111.

78. Pritchard, *Ancient Near Eastern Texts Relating to the Old Testament*, 368.

79. Luckert, *Egyptian Light and Hebrew Fire*, 112.

80. Sheafer, *Ramses the Great*, 55.

81. Traunecker, *The Gods of Egypt*, 88–89.

82. Luckert, *Egyptian Light and Hebrew Fire*, 130.

83. Cited in Gnuse, *No Other Gods*, 165.

84. Luckert, *Egyptian Light and Hebrew Fire*, 135.

85. Schama, *The Story of the Jews*, 35–36.

86. John Day, *Yahweh and the Gods and Goddesses of Canaan*, 228.

CHAPTER TWO. THE DIVINE CONSORT

1. Dever, *Did God Have a Wife?*, 208.

2. Exodus 34:13.

3. Deuteronomy 16:21.

4. Dever, *Did God Have a Wife?*, 215.

5. Patai, *Hebrew Goddess*, 25.

6. Olyan, *Asherah and the Cult of Yahweh in Israel*, 16.

7. Olyan, *Asherah and the Cult of Yahweh in Israel*, 3.

8. Mark S. Smith, *Early History of God*, 80.

9. Korpel, "Asherah outside Israel," 130.

10. Korpel, "Asherah outside Israel," 137.

11. Becking and Dijkstra, introduction to *Only One God?*, 13.

12. 2 Kings 21:7.

13. Olyan, *Asherah and the Cult of Yahweh in Israel*, 5–6.

14. Mark S. Smith, *Origins of Biblical Monotheism*, 47.

15. Dever, *Did God Have a Wife?*, 225.

16. Dever, *Did God Have a Wife?*, 227.

17. Ackerman, *Under Every Green Tree*, 191.

18. Hadley, *The Cult of Asherah in Ancient Israel and Judah*, 187.

19. Dijkstra, "I Have Blessed You by YHWH of Samaria and his Asherah," 33.

20. Lemaire, "Date et origine des Inscriptions Hebraiques et Pheniciennes de Kuntillet 'Ajrud," 139.

21. Dever, *Did God Have a Wife?*, 163.

22. Dijkstra, "I Have Blessed You by YHWH of Samaria and his Asherah," 27.

23. Dijkstra, "I Have Blessed You by YHWH of Samaria and his Asherah," 27.

24. Schama, *The Story of the Jews*, 16.

25. Freedman, "'Who Is Like Thee Among the Gods?,'" 322.

26. Genesis 49:25.

27. Freedman, "'Who Is Like Thee Among the Gods?,'" 325.

28. Deuteronomy 33:2.

29. Dijkstra, "El, the God of Israel," 115.

30. Dijkstra, "El, the God of Israel," 115.

31. Ackerman, *Under Every Green Tree*, 35.

32. Olyan, *Asherah and the Cult of Yahweh in Israel*, 34.

33. 1 Kings 3:2–3.

34. Luckert, *Egyptian Light and Hebrew Fire*, 143.

35. Luckert, *Egyptian Light and Hebrew Fire*, 157.

36. 1 Kings 7:19.

37. Dever, *Biblical Writers*, 152.

38. Patai, *Hebrew Goddess*, 72.

39. Keel, *The Symbolism of the Biblical World*, 166.

40. 1 Kings 11:4.

41. 1 Samuel 9:9.

42. Andersen and Freedman, *Hosea,* 31.

43. Lang, *Monotheism,* 54.

44. Morton Smith, *Palestinian Parties and Politics that Shaped the Old Testament,* 31.

45. Lang, *Monotheism,* 30.

46. Micah 4:5.

47. 1 Kings 14:15.

48. 2 Kings 23:15.

49. Patai, *Hebrew Goddess,* 42.

50. Freedman, "'Who Is Like Thee Among the Gods?,'" 326.

51. Cross, *Canaanite Myth and Hebrew Epic,* 75.

52. E.g., 2 Kings 17:10.

53. 1 Kings 16:33.

54. 1 Kings 18:19.

55. Olyan, *Asherah and the Cult of Yahweh in Israel,* 8.

56. Hackett, "Jezebel," 150.

57. 2 Kings 13:6.

58. Patai, *Hebrew Goddess,* 43.

59. Olyan, *Asherah and the Cult of Yahweh in Israel,* 7.

60. Becking, *The Fall of Samaria,* 29.

61. 1 Kings 14:23–24.

62. 1 Kings 15:13.

63. 2 Chronicles 15:8.

64. 2 Chronicles 17:6.

65. 2 Chronicles 24:18.

66. 2 Kings 18:4.

67. 2 Kings 21:7.

68. Dever, *Did God Have a Wife?,* 212.

69. Ackerman, *Under Every Green Tree,* 212.

70. Patai, *Hebrew Goddess,* 50.

71. Dever, *Biblical Writers,* 197.

72. Lemche, *Ancient Israel,* 165.

73. Gnuse, *No Other Gods,* 177.

74. Patai, *Hebrew Goddess,* 50.

75. 2 Kings 21:7.

76. Dever, *Did God Have a Wife?,* 213–14.

77. 1 Kings 14:23–24.

CHAPTER 3. ISRAEL'S HIDDEN PRIESTESSES

1. Deuteronomy 23:17.
2. Ackerman, *Warrior, Dancer, Seductress, Queen,* 138–39.
3. Ackerman, *Warrior, Dancer, Seductress, Queen,* 154.
4. Bird, "The Place of Women in the Israelite Cultus," 407.
5. Camp, *Wisdom and the Feminine,* 116.
6. Quoted in Lang, *Wisdom,* 126.
7. Bird, "The Place of Women in the Israelite Cultus," 407.
8. Meyers, *Discovering Eve,* 91.
9. de Boer, "The Counsellor," 43.
10. de Boer, "The Counsellor," 59.
11. de Boer, "The Counsellor," 59.
12. 2 Samuel 20:14–22.
13. de Boer, "The Counsellor," 60.
14. 2 Samuel 14.
15. Camp, "Wise Women of 2 Samuel," 24.
16. 2 Samuel 20:19, 14:13.
17. Camp, "Wise Women of 2 Samuel," 14–15.
18. Quoted in Patai, *Hebrew Goddess,* 86.
19. Mann and Lyle, *Sacred Sexuality,* 6.
20. Mann and Lyle, *Sacred Sexuality,* 8.
21. Qualls-Corbett, *The Sacred Prostitute,* 39.
22. Mann and Lyle, *Sacred Sexuality,* 114.
23. Exodus 34:15; Jeremiah 3:9.
24. 1 Kings 14:24.
25. 1 Kings 15:12, 22:46.
26. 2 Kings 23:7.
27. Job 36:13–14.
28. Genesis 38:6–26.
29. van der Toorn, *From Her Cradle to Her Grave,* 103.
30. Hosea 4:14.
31. Dever, *Did God Have a Wife?,* 217.
32. Dijkstra, "El, the God of Israel," 116.
33. Dijkstra, "Women and Religion in the Old Testament," 177.
34. Bird, "The End of the Male Cult Prostitute," 46.
35. Haar, *Simon Magus,* 270.

36. Haar, *Simon Magus,* 270.

37. Hosea 2:2.

38. Scott, *Sophia and the Johannine Jesus,* 45.

39. Scott, *Sophia and the Johannine Jesus,* 45.

40. Ruether, *Sexism and God-Talk,* 25.

CHAPTER FOUR. GODDESSES TO BE RECKONED WITH

1. Jeremiah 3:9.

2. Jeremiah 2:20.

3. Jeremiah 3:11.

4. Jeremiah 44:15–19.

5. John Day, *Yahweh and the Gods and Goddesses of Canaan,* 148.

6. Jeremiah 7:16–18.

7. John Day, *Yahweh and the Gods and Goddesses of Canaan,* 131; Dever, *Did God Have a Wife?,* 133; Ackerman, *Under Every Green Tree,* 20–28.

8. Patai, *Hebrew Goddess,* 54–55.

9. Handy, *Among the Host of Heaven,* 103.

10. Niehr, "In Search of YHWH's Cult Statue in the First Temple," 79.

11. Porten et al., *The Elephantine Papyri in English,* 125.

12. MacLaurin, "Date of the Foundation of the Jewish Colony at Elephantine," 92.

13. MacLaurin, "Date of the Foundation of the Jewish Colony at Elephantine," 90.

14. John Day, *Yahweh and the Gods and Goddesses of Canaan,* 143–44.

15. van der Toorn, "Goddesses in Early Israelite Religion," 87.

16. Patai, *Hebrew Goddess,* 60–61.

17. Patai, *Hebrew Goddess,* 61.

18. Dever, *Did God Have a Wife?,* 270.

19. Quoted in Mark S. Smith, *Early History of God,* 61–62.

20. Quoted in Walls, *The Goddess Anat in Ugaritic Myth,* 178.

21. Cross, *Canaanite Myth and Hebrew Epic,* 118.

22. Patai, *Hebrew Goddess,* 61.

23. Westenholz, "Goddesses in the Ancient Near East 3000–1000 BC," 79.

24. Walls, *The Goddess Anat in Ugaritic Myth,* 203.

25. Albright, *Yahweh,* 112.

26. Albright, *Yahweh,* 114.

27. Walls, *The Goddess Anat in Ugaritic Myth,* 53.

28. Walls, *The Goddess Anat in Ugaritic Myth,* 53.

29. Dijkstra, "Women and Religion in the Old Testament," 178.

30. Peggy L. Day, "Anat," 181.

31. Peggy L. Day, "Anat," 188–89.

32. Peggy L. Day, "Anat," 189.

33. Mark S. Smith, *Early History of God,* 61.

34. Ackerman, *Warrior, Dancer, Seductress, Queen,* 51.

35. Judges 1:33.

36. Judges 3:31.

37. Judges 5:6–8.

38. Schloen, "Caravans, Kenites, and *Casus Belli,*" 20.

39. Meindert Dijkstra, "Women and Religion in the Old Testament," in Becking, *Only One God?* 178.

40. Brenner, *The Israelite Woman,* 52.

41. 1 Samuel 18:6.

42. Dijkstra, "Women and Religion in the Old Testament," in Becking, *Only One God?* 179–80.

43. Dijkstra, "Women and Religion in the Old Testament," in Becking, *Only One God?* 178.

44. Judges 4:4.

45. Judges 4:9.

46. Ackerman, *Warrior, Dancer, Seductress, Queen,* 58–59.

47. Mazar, "The Sanctuary of Arad and the Family of Hobab the Kenite," 301–2.

48. Ackerman, *Warrior, Dancer, Seductress, Queen,* 92–96.

49. Mazar, "The Sanctuary of Arad and the Family of Hobab the Kenite," 302.

50. Judges 5:24–27.

51. Niditch, "Eroticism and Death in the Tale of Jael," 45.

52. Niditch, "Eroticism and Death in the Tale of Jael," 47.

53. Niditch, "Eroticism and Death in the Tale of Jael," 47.

54. Niditch, "Eroticism and Death in the Tale of Jael," 47.

55. Niditch, "Eroticism and Death in the Tale of Jael," 49.

56. Jeremiah 4:30.

57. Niditch, "Eroticism and Death in the Tale of Jael," 50.

58. Niditch, "Eroticism and Death in the Tale of Jael," 45.

59. Judges 5:30.

60. Dempster, "Mythology and History in the Song of Deborah," 43–44.

61. Ackerman, *Warrior, Dancer, Seductress, Queen,* 61.

62. Ackerman, *Warrior, Dancer, Seductress, Queen,* 5.

CHAPTER FIVE. SOPHIA'S SECRETS

1. McEvenue, "Who Was Second Isaiah?" 215–16.

2. McLaughlin, *What Are They Saying about Ancient Israelite Religion?*, 91.

3. Gnuse, *No Other Gods,* 208, 223.

4. McLaughlin, *What Are They Saying about Ancient Israelite Religion?*, 97.

5. Lemche, *Ancient Israel,* 177; Albertz, *A History of Israelite Religion,* 2:369–72.

6. Ackerman, *Under Every Green Tree,* 214.

7. Ackerman, *Under Every Green Tree,* 216.

8. Camp, *Wise, Strange and Holy,* 30.

9. Camp, *Wise, Strange and Holy,* 30–31.

10. Nehemiah 6:14.

11. Nehemiah 9:6.

12. Stern, "What Happened to the Cult Figurines?," 54.

13. Schama, *The Story of the Jews,* 36.

14. Camp, *Wise, Strange and Holy,* 32.

15. Camp, *Wise, Strange and Holy,* 40–41.

16. Schama, *The Story of the Jews,* 41.

17. Ackerman, "'And the Women Knead Dough,'" 118.

18. Quoted in Pope, *Song of Songs,* 19.

19. Ruether, *Sexism and God-Talk,* 139–40.

20. Marttila and Pajunen, "Wisdom, Israel and Other Nations," 6.

21. Lang, "Wisdom," 901.

22. Lang, "Wisdom," 900.

23. Hadley, "Wisdom and the Goddess," 236.

24. Handy, *Among the Host of Heaven,* 82–83.

25. Proverbs 3:18.

26. Proverbs 3:19.

27. Murphy, "The Personification of Wisdom," 229.

28. Proverbs 8:22–26.

29. Hadley, "Wisdom and the Goddess," 237.

30. Proverbs 8:30–31.

31. Lang, "Wisdom," 65–66; Murphy, "The Personification of Wisdom," 225.

32. See Hadley, "Wisdom and the Goddess," 238.

33. Lang, "Wisdom," 79.

34. Camp, *Wise, Strange and Holy,* 13–14.

35. Camp, *Wise, Strange and Holy,* 14.

36. Camp, *Wise, Strange and Holy*, 44.

37. Proverbs 7:14–15.

38. Proverbs 7:22–23.

39. Proverbs 8:35.

40. Proverbs 9:10.

41. Murphy, "The Personification of Wisdom," 236.

42. Proverbs 8:15–16.

43. Camp, *Wise, Strange and Holy*, 33.

44. Lang, "Wisdom," 903.

45. Albertz and Becking, *Yahwism After the Exile*, xi.

46. Kloppenborg, "Isis and Sophia in the Book of Wisdom," 58.

47. Patai, *Hebrew Goddess*, 26.

48. Assmann, "Isis," 457.

49. Assmann, "Isis," 457.

50. Murphy, "The Personification of Wisdom," 223.

51. Kloppenborg, "Isis and Sophia in the Book of Wisdom," 67.

52. Wisdom of Solomon 7:21. References to the Wisdom of Solomon and Book of Ben Sira are from the Catholic Public Domain Version of the Bible (CPDV).

53. Hurtado, *One God, One Lord*, 44.

54. Ringgren, *Word and Wisdom*, 115.

55. Ringgren, *Word and Wisdom*, 115.

56. Wisdom of Solomon 8:3.

57. Murphy, "The Personification of Wisdom," 230.

58. Wisdom of Solomon 8:9.

59. Kloppenborg, "Isis and Sophia in the Book of Wisdom," 76; Lang, "Wisdom," 900.

60. Kloppenborg, "Isis and Sophia in the Book of Wisdom," 78.

61. Marttila and Pajunen, "Wisdom, Israel and Other Nations," 10; Ringgren, *Word and Wisdom*, 145–46.

62. Sirach 24:22.

63. Sirach 24:5, 24:14.

64. Hurtado, *One God, One Lord*, 42.

65. Hurtado, *One God, One Lord*, 44.

66. Sirach 24:12–13.

67. Ringgren, *Word and Wisdom*, 124.

68. Philo, *Questions and Answers on Genesis*, 150.

69. Deuteronomy 34:9.

70. Geo Widengren, quoted in Ringgren, *Word and Wisdom*, 165.

71. Genesis 1:2.
72. Sirach 1:9.
73. Wisdom of Solomon 7:25.
74. Wisdom of Solomon 9:17.
75. Sirach 50:28.
76. The Testament of Levi, quoted in Purvis, "Ben Sira and the Foolish People of Shechem," 89.
77. Knoppers, *Jews and Samaritans,* 5.
78. Knoppers, *Jews and Samaritans,* 32; Cogan, *Imperialism and Religion,* 111.
79. 1 Maccabees 14:41 (RSV).
80. Deuteronomy 18:15.

CHAPTER SIX. "THE GREAT REVELATION"

1. Cartlidge, "The Fall and Rise of Simon Magus," 24.
2. Cartlidge, "The Fall and Rise of Simon Magus," 26.
3. Cartlidge, "The Fall and Rise of Simon Magus," 24–26.
4. Ambrose, "The Fall of Simon Magus on a Capital at Vézelay," 157.
5. Price, *The Pre-Nicene New Testament,* 38–40.
6. Price, *The Pre-Nicene New Testament,* 38–39.
7. Price, *The Pre-Nicene New Testament,* 38.
8. Mead, *Simon Magus,* 20.
9. Price, *The Pre-Nicene New Testament,* 44.
10. Morton Smith, "The Account of Simon Magus in Acts 8," in Lieberman, Spiegel, Strauss and Hyman, 2:742.
11. Luckert, *Egyptian Light and Hebrew Fire,* 300–304.
12. Jonas, *The Gnostic Religion,* 105.
13. Price, *The Pre-Nicene New Testament,* 41.
14. Price, *The Pre-Nicene New Testament,* 41.
15. Mead, *Simon Magus,* 19.
16. Price, *The Pre-Nicene New Testament,* 45.
17. Mead, *Simon Magus,* 21.
18. Mead, *Simon Magus,* 21.
19. Price, *The Pre-Nicene New Testament,* 43.
20. Luke 3:9; Matthew 3:10.
21. Mead, *Simon Magus,* 48.
22. See Picknett and Prince, *Masks of Christ,* 293–94, 362.

23. Acts 8:9–24.

24. Morton Smith, "The Account of Simon Magus in Acts 8," in Lieberman, Spiegel, Strauss and Hyman, 2:741.

25. See Kent, "Curses in Acts."

26. Strelan, *Strange Acts,* 213.

27. Conner, *Magic in Christianity,* 346.

28. Haar, *Simon Magus,* 192.

29. Haar, *Simon Magus,* 193.

30. Haar, *Simon Magus,* 158.

31. Cartlidge, "The Fall and Rise of Simon Magus," 26–27.

32. Conner, *Magic in Christianity,* 407.

33. See Picknett and Prince, *Masks of Christ,* 200–201, 222–24. For the current state of research in this area, see Conner, *Magic in Christianity.*

34. Cartlidge, "The Fall and Rise of Simon Magus," 27–28.

35. Black, *The Scrolls and Christian Origins,* 64, 81.

36. Lüdemann, "The Acts of the Apostles," 424.

37. Haar, *Simon Magus,* 263.

38. Haar, *Simon Magus,* 2.

39. Mead, *Simon Magus,* 9–10.

40. Quoted in Haar, *Simon Magus,* 267.

41. Quoted in Haar, *Simon Magus,* 278.

42. Quoted in Haar, *Simon Magus,* 129.

43. Quoted in Haar, *Simon Magus,* 2.

44. Haar, *Simon Magus,* 102.

45. Origen, *Contra Celsum,* 53, 325.

46. Quoted in Pummer, *Early Christian Authors,* 122.

47. Mead, *Simon Magus,* 24.

48. Quoted in Haar, *Simon Magus,* 106.

49. Mead, *Simon Magus,* 25.

50. Quoted in Haar, *Simon Magus,* 104.

51. Fossum, "Simonian Sophia Myth," 185.

52. Quoted in Cartlidge, "The Fall and Rise of Simon Magus," 28.

53. Pick, *The Apocryphal Acts of Paul, Peter, John, Andrew and Thomas,* 93.

54. Haar, *Simon Magus,* 275.

55. Jones, *An Ancient Jewish Christian Source on the History of Christianity,* 2.

56. Pummer, *Early Christian Authors,* 103.

57. Eisenmann, *James the Brother of Jesus,* 603.

58. Schneemelcher, *New Testament Apocrypha,* 2:512.

59. Schneemelcher, *New Testament Apocrypha,* 2:513.

60. Schneemelcher, *New Testament Apocrypha,* 2:513.

61. Schneemelcher, *New Testament Apocrypha,* 2:515.

62. Schneemelcher, *New Testament Apocrypha,* 2:515.

63. Schneemelcher, *New Testament Apocrypha,* 2:516.

64. Schneemelcher, *New Testament Apocrypha,* 2:516.

65. Haar, *Simon Magus,* 285.

66. Fossum, "Simonian Sophia Myth," 186.

67. Salles-Dabadie, *Recherche sur Simon le Mage,* 84–88.

68. Haar, *Simon Magus,* 287–89; Daniélou, *A History of Early Christian Doctrine Before the Council of Nicaea,* 72.

69. Luckert, *Egyptian Light and Hebrew Fire,* 300.

70. See Picknett and Prince, *Forbidden Universe,* chapter 7.

71. Luckert, *Egyptian Light and Hebrew Fire,* 303.

72. Fossum, "Simonian Sophia Myth," 191.

73. Mead, *Simon Magus,* 39.

74. Fossum, "Simonian Sophia Myth," 188.

75. Haar, *Simon Magus,* 88.

76. Fossum, "Simonian Sophia Myth," 188.

77. Haar, *Simon Magus,* 267.

78. Fossum, "Simonian Sophia Myth," 194.

79. Fossum, "Simonian Sophia Myth," 194.

80. Luckert, *Egyptian Light and Hebrew Fire,* 307.

81. Luckert, *Egyptian Light and Hebrew Fire,* 305.

82. Origen, *Contra Celsum,* 52.

83. Quoted by Chadwick in note in Origen, *Contra Celsum,* 325.

84. Quoted by Chadwick in note in Origen, *Contra Celsum,* 325.

85. MacDonald, *The Theology of the Samaritans,* 34.

86. See Picknett and Prince, *Masks of Christ,* 251–54.

87. Pummer, *The Samaritans,* 120.

88. Schneemelcher, *New Testament Apocrypha,* 2:512–13.

89. Origen, *Contra Celsum,* 325.

90. Fossum, *Name of God,* 55; Haar, *Simon Magus,* 275.

91. Fossum, *Name of God,* 120.

92. Fossum, *Name of God,* 114.

93. Roberts and Donaldson, *Ante-Nicene Christian Library,* 3:197.

94. Jonas, *The Gnostic Religion,* 109.

95. This is discussed more fully in Picknett and Prince, *Masks of Christ,* 384–86.

96. See Picknett and Prince, *Masks of Christ,* chapter 7.

97. Acts 18:24–28, 19:1–7.

98. See Picknett and Prince, *Templar Revelation,* chapter 15; Picknett and Prince, *Masks of Christ,* 254–60.

99. Morton Smith, "The Account of Simon Magus in Acts 8," in Lieberman, Spiegel, Strauss and Hyman, 2:739.

100. See Picknett and Prince, *Masks of Christ,* 143–44.

101. Haar, *Simon Magus,* 1.

102. Jonas, *The Gnostic Religion,* 110.

103. Morton Smith, "The Account of Simon Magus in Acts 8," in Lieberman, Spiegel, Strauss, and Hyman, 2:737.

104. Haar, *Simon Magus,* 33.

105. Luckert, *Egyptian Light and Hebrew Fire,* 299.

106. Luckert, *Egyptian Light and Hebrew Fire,* 299–300.

CHAPTER SEVEN. JESUS AND HIS GODDESS

1. Romer, *Testament,* 194.

2. See Laible, "Jesus Christ in the Talmud."

3. Fiorenza, *In Memory of Her,* 134.

4. Scott, *Sophia and the Johannine Jesus,* 83.

5. Scott, *Sophia and the Johannine Jesus,* 86.

6. Crossan, *Who Killed Jesus?,* 26.

7. Luke 11:49.

8. Matthew 23:34.

9. See Picknett, *Mary Magdalene,* prologue.

10. 1 Corinthians 5:8.

11. Mark 15:40.

12. Phipps, *Sexuality of Jesus,* 53.

13. Luke 8:3.

14. E.g., Luke 12:33.

15. E.g., Witherington, *Women in the Ministry of Jesus,* 117.

16. On the problems with the bloodline theory, see Picknett and Prince, *Sion Revelation,* 273–81.

17. Quoted in Phipps, *Was Jesus Married?,* 1.

18. Starbird, *The Woman with the Alabaster Jar,* 41–43.

19. Baigent, Leigh, and Lincoln, *Holy Blood, Holy Grail,* 333–34.

20. Witherington, *Women in the Ministry of Jesus,* 101; Scott, *Sophia and the Johannine Jesus,* 200.

21. Luke 10:39. On it meaning "disciple," see Witherington, *Women in the Ministry of Jesus,* 101.

22. Luke 7:37.

23. Phipps, *Sexuality of Jesus,* 69.

24. Fiorenza, *In Memory of Her,* xiii.

25. Scott, *Sophia and the Johannine Jesus,* 210–11.

26. Ruth 3:7.

27. Robinson, *The Nag Hammadi Library in English,* 525.

28. Robinson, *The Nag Hammadi Library in English,* 524.

29. Leloup, *The Gospel of Mary Magdalene,* 6.

30. *Pistis Sophia,* 135.

31. Robinson, *The Nag Hammadi Library in English,* 138.

32. Cullmann, "The Significance of the Qumran Texts for Research into the Beginnings of Christianity," 19. (Originally published in the *Journal of Biblical Literature* in 1955.)

33. Schneemelcher, *New Testament Apocrypha,* 2:532.

34. Matthew 11:11. The phrase (worded slightly differently) is also in Luke (7:28), showing that it was originally in Q.

35. Roberts and Donaldson, *Ante-Nicene Christian Library,* 3:182.

36. Jones, *An Ancient Jewish Christian Source on the History of Christianity,* 129. See also Fossum, *Name of God,* 114–15.

37. Price, *The Pre-Nicene New Testament,* 999.

38. Wilson, *The Gospel of Philip,* 35.

39. Wilson, *The Gospel of Philip,* 41.

40. Wilson, *The Gospel of Philip,* 39–40.

41. Haar, *Simon Magus,* 270.

42. Revelation 2:14–16.

43. Revelation 2:6.

44. Acts 6:5.

45. Williams, *The Panarion of Epiphanius of Salamis,* 77.

46. Robinson, *The Nag Hammadi Library in English,* 295.

47. Layton, *The Gnostic Scriptures,* 77–78.

48. Price, *The Pre-Nicene New Testament,* 788.

49. Layton, *The Gnostic Scriptures,* 80.

50. Robinson, *The Nag Hammadi Library in English,* 295.

51. Haar, *Simon Magus,* 269.

52. Haar, *Simon Magus,* 269.

53. Luckert, *Egyptian Light and Hebrew Fire,* 307.

54. Mark 2:19; Luke 5:34; Matthew 9:15.

55. Wilson, *The Gospel of Philip,* 21.

56. Scott, *Sophia and the Johannine Jesus,* 14.

57. Scott, *Sophia and the Johannine Jesus,* 129.

58. Scott, *Sophia and the Johannine Jesus,* 114.

59. John 1:1–3.

60. Black, *Aramaic Approach,* 149–50; Dodd, *The Interpretation of the Fourth Gospel,* 9.

61. See Picknett and Prince, *Masks of Christ,* 48–50.

62. George Witterschein, introduction to Gaus, *The Unvarnished New Testament,* 15–16.

63. John 4:1–42.

64. Scott, *Sophia and the Johannine Jesus,* 191.

65. Scott, *Sophia and the Johannine Jesus,* 188, 196.

66. John 4:37–38.

67. Lincoln, *The Gospel According to Saint John,* 171–81; Scott, *Sophia and the Johannine Jesus,* 239.

68. Lincoln, *The Gospel According to Saint John,* 172.

69. John 20:17.

70. Phipps, *Sexuality of Jesus,* 59.

71. 1 Corinthians 7:1.

72. Scott, *Sophia and the Johannine Jesus,* 238–39.

73. Scott, *Sophia and the Johannine Jesus,* 239.

74. Luke 12:10.

75. Price, *The Pre-Nicene New Testament,* 807–8.

76. Wilson, *The Gospel of Philip,* 31.

EPILOGUE. EQUAL RITES

1. Fox, *Pagans and Christians,* 373.

2. Fox, *Pagans and Christians,* 355.

3. Fox, *Pagans and Christians,* 308–10.

4. Cullmann, "The Significance of the Qumran Texts for Research into the Beginnings of Christianity," 26.

5. Black, *The Scrolls and Christian Origins*, 5.

6. Fox, *Pagans and Christians*, 266.

7. Fox, *Pagans and Christians*, 205.

8. Freeman, *AD 381*, 199.

9. Schaberg, *The Illegitimacy of Jesus*, 12.

10. Fiorenza, "Wisdom Mythology and the Christological Hymns of the New Testament," 35.

11. See Picknett and Prince, *Templar Revelation*, chapters 3 and 4.

12. Newman, *From Virile Woman to WomanChrist*, 172–81.

13. Quoted in Patai, *Hebrew Goddess*, 295.

14. Patai, *Hebrew Goddess*, 32.

15. Novick, *On the Wings of Shekhinah*, 7–8.

16. Patai, *Hebrew Goddess*, 118, 123.

17. Patai, *Hebrew Goddess*, 139.

18. Patai, *Man and Temple*, 92–93.

19. Dever, *Did God Have a Wife?*, 303.

Bibliography

Ackerman, Susan. "'And the Women Knead Dough': The Worship of the Queen of Heaven in Sixth-Century Judah." In *Gender Difference in Ancient Israel,* edited by Peggy L. Day. Minneapolis, Minn.: Fortress Press, 1989.

———. *Under Every Green Tree: Popular Religion in Sixth-Century Judah.* Atlanta, Ga.: Scholars Press, 1992.

———. *Warrior, Dancer, Seductress, Queen: Women in Judges and Biblical Israel.* New York: Doubleday, 1998.

Albertz, Rainer. *A History of Israelite Religion in the Old Testament Period.* 2 vols. London: SCM Press, 1994.

Albertz, Rainer, and Bob Becking. *Yahwism After the Exile: Perspectives on Israelite Religion in the Persian Era.* Assen, Netherlands: Royal Van Gorgum, 2003.

Albright, William Foxwell. *From the Stone Age to Christianity: Monotheism and the Historical Process.* Baltimore, Md.: Johns Hopkins Press, 1957.

———. *Yahweh and the Gods of Canaan: A Historical Analysis of Two Contrasting Faiths.* London: Athlone Press, 1968.

Ambrose, Kirk. "The Fall of Simon Magus on a Capital at Vézelay." *Gazette des Beaux-Arts* 137, no. 1587 (2001): 151–66.

Andersen, Francis I., and David Noel Freedman. *Hosea: A New Translation with Introduction and Commentary.* New Haven, Conn.: Yale University Press, 1980.

Assmann, Jan. "Isis." In *Dictionary of Deities and Demons in the Bible,* edited by Karel van der Toorn, Bob Becking, and Pieter W. van der Horst. Grand Rapids, Mich.: William B. Eerdmans Publishing, 1995.

Baigent, Michael, Richard Leigh, and Henry Lincoln. *Holy Blood, Holy Grail.* New York: Dell, 1983.

Becking, Bob. *The Fall of Samaria: An Historical and Archaeological Study.* Leiden, Netherlands: E.J. Brill, 1992.

Becking, Bob, Meindert Dijkstra, Marjo C. A. Korpel, and Karel J. H. Vriezen. *Only One God?: Monotheism in Ancient Egypt and the Veneration of the Goddess Asherah.* New York: Sheffield Academic Press, 2001.

Bird, Phyllis. "The End of the Male Cult Prostitute: A Literary-Historical and Sociological Analysis of Hebrew *Qades-Qedesim.*" In *Congress Volume: Cambridge 1995,* edited by J. A. Emerton. Leiden, Netherlands: Brill, 1997.

———. "The Place of Women in the Israelite Cultus." In *Ancient Israelite Religion: Essays in Honor of Frank Moore Cross,* edited by Patrick D. Miller Jr., Paul D. Hanson, and S. Dean McBride. Philadelphia: Fortress Press, 1987.

Black, Matthew. *An Aramaic Approach to the Gospels and Acts.* Rev ed. Oxford, U.K.: Clarendon Press, 1967.

———. *The Scrolls and Christian Origins: Studies in the Jewish Background of the New Testament.* Chico, Calif.: Scholars Press, 1981.

Black, Matthew, and H. H. Rowley, eds. *Peake's Commentary on the Bible.* London: Thomas Nelson and Sons, 1962.

Botterweck, G. Johannes, Helmer Ringgren, and Heinz-Josef Fabry, eds. *Theological Dictionary of the Old Testament.* Grand Rapids, Mich.: William B. Eerdmans Publishing, 1995.

Brenner, Athalya. *The Israelite Woman: Social Role and Literary Type in Biblical Narrative.* Sheffield, U.K.: JSOT Press, 1985.

Camp, Claudia V. *Wisdom and the Feminine in the Book of Proverbs.* Sheffield, U.K.: Almond, 1985.

———. *Wise, Strange and Holy: The Strange Woman and the Making of the Bible.* Sheffield, U.K.: Sheffield Academic Press, 2000.

———. "The Wise Women of 2 Samuel: A Role Model for Woman in Early Israel." *Catholic Bible Quarterly* 43, no. 1 (1981): 14–29.

Cartlidge, David R. "The Fall and Rise of Simon Magus: How the Worst Man in Christendom Saved the Church." *Bible Review* 21, no. 4 (2005): 24–36.

Cogan, Morton. *Imperialism and Religion: Assyria, Judah and Israel in the Eighth and Seventh Centuries B.C.E.* Missoula, Mont.: Society of Biblical Literature/ Scholars Press, 1974.

Conner, Robert. *Magic in Christianity: From Jesus to the Gnostics.* Oxford, U.K.: Mandrake, 2014.

Coogan, Michael D., ed. *The Oxford History of the Biblical World.* New York: Oxford University Press, 1998.

Cornelius, Izak. "The Many Images of God: Divine Images and Symbols in Ancient Near Eastern Religions." In *The Image and the Book: Iconic Cults, Aniconism, and the Rise of Book Religion in Israel and the Ancient Near East,* edited by Karel van der Toorn. Leuven, Belgium: Peeters, 1997.

Cross, Frank Moore. *Canaanite Myth and Hebrew Epic.* Cambridge, Mass.: Harvard University Press, 1973.

Crossan, John Dominic. *Who Killed Jesus? Exploring the Roots of Anti-Semitism in the Gospel Story of the Death of Jesus.* San Francisco: HarperSanFrancisco, 1995.

Cullmann, Oscar. "The Significance of the Qumran Texts for Research into the Beginnings of Christianity." In *The Scrolls and the New Testament,* edited by Krister Stendahl and James H. Charlesworth. New York: Crossroad Publishing, 1992.

Dalman, Gustaf. *Jesus Christ in the Talmud, Midrash, Zohar, and in the Liturgy of the Synagogue: Texts and Translations.* London: Deighton, Bell and Co., 1893.

Daniélou, Jean. *A History of Early Christian Doctrine Before the Council of Nicaea.* 3 vols. Philadelphia: Westminster Press, 1964–77.

Day, John. *Yahweh and the Gods and Goddesses of Canaan.* Sheffield, U.K.: Sheffield Academic Press, 2000.

Day, John, Robert P. Gordon, and H. G. M. Williamson, eds. *Wisdom in Ancient Israel: Essays in Honour of J. A. Emerton.* New York: Cambridge University Press, 1995.

Day, Peggy L. "Anat: Ugarit's 'Mistress of Animals.'" *Journal of Near Eastern Studies* 51, no. 3 (1992): 181–190.

———, ed. *Gender Difference in Ancient Israel.* Minneapolis, Minn.: Fortress Press, 1989.

de Boer, P. A. H. "The Counsellor." In *Wisdom in Israel and in the Ancient Near East,* edited by M. Noth and D. Winton Thomas. Leiden, Netherlands: E. J. Brill, 1955.

Dempster, Stephen G. "Mythology and History in the Song of Deborah." *Westminster Theological Journal* 41, no. 1 (1978): 33–53.

Dever, William G. *Did God Have a Wife? Archaeology and Folk Religion in Ancient Israel.* Grand Rapids, Mich.: William B. Eerdmans Publishing, 2005.

———. *What Did the Biblical Writers Know and When Did They Know It? What Archaeology Can Tell Us about the Reality of Ancient Israel.* Grand Rapids, Mich.: William B. Eerdmans Publishing, 2001.

———. *Who Were the Early Israelites and Where Did They Come From?* Grand Rapids, Mich.: William B. Eerdmans Publishing, 2003.

Dijkstra, Meindert. "El, the God of Israel—Israel, the People of YHWH: On the Origins of Ancient Israelite Yahwism." In *Only One God?: Monotheism in Ancient Egypt and the Veneration of the Goddess Asherah,* by Bob Becking, Meindert Dijkstra, Marjo C. A. Korpel, and Karel J. H. Vriezen, 81–126. New York: Sheffield Academic Press, 2001.

———. "I Have Blessed You by YHWH of Samaria and his Asherah: Texts with Religious Elements from the Soil Archive of Ancient Israel." In *Only One God?: Monotheism in Ancient Egypt and the Veneration of the Goddess Asherah,* by Bob Becking, Meindert Dijkstra, Marjo C. A. Korpel, and Karel J. H. Vriezen, 17–44. New York: Sheffield Academic Press, 2001.

———. "Women and Religion in the Old Testament." In *Only One God?: Monotheism in Ancient Egypt and the Veneration of the Goddess Asherah,* by Bob Becking, Meindert Dijkstra, Marjo C. A. Korpel, and Karel J. H. Vriezen, 164–88. New York: Sheffield Academic Press, 2001.

Dodd, C. H. *The Interpretation of the Fourth Gospel.* Cambridge, U.K.: Cambridge University Press, 1953.

Eisenmann, Robert. *James the Brother of Jesus: The Key to Understanding the Secrets of Early Christianity and the Dead Sea Scrolls.* London: Watkins, 2002.

Emerton, J. A., ed. *Congress Volume: Cambridge 1995.* Leiden, Netherlands: Brill, 1997.

Exum, J. Cheryl. "Judges." In *Harper's Bible Commentary,* edited by James L. Mays. San Francisco: HarperSanFrancisco, 1988.

Feather, Robert. *Where Moses Stood.* London: Copper Scroll, 2014.

Finkelstein, Israel, and Neil Asher Silberman. *The Bible Unearthed: Archaeology's New Vision of Ancient Israel and the Origin of Its Sacred Texts.* New York: Free Press, 2001.

Fiorenza, Elizabeth Schüssler. *In Memory of Her: A Feminist Theological Reconstruction of Christian Origins.* London: SCM Press, 1983.

———. "Wisdom Mythology and the Christological Hymns of the New Testament." In *Aspects of Wisdom in Judaism and Early Christianity,* edited by Robert L. Wilken. Notre Dame, Ind.: University of Notre Dame Press, 1975.

Fossum, Jarl E. *The Name of God and the Angel of the Lord: Samaritan and Jewish Concepts of Intermediation and the Origin of Gnosticism.* Tübingen, Germany: J.C.B. Mohr, 1985.

———. "The Simonian Sophia Myth." *Studi e Materiali di Storia delle Religione* 53, no. 2 (1987): 185–198.

Fox, Robin Lane. *Pagans and Christians.* London: Penguin, 2006.

Freedman, David Noel. "'Who Is Like Thee Among the Gods?' The Religion of Early Israel." In *Ancient Israelite Religion: Essays in Honor of Frank Moore Cross,* edited by Patrick D. Miller Jr., Paul D. Hanson, and S. Dean McBride. Philadelphia: Fortress Press, 1987.

Freeman, Charles. *AD 381: Heretics, Pagans and the Christian State.* London: Pimlico, 2008.

Gaus, Andy. *The Unvarnished New Testament.* Grand Rapids, Mich.: Phanes Press, 1991.

Gnuse, Robert Karl. *No Other Gods: Emergent Monotheism in Israel.* Sheffield, U.K.: Sheffield Academic Press, 1997.

Goodison, Lucy, and Christine Morris, eds. *Ancient Goddesses: The Myths and the Evidence.* London: British Museum Press, 1998.

Haar, Stephen. *Simon Magus: The First Gnostic?* New York: Walter de Gruyter, 2003.

Hackett, Jo Ann. "Jezebel." In *The Oxford Guide to People and Places of the Bible,* edited by Bruce M. Metzger and Michael D. Coogan. New York: Oxford University Press, 2001.

Hadley, Judith M. *The Cult of Asherah in Ancient Israel and Judah: Evidence for a Hebrew Goddess.* Cambridge, U.K.: Cambridge University Press, 2000.

———. "Wisdom and the Goddess." In *Wisdom in Ancient Israel: Essays in Honour of J. A. Emerton,* edited by John Day, Robert P. Gordon, and H. G. M. Williamson. New York: Cambridge University Press, 1995.

Hancock, Graham. *The Sign and the Seal: A Quest for the Lost Ark of the Covenant.* London: Heinemann, 1992.

Handy, Lowell K. *Among the Host of Heaven: The Syro-Phoenician Pantheon as Bureaucracy.* Winona Lake, Ind.: Eisenbrauns, 1994.

Haskins, Susan. *Mary Magdalen.* London: HarperCollins, 1993.

Hestrin, Ruth. "The Lachish Ewer and the 'Asherah." *Israel Exploration Journal* 37, no. 4 (1987): 212–23.

Hooke, S. H. "Genesis." In *Peake's Commentary on the Bible,* edited by Matthew Black and H. H. Rowley. London: Thomas Nelson and Sons, 1962.

Hurtado, Larry W. *One God, One Lord: Early Christian Devotion and Ancient Jewish Monotheism.* Edinburgh: T&T Clark, 1998.

Jonas, Hans. *The Gnostic Religion: The Message of the Alien God and the Beginnings of Christianity.* Rev. ed. London: Routledge, 1992.

Jones, F. Stanley. *An Ancient Jewish Christian Source on the History of Christianity: Pseudo-Clementine Recognitions 1.27-71.* Atlanta, Ga.: Scholars Press, 1995.

Keel, Othmar. *The Symbolism of the Biblical World: Ancient Near Eastern*

Iconography and the Book of Psalms. Rev. ed. Winona Lake, Ind.: Eisenbrauns, 1997.

Kent, Benedict H. M. "Curses in Acts: Hearing the Apostles' Words of Judgment Alongside 'Magical' Spell Texts." *Journal for the Study of the New Testament* 39, no. 4 (2017): 412–40.

King, Karen L. *The Gospel of Mary of Magdala: Jesus and the First Woman Apostle.* Salem, Ore.: Polebridge Press, 2003.

Kitchen, K. A. Review of *Egypt, Canaan, and Israel in Ancient Times,* by Donald B. Redford. *Journal of Semitic Studies* 41, no. 1 (1996): 121–25.

Kloppenborg, John S. "Isis and Sophia in the Book of Wisdom." *Harvard Theological Review* 75, no. 1 (1982): 57–84.

Knoppers, Gary N. *Jews and Samaritans: The Origins and History of Their Early Relations.* New York: Oxford University Press, 2013.

Korpel, Marjo C. A. "Asherah outside Israel." In *Only One God?: Monotheism in Ancient Egypt and the Veneration of the Goddess Asherah,* by Bob Becking, Meindert Dijkstra, Marjo C. A. Korpel, and Karel J. H. Vriezen, 127–150. New York: Sheffield Academic Press, 2001.

Laible, Henry. "Jesus Christ in the Talmud." In *Jesus Christ in the Talmud, Midrash, Zohar, and in the Liturgy of the Synagogue: Texts and Translations,* by Gustaf Dalman. London: Deighton, Bell and Co., 1893.

Lang, Bernhard. *The Hebrew God: Portrait of the Ancient Deity.* New York: Yale University Press, 2002.

———. *Monotheism and the Prophetic Minority: An Essay in Biblical History and Sociology.* Sheffield, U.K.: Almond Press, 1983.

———. "Wisdom." In *Dictionary of Deities and Demons in the Bible,* edited by Karel van der Toorn, Bob Becking, and Pieter W. van der Horst. Grand Rapids, Mich.: William B. Eerdmans Publishing, 1995.

———. *Wisdom and the Book of Proverbs: A Hebrew Goddess Redefined.* New York: Pilgrim Press, 1986.

Layton, Bentley, *The Gnostic Scriptures.* London: SCM Press, 1987.

Leloup, Jean. *The Gospel of Mary Magdalene.* Rochester, Vt.: Inner Traditions, 2002.

Lemaire, André. "Date et origine des Inscriptions Hebraiques et Pheniciennes de Kuntillet 'Ajrud." *Studi Epigrafici e Linguistici sul Vicino Oriente antico* 1 (1984): 131–43.

Lemche, Niels Peter. *Ancient Israel: A New History of Israelite Society.* Sheffield, U.K.: JSOT Press, 1988.

Lieberman, Saul, Shalom Spiegel, Leo Strauss and Arthur Hyman. *Harry Austryn*

Wolfson: Jubilee Volume. 3 vols. Jersalem: American Academy for Jewish Research, 1965.

Lincoln, Andrew T. *The Gospel According to Saint John.* New York: Continuum, 2005.

Luckert, Karl W. *Egyptian Light and Hebrew Fire: Theological and Philosophical Roots of Christendom in Evolutionary Perspective.* New York: State University of New York Press, 1991.

Lüdemann, G. "The Acts of the Apostles and the Beginnings of Simonian Gnosis." *New Testament Studies* 33, no. 3 (1987): 420–26.

MacDonald, John. *The Theology of the Samaritans.* London: SCM Press, 1964.

MacLaurin, E. C. B. "Date of the Foundation of the Jewish Colony at Elephantine." *Journal of Near Eastern Studies* 27, no. 2 (1968): 89–96.

Mann, A. T., and Jane Lyle. *Sacred Sexuality.* Rockport, Mass.: Element Books, 1995.

Marttila, Marko, and Mika S. Pajunen. "Wisdom, Israel and Other Nations." *Journal of Ancient Judaism* 4, no. 1 (2013): 2–26.

Mays, James L. ed. *Harper's Bible Commentary.* San Francisco: HarperSanFrancisco, 1988.

Mazar, B. "The Sanctuary of Arad and the Family of Hobab the Kenite." *Journal of Near Eastern Studies* 24, no. 3 (1965): 297–303.

McCarter, P. Kyle. "Exodus." In *Harper's Bible Commentary,* edited by James L. Mays. San Francisco: HarperSanFrancisco, 1988.

McEvenue, S. "Who Was Second Isaiah?" In *Studies in the Book of Isaiah: Festschrift Willem A.M. Beuken,* by J. Van Ruiten and M. Vervenne. Leuven, Belgium: Leuven University Press, 1997.

McLaughlin, John L. *What Are They Saying about Ancient Israelite Religion?* New York: Paulist Press, 2016.

Mead, G. R. S. *Simon Magus: An Essay.* New York: Theosophical Publishing Society, 1892.

Metzger, Bruce M., and Michael D. Coogan, eds. *The Oxford Guide to People and Places of the Bible.* New York: Oxford University Press, 2001.

Meyers, Carol. *Discovering Eve: Ancient Israelite Women in Context.* New York: Oxford University Press, 1988.

Miller Jr., Patrick D., Paul D. Hanson, and S. Dean McBride, eds. *Ancient Israelite Religion: Essays in Honor of Frank Moore Cross.* Philadelphia: Fortress Press, 1987.

Murphy, Roland E. "The Personification of Wisdom." In *Wisdom in Ancient Israel: Essays in Honour of J. A. Emerton,* edited by John Day, Robert P. Gordon, and H. G. M. Williamson. New York: Cambridge University Press, 1995.

Newman, Barbara. *From Virile Woman to WomanChrist: Studies in Medieval Religion and Literature*. Philadelphia: University of Pennsylvania Press, 1995.

Niditch, Susan. "Eroticism and Death in the Tale of Jael." In *Gender Difference in Ancient Israel*, edited by Peggy L. Day. Minneapolis, Minn.: Fortress Press, 1989.

Niehr, Herbert. "In Search of YHWH's Cult Statue in the First Temple." In *The Image and the Book: Iconic Cults, Aniconism, and the Rise of Book Religion in Israel and the Ancient Near East*, edited by Karel van der Toorn. Leuven, Belgium: Peeters, 1997.

Noth, M., and D. Winton Thomas, eds. *Wisdom in Israel and in the Ancient Near East*. Leiden, Netherlands: E. J. Brill, 1955.

Novick, Rabbi Léah. *On the Wings of Shekhinah: Rediscovering Judaism's Divine Feminine*. Wheaton, Ill.: Quest Books, 2008.

Olyan, Saul M. *Asherah and the Cult of Yahweh in Israel*. Atlanta, Ga.: Scholars Press, 1988.

Origen. *Contra Celsum*. Translated by Henry Chadwick. Rev. ed. Cambridge, U.K.: Cambridge University Press, 1965.

Patai, Raphael. *The Hebrew Goddess*. Expanded ed. Detroit, Mich.: Wayne State University Press, 1990.

———. *Man and Temple: In Ancient Jewish Myth and Ritual*. New York: Thomas Nelson and Sons, 1947.

Philo. *Questions and Answers on Genesis*. Translated by Ralph Marcus. Cambridge, Mass.: Harvard University Press, 1953.

Phipps, W. E. *Was Jesus Married? The Distortion of Sexuality in the Christian Tradition*. New York: Harper and Row, 1970.

———. *The Sexuality of Jesus: Theological and Literary Perspectives*. New York: Harper and Row, 1973.

Pick, Bernhard. *The Apocryphal Acts of Paul, Peter, John, Andrew and Thomas*. Chicago, Ill.: Open Court Publishing, 1909.

Picknett, Lynn. *Mary Magdalene: Christianity's Hidden Goddess*. Rev. ed. London: Constable, 2004.

———. *The Secret History of Lucifer: The Ancient Path to Knowledge and the Real Da Vinci Code*. London: Constable, 2003.

Picknett, Lynn, and Clive Prince. *The Forbidden Universe: The Occult Origins of Science and the Search for the Mind of God*. London: Constable, 2011.

———. *The Masks of Christ: Behind the Lies and Cover-Ups About the Man Believed to Be God*. London: Sphere, 2008.

———. *The Sion Revelation: The Truth About the Guardians of Christ's Sacred Bloodline.* New York: Touchstone, 2006.

———. *The Templar Revelation: Secret Guardians of the True Identity of Christ.* New York: Touchstone, 1997.

Pistis Sophia. Translated by G. R. S. Mead. London: J. M. Watkins, 1921.

Pope, Marvin H. *Song of Songs: A New Translation with Introduction and Commentary.* Garden City, N.Y.: Doubleday, 1977.

Porten, Bazalel, with J. Joel Farber, Cary J. Martin, Günter Vittmann, Leslie S. B. MacCoull, and Sarah Clackson. *The Elephantine Papyri in English: Three Millennia of Cross-Cultural Continuity and Change.* Leiden, Netherlands: E. J. Brill, 1996.

Price, Robert M. *The Pre-Nicene New Testament: Fifty-four Formative Texts.* Salt Lake City, Utah: Signature Books, 2006.

Pritchard, James B. *Ancient Near Eastern Texts Relating to the Old Testament.* Princeton, N.J.: Princeton University Press, 1969.

Pummer, Reinhard. *Early Christian Authors on Samaritans and Samaritanism: Texts, Translations and Commentary.* Tübingen, Germany: Mohr Siebeck, 2002.

———. *The Samaritans: A Profile.* Grand Rapids, Mich.: William B. Eerdmans Publishing, 2016.

Purvis, James D. "Ben Sira and the Foolish People of Shechem." *Journal of Near Eastern Studies* 24, no. 1 & 2 (1965): 88–94.

Qualls-Corbett, Nancy. *The Sacred Prostitute: Eternal Aspect of the Sacred Feminine.* Toronto: Inner City Books, 1988.

Rast, Walter. "Joshua." In *Harper's Bible Commentary,* edited by James L. Mays. San Francisco: HarperSanFrancisco, 1988.

Redford, Donald B. *Egypt, Canaan, and Israel in Ancient Times.* Princeton, N.J.: Princeton University Press, 1992.

Ringgren, Helmer. *Word and Wisdom: Studies in the Hypostatization of Divine Qualities and Functions in the Ancient Near East.* Lund, Sweden: Häkan Ohlssons Boktryckeri, 1947.

Roberts, Rev. Alexander, and James Donaldson, eds. *Ante-Nicene Christian Library: Translations of the Writings from the Fathers Down to AD 325.* 25 vol. Edinburgh: T. & T. Clark, 1867–97.

Robinson, James M., ed. *The Nag Hammadi Library in English.* Leiden, Netherlands: E. J. Brill, 1996.

Romer, John. *Testament: The Bible and History.* London: Michael O'Mara, 1988.

Ruether, Rosemary Radford. *Sexism and God-Talk: Toward a Feminist Theology.* London: SCM Press, 1983.

Salles-Dabadie, J. M. A. *Recherche sur Simon le Mage, I: L'"Apophasis megalè."* Paris: J. Gabalda et Cie., 1969.

Sanders, Paul. *The Provenance of Deuteronomy 32.* Leiden, Netherlands: E. J. Brill, 1996.

Schaberg, Jane. *The Illegitimacy of Jesus: A Feminist Theological Interpretation of the Infancy Narratives.* Sheffield, U.K.: Sheffield Academic Press, 1995.

Schama, Simon. *The Story of the Jews: Finding the Words—1000 BCE-1492 CE.* London: Bodley Head, 2013.

Schloen, J. David. "Caravans, Kenites, and *Casus Belli*: Enmity and Alliance in the Song of Deborah." *Catholic Bible Quarterly* 55, no. 1 (1993): 18–38.

Schneemelcher, Wilhelm, ed. *New Testament Apocrypha.* 2 vols. Louisville, Ky.: John Knox Press, 1991–92.

Scott, Martin. *Sophia and the Johannine Jesus.* Sheffield, U.K.: Sheffield Academic Press, 1992.

Sheafer, Silvia Anne. *Ramses the Great.* New York: Chelsea House, 2009.

Smith, Mark S. *The Early History of God: Yahweh and the Other Deities of Ancient Israel.* San Francisco: HarperSanFrancisco, 1990.

———. *The Origins of Biblical Monotheism: Israel's Polytheistic Background and the Ugaritic Texts.* New York: Oxford University Press, 2001.

Smith, Morton. *Palestinian Parties and Politics that Shaped the Old Testament.* London: SCM Press, 1987.

Stager, Lawrence E. "Forging an Identity: The Emergence of Ancient Israel." In *The Oxford History of the Biblical World,* edited by Michael D. Coogan, 123–75. New York: Oxford University Press, 1998.

Starbird, Margaret. *The Woman with the Alabaster Jar.* Santa Fe, N. Mex: Bear & Co., 1993.

Stendahl, Krister, and James H. Charlesworth, eds. *The Scrolls and the New Testament.* New York: Crossroad Publishing, 1992.

Stern, Ephraim. "What Happened to the Cult Figurines? Israelite Religion is Purified After the Exile." *Biblical Archaeology Review* 15, no. 4 (1989): 22–25, 53–54.

Strelan, Rick. *Strange Acts: Studies in the Cultural World of the Acts of the Apostles.* New York: Walter de Gruyter, 2004.

Traunecker, Claude. *The Gods of Egypt.* Ithaca, N.Y.: Cornell University Press, 2001.

Trible, Phyllis. "Depatriarchalizing in Biblical Interpretation." *Journal of the American Academy of Religion* 41, no. 1 (1973): 30–48.

van der Toorn, Karel. *From Her Cradle to Her Grave: The Role of Religion in the Life of the Israelite and the Babylonian Woman.* Sheffield, U.K.: JSOT Press, 1994.

———. "Goddesses in Early Israelite Religion." In *Ancient Goddesses: The Myths and the Evidence,* edited by Lucy Goodison and Christine Morris. London: British Museum Press, 1998.

———, ed. *The Image and the Book: Iconic Cults, Aniconism, and the Rise of Book Religion in Israel and the Ancient Near East.* Leuven, Belgium: Peeters, 1997.

van der Toorn, Karel, Bob Becking, and Pieter W. van der Horst, eds. *Dictionary of Deities and Demons in the Bible.* Grand Rapids, Mich.: William B. Eerdmans Publishing, 1995.

Van Ruiten, J., and M. Vervenne. *Studies in the Book of Isaiah: Festschrift Willem A. M. Beuken.* Leuven, Belgium: Leuven University Press, 1997.

Walls, Neal H. *The Goddess Anat in Ugaritic Myth.* Atlanta, Ga.: Scholars Press, 1992.

Westenholz, Joan Goodnick. "Goddesses in the Ancient Near East 3000–1000 BC." In *Ancient Goddesses: The Myths and the Evidence,* edited by Lucy Goodison and Christine Morris. London: British Museum Press, 1998.

Wilken, Robert L., ed. *Aspects of Wisdom in Judaism and Early Christianity.* Notre Dame, Ind.: University of Notre Dame Press, 1975.

Williams, Frank. *The Panarion of Epiphanius of Salamis: Book I (Sects 1-46).* Leiden, Netherlands: E. J. Brill, 1987.

Wilson, R. Mc L. *The Gospel of Philip: Translated from the Coptic Text, With an Introduction and Commentary.* London: A.R. Mowbray & Co., 1962.

Witherington III, Ben. *Women in the Ministry of Jesus: A Study of Jesus' Attitudes to Women and their Roles as Reflected in His Earthly Life.* New York: Cambridge University Press, 1984.

Index